American Architecture 1607–1860

Marcus Whiffen

AMERICAN ARCHITECTURE
Volume 1
1607–1860

The MIT Press
Cambridge, Massachusetts

Second paperback edition, 1984

This book was set in VIP Aldus and VIP Palatino Bold Italic by DEKR Corporation and printed and bound by Halliday Lithograph in the United States of America.

Library of Congress Cataloging in Publication Data

Whiffen, Marcus.
    American architecture.

    Reprint. Originally published: American architecture, 1607–1976.
    Bibliography: p.
    Includes index.
    Contents: v. 1. 1607–1860—v. 2. 1860–1976.
    1. Architecture—United States. I. Koeper, Frederick. II. Title.
NA705.W473   1983   720'.973   83–5403
ISBN 0–262–73069–3 (v. 1)
        0–262–73070–7 (v. 2)

To Inge

Contents

Contents
Volume 2
1860–1976
Frederick Koeper

Foreword

The American architecture of the title of this book is architecture in that part of the North American continent which before the admission of Hawaii and Alaska to the Union constituted the geographical entity of the United States. Thus the adjective *American* is applied in a purely geographical sense to what was created—most obviously in colonial times, but no less in more recent—by men of many diverse national origins and cultures.

Can *American*, applied to architecture, have another sense? That is to say, does American architecture, as the product of the special conditions of a geographical area and the needs and beliefs and ideals of its inhabitants, have qualities that distinguish it from other architectures of the western world, so that we might remark, for instance, that such-and-such a building is "very American"? The pursuit of national characteristics in the arts has led some of the best scholars and critics on to perilous quicksands of generalization. Yet the question is one that the reader may fairly expect some thoughts on, if not a definitive answer to.

The fact that for the greater part of its history American architecture has been dependent on external sources, generally European, for both tradition and innovation should make it easier to detect the specifically American elements in it, if there are any. It is not easy. The church architecture of Spanish New Mexico was unique, and so was the eighteenth-century domestic architecture of the French Mississippi Valley. But both were regional developments and therefore provide no clues to Americanness. British colonial architecture, however, does have a characteristic that may fairly be called American. The wooden houses of seventeenth-century New England are perceptibly more spacious, with higher rooms, than their counterparts in the mother country. The same is true of the eighteenth-century houses of the South. None of them is really large by the English standards of the age; many of them are almost noble in scale. Singleton Moorehead of the Williamsburg restoration used to show visiting architects an elevation of the George Wythe House, a typical "double pile" built about 1750, and ask them to sketch a man at the front door. The men depicted were never less than seven feet tall. Is it permissible to see here the beginning of that enlargement of scale which by the early twentieth century had made the centers of New York and Chicago virtually different in kind from any city in Europe? The early New England house was more spacious because of the abundance of timber, no doubt. But that is no argument against the connection, for it must have been the vast forests of the new continent that implanted in the minds of the first settlers that faith in the limitlessness of natural resources which until very re-

cently was an integral and conspicuous part of the American men-
tality, and to which the optimism that inspired the unprecedented
scale of American cities was in great part due.

A clean-cut clarity of external form, without wings, porches, or
other excrescences, is another characteristic of the colonial house
which recurs often enough—for example, in the temple-form buildings of the Greek Revival, in the "neo-formalist" buildings of the
1950s and 1960s, and in an extreme degree in certain buildings
discussed in the last chapter of this book—to encourage one to risk
the attachment of the adjective American to it. Certainly Frank Lloyd
Wright recognized it as an American characteristic when he set out
to "eliminate the box" and give America an architecture embodying
his own conception of space. Or was it an *American* conception of
space, hitherto unformulated in architectural terms, which he re-
vealed to his countrymen? One American critic has written: "The
conception of space as flowing with a ground line, wherein the
architectural shelter is only a more defined and more complex part
of a great continuous whole, is as foreign to European thought as
their conception of space as an isolated volume is to ours."[1] If this
contention is true—and there are many twentieth-century buildings
that could be cited in evidence, as well as the importance of the road
as an image and metaphor in American literature—the difference
described may surely be accounted for by the sheer size of America
and the seeming endlessness of its landscapes, which even today are
unimaginable by Europeans who have not experienced them.

Empiricism and pragmatism are often named as typically American
attitudes of mind. Empirical considerations must play a part in the
design of any building; nevertheless a good case can be made for the
view that American architects have been more empirically-minded
than their European colleagues. At the highest level Wright, in his
insistence on the integration of house and site, was an empiricist,
however he might try to idealize his approach to design as organi-
cism; by contrast, Le Corbusier was undismayed when an Indian
client sold the working drawings for a house and it was built in
another place, for he always designed his Indian houses, he said, for
the sun and prevailing winds of India and not for individual sites.
However, it is in the history of the structural system that made
possible that entirely American creation, the skyscraper, that evidence of the prevalence of empiricism, with its limitations, may most
easily be seen. The metal frame was introduced in Chicago by Jenney,
an engineer by training. It was accepted gladly by the architects of
high buildings as a means of lightening them—that is, as an empirical
device. Not one of these architects gave it any thought as an archi-

tectural form with its own esthetic; the greatest, Sullivan, in his finest buildings concealed it within an envelope that obeyed the classical rules of composition. It was left to architects in Europe to recognize its spatial implications, and it was a European, Mies van der Rohe, who made it the most subtle modulator of architectural design since the Greek and Roman orders and who employed it as such in a number of masterpieces in the city of its youth.

The reader of the following pages will doubtless arrive at generalizations of his own, perhaps more valid than the authors'. He will find that, as is necessary in a book of this scope if it is to be more than a chronicle, the treatment of the subject is a compromise between the chronological and the thematic; different aspects of a period are sometimes dealt with in separate chapters and there are some considerable overlappings of time. The reader will also find that in order to avoid overloading the text with dates, those of the birth and death of all architects mentioned in it who built in America are, when known, given in the index, while to save him from disappointments of a kind so often experienced by lovers of architecture visiting new places the fact that a building no longer exists is indicated there too. (Such disappointments cannot be prevented altogether; although the rage for destruction may have abated as a result of recent legislation and changed attitudes, important buildings disappear every week.) If the reader gains pleasure or profit from the book, he should be grateful, as are the authors, to all those whose help has made it a better book than it would have been without it, especially Cynthia E. Cobb, who drew all the plans except those reproduced from architects' originals; Diane Gingold, who searched for photographs in the Library of Congress; William H. Pierson, Jr., who was most generous with his excellent photographs; Julian Silva, who read volume 2 in manuscript and made suggestions relating to matters of style; and Robert L. Sweeney, who helped in matters relating to twentieth-century architects in general and Frank Lloyd Wright in particular.

I   *1607–1860*

Marcus Whiffen

"The Towne itself by the care and providence of Sir Thomas Gates is reduced into a handsome forme, and hath in it two faire rowes of howses, all of framed timber, two stories, and an upper Garret, or Corne loft high." The town was Jamestown, the year 1615. There could be no better illustration of the general rule that the prime object of settlers in a new land is to reproduce as nearly as possible the living conditions of their old, to build themselves homes away from home, than that the first permanent British settlement in America should have had row houses, of the form (as archaeology has confirmed) of the English urban unit-house, about twice as deep as it was broad and with rooms back and front on each floor. The type had been developed in medieval towns where space was restricted—that is, for conditions that could only be produced artificially on the edge of the vast American continent. As one writer has remarked, "in English minds Jamestown was to be a city of continuous and adjacent habitations, like Oxford and Chipping Camden." [1] And, one might add, London. Early in the eighteenth century, the Reverend Hugh Jones, who had been professor of mathematics at William and Mary, noted: "The habits, life, customs, computations, etc. of the Virginians are much the same as about London, which they esteem their home." No doubt it had been so from the early days of the colony.

Row houses were specified in Lord Baltimore's instructions for laying out St. Mary's City, capital of Maryland, in 1634, but few were built. In the seventeenth century all but a handful of Americans lived in free-standing dwellings. At first these neither stood very high nor were constructed of such materials as to stand very long. Several primitive types were employed in the early days of settlement. The three commonest seem to have been, first, the cabin, with walls of wattle and daub (woven osier withies coated with mud) and a thatched roof whose ridgepole was supported by cratchets (forked posts); second, the English wigwam, with a framework of poles bent over into hoop form and thatched—the thatch and a door and a wooden chimney distinguishing it from the Indian wigwam with its smoke hole and covering of mats or bark skins; and third, the dugout. The use and manner of construction of the last were described by a New England settler: "They burrow themselves in the Earth for their first shelter under some Hill side, casting the Earth aloft upon Timber; they make a smoky fire against the Earth at its highest side. . . . yet in these poor *Wigwames* they sing Psalms, pray, and praise their God till they can provide them houses." (Wigwam is here used as a generic term for any primitive dwelling.)

Even if the English wigwam owed its form as well as its name to the Indians—a moot point—all the techniques employed in it were known in rural England, where in the seventeenth century houses of various primitive types were still home to countrymen in remote districts. In any case settlers of all classes were soon able to move up to better things. Our authority for the New England dugout recorded the improvement in the Massachusetts Bay Colony in 1654: "The Lord hath been pleased to turn all the wigwams, huts, and hovels the English dwelt in at their first coming into orderly, fair and well built houses."

Building with Wood

Not every settler might have been ready to recognize the direct participation of the Almighty in the provision of housing; none could deny that He had been most munificent in providing the new continent with the traditional building material of England, wood. The great majority of the "well built houses" of British America, in the South as well as in New England, were timber-framed in the seventeenth century and for long after. Most Americans preferred frame houses to those of masonry. Thomas Jefferson, toward the end of the eighteenth century, complained of "the unhappy prejudice . . . that houses of brick or stone" were "less wholesome than those of wood," while as late as the mid-nineteenth century the prejudice found expression on certain Texas plantations where the slave quarters were built of the admirable local limestone and the great house was built of timber laboriously hauled overland from the port of Galveston.

The traditional English house frame, as used in America for two and a half centuries, was a work of art rather than science. Although its parts—sills, posts, studs, joists, girts, summers, and plates—were graded in size or scantling according to their functions, the stability of the whole derived in the final analysis from the carpenter's skill in cutting and fitting the joints—mortice and tenon, tusk and tenon, dovetail lap, fastened with wooden pegs or treenails—and to a degree from the sheer weight of material rather than from adherence to structural principles. The use of diagonal bracing was minimal, being limited usually to a pair of braces to each corner post. In seventeenth-century New England the walls of frame houses were sometimes covered with plaster, sometimes with flush siding, more often with wooden shingles; before the end of the century clapboards, made by splitting rather than sawing the log, were in general use. In the South sawn boards, which had the advantage of greater length and breadth, were the rule, split boards being employed only for service buildings. (All boards nailed to walls with an overlap, split or sawn, were called clapboards.)

On roofs thatch was soon superseded by shingles, which became the commonest roof covering, north and south. Their use represented a return to earlier English practice, for shingles had been a common roof covering in the Middle Ages until the rising price of wood led to the substitution of earthen tiles and stone slates. Two forms of roof were in general use, the steep-pitched **A** roof and the gambrel, which has two slopes on each side. Roof frames were broadly divisible into two classes, those having framed principals, or trusses, and those which had common rafters only. They were much more varied than house frames. In trussed roofs not only was there the choice between the king-post truss (with a single vertical post from the tie beam to the ridge), the queen-post truss (with two posts), and the simple truss without any post at all but with a collar or wind beam; there were also different ways of relating the purlins (the horizontal members joining the trusses) to the rafters and distributing the diagonal braces which stiffened the frame longitudinally. In making his choices the colonial carpenter might be influenced by individual preference or regional practice—regional here being understood to refer to England as well as to America. For example, the unusual position of the braces in the roof of the Fairbanks House (1637) the oldest wooden house in America, was standard practice in that part of East Anglia from which the Dedham carpenters came. The only feature of the colonial roof frame that can be described as un-English is a negative one, namely, the omission of the ridgepole. It was an omission that followed logically, or at least commonsensically, from the abandonment of thatch, which needs a ridgepole to hang from.

Regional Differences   When we turn from the construction of the seventeenth-century house in the British colonies to its plan and general design, it becomes more difficult to generalize; significant differences between New England and the South force themselves upon the attention. What can be said of both regions is that when a house had one room only, as many of the early houses did, that room was always called the hall, and when it had two the second was nearly always called the parlor. The hall was the original all-purpose room of the early medieval English house, retained as the essential nucleus in all elaborations of plan. In houses in the country its long axis lay parallel with the front of the house and it was entered near one end, the "lower" end, through one of its long sides; the chimney stood at the other, "upper" end. The parlor was described by a seventeenth-century English author as "a fair lower Room designed for the Entertainment of company"—which did not prevent it containing a bed, in England or America. The term, of monastic provenance, had come into use in the fourteenth century in the Midlands and the North; in southern England, where the two-room house became common rather earlier, the second room had been called the chamber since the twelfth century. South-of-England usage was occasionally followed in the colonies, as inventories show, but where there is no indication to the contrary it may be assumed that a chamber was a bedroom on the upper floor.

In the location of the parlor New England and the South differed radically. In New England the parlor adjoined the upper end of the hall, with which it shared a massive axial chimney; in the South it was placed at the lower end and had its own chimney. Both arrangements had English precedents. The New England plan originated in Essex and East Anglia as a product of the housing revolution which brought about so great an improvement in rural living conditions in the reign of Elizabeth I. In England there remain transitional examples in which entrance is still directly into the hall after the medieval fashion; the placing of the door in the center of the front opposite the chimney made for convenience, providing as it did easy access from outside to the hall, parlor, and stairs; it also facilitated the achievement of external symmetry, which by the seventeenth century had come to be valued even in relatively modest houses. The gable-end chimneys of the South, with their tapered offsets, were probably introduced by builders from the West Midlands, for such chimneys were characteristics of the farmhouses of that region. External symmetry was no problem in the southern type, since the door at the lower end of the hall naturally fell in the middle of the front. (Nonetheless, approximate symmetry was often considered good enough.) In early houses, such as the Adam Thoroughgood House near Norfolk, Virginia, the stair was in the hall, opposite the front door (1). A major improvement was effected when a partition was built across the lower end of the hall and the stair placed in the passage so formed. This resulted in the hall-passage-parlor plan of innumerable houses in the South built in colonial times and well into the nineteenth century.

In the early days plans were not as standardized by region as they became later; central-chimney houses were built in the South and, if more rarely, end-chimney houses in New England. It was, no doubt, a matter of the survival of the fittest, with climate as the chief determinant. In the northeastern winters the chimney of the New England house could warm two rooms on each floor—three on the

1
*Adam Thoroughgood
House, Princess Anne
County, Virginia. 1636.
View from southwest.*

first floor when a kitchen lean-to was added to the basic plan—while the passage through the middle of the Southern house created, as Hugh Jones observed in 1724, "an air-draught in summer." That is to say, the key to the success of the one plan was central heating; of the other, central cooling.

The buildings that stand today do not give a true picture of seventeenth-century housing in either New England or in the South, for it is always the better houses that tend to survive. One thinks of the two-storied Capen and Boardman houses as "typical of New England," and in one sense they are; yet such houses were certainly outnumbered by those of one or one and a half stories. Then brick is a material with greater powers of survival than wood, and in the South nearly all the seventeenth-century houses that have survived are of brick, although most Southern houses were of wood throughout the colonial period. (It is true that there were always more brick houses in the South than in New England.)

North and south, seventeenth-century houses were only one room deep under the main roof; if there was a second range of rooms at the back it was sheltered by a lean-to or shed roof, resulting in what in New England came to be known as the salt box house (2, 3). (The

2
Boardman House, Saugus,
Massachusetts. Circa
1686. West end.

3
Boardman House, Saugus,
Massachusetts. Plan
of first floor.

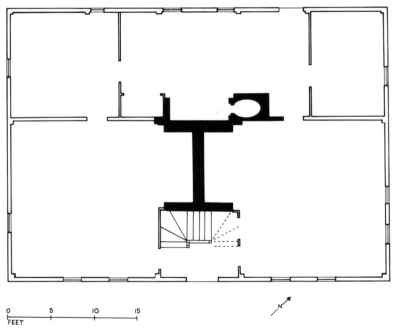

0   5   10   15
FEET

N

three known exceptions to the rule, two in New England and one in the South, will be mentioned presently.) North and south, they present themselves, compositionally, as arrangements of rectangles and triangles. Much of their character derived from their steep-pitched roofs, especially when, as in the John Ward House at Salem, Massachusetts, there were cross gables (4). In general, the upper parts of the New England house were more complex and had a greater visual impact than the ground story. A feature that often contributed to this was the framed overhang or jetty, in which the girts projected a foot or more beyond the wall below to carry the second-floor posts and wall frame. It is a feature about whose origin and purpose there has been much dispute. It may have been devised to avoid weakening the girts by making mortices in them from three directions at one point to receive the tenons of another girt and the first- and second-floor posts; in town houses it could be used to "steal" space over the street, whether or not this was its first func-

4
John Ward House, Salem, Massachusetts. 1684 (west half) and later. View from southwest.

tion. But in many cases the reason for its use must have been esthetic. That this was so is suggested by the random way in which jetties were disposed—sometimes on all four sides of a house, sometimes on two or three, sometimes on one only—and above all by the fact that they were rarely used after taste changed in the eighteenth century. The same is true of the hewn overhang, in which a much slighter projection of the upper story was produced by cutting away the lower part of the two-story posts and carving the transition between the upper and lower parts into the semblance of a bracket.

Some Notable Houses

In the Southern house chimney offsets and dormer windows went some way toward supplying the complexity achieved in New England with cross gables and jetties. In the seventeenth century Southern architecture was more varied than that of New England, and a number of houses that depart in one way or another from the ubiquitous hall-and-parlor and hall-passage-parlor types still survive (or survived long enough to be recorded) or are known from excavation. The so-called Governor's Castle at St. Mary's City, Maryland, built in 1634–39, was the most unusual. A brick structure of two stories, exactly square on plan, it had eight rooms on the ground floor grouped with a military symmetry; it is possible to regard it as the first American example of a "double-pile" house, though its plan has an arbitrary quality which gives it more in common with the architectural "conceits" of the sixteenth century than with the standard double-pile house of the eighteenth. Another two-story house of considerable size by American standards was Sir William Berkeley's Green Spring, near Jamestown, built around 1646. This was a long shallow house with a central chimney between the hall and parlor. A sketch made by the architect Latrobe in 1796 shows that it had a porch with a shaped gable of the kind to be seen in Bacon's Castle.

Bacon's Castle was built around 1655 by one Arthur Allen, who had arrived from England in 1649, and takes its name from Nathaniel Bacon of the 1676 Rebellion (5, 6). It is a house that might have been built in England at any time during the first four decades of the century. The shaped gable was a feature which reached England from the Low Countries just before 1600; the rows of chimney stacks, set diagonally, had a longer history going back to a time in the sixteenth century when chimneys were still relatively rare and a display of them denoted wealth and superior social status. The placing of the stairs in a tower, which balances the two-story porch and turns the plan into a cross, was a medieval arrangement that persisted down to the reign of James I; their form, that of the open-well staircase, did not appear in England until that reign.

5
*Bacon's Castle, Surry
County, Virginia. Circa
1655. From west.*

6
*Bacon's Castle, Surry
County, Virginia. Plan of
first floor.*

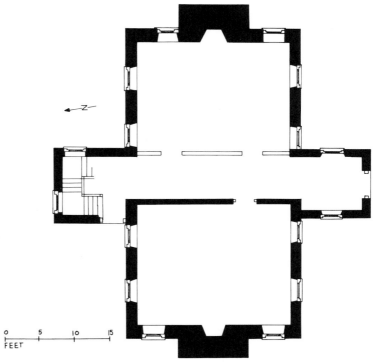

0   5   10   15
FEET

Two other seventeenth-century houses still standing in Virginia have porches with chambers above: Foster's Castle and Christ's Cross, both in New Kent County and built around 1690. They are both of brick, as was Malvern Hall in Henrico County, but the finest seventeenth-century house in the South, after Bacon's Castle, to have survived into the twentieth century was of wood. Bond Castle, in Calvert County, Maryland, was built sometime in the last quarter of the century. It had a two-story porch on either front with jettied sides and gables; the stairs were in the central passage. In its final form Bond Castle had a second parlor or chamber at one end and a kitchen at the other. This is a late example of the kitchen being incorporated in the house itself; in the eighteenth century the outhouse kitchen became the rule—a return to medieval practice encouraged by slave-owning.

With the exception of the Governor's Castle at St. Mary's, classifiable only as a sport, these houses in Virginia and Maryland are all late examples of an English tradition of house design that was at least as old as the century. In New England, the 1670s saw the building of three brick houses, which, in that they were two rooms deep under the main roof and thus "double piles," were closer to contemporary developments in the mother country. The Peter Sergeant House in Boston, completed by 1679, was large but, with its shaped gables and diamond chimneys, distinctly old-fashioned. The Peter Tufts House at Medford, which was under construction in 1675, is, with its gambrel roof, end chimneys in the thickness of the wall, and two rooms on either side of the central passage on each floor, far more prophetic of the shape of things to come, or more precisely of the shape of countless eighteenth-century houses from Maine to South Carolina.

The Boston house of the rich merchant John Foster, which in the eighteenth century came into the possession of Governor Thomas Hutchinson, was a much grander affair—very grand indeed for its time and place. Built in 1689–92, it had Ionic pilasters, of Portland stone, rising through its three stories on the street front—the first giant order in the English colonies. The discontinuance of the frieze and architrave between the pilasters to accommodate the third-story windows was a device frequently employed in the English Baroque of the early eighteenth century, but in all other respects the house represented a type of classicism owing much to Holland which had flourished in England for fifty years. The garlanded pilaster capitals, which must have been carved in England, can be paralleled in numerous buildings of the middle third of the seventeenth century in England and Holland; the cantilevered balcony was a feature more common in Holland than in England. Until 1765, when it was hacked down by a mob protesting the Stamp Act, a cupola intensified the Dutch character of the building.

In Philadelphia the largest seventeenth-century house was of H-form plan. Owned by the merchant Samuel Carpenter, on account of the rarity in America of the material used for its roof it came to be known as the Slate Roof House. It was designed and built, around 1690, by James Portues, a house carpenter who, like many colonial craftsmen, came from England as an indentured servant and set up on his own when he had satisfied the terms of his contract. With hipped roofs, Flemish-bond brickwork, and a pedimented doorway, the Slate Roof House showed a close adherence to London building practices in a city which was to continue to adhere to them more closely than any other in America.

Public Buildings in the English Colonies

For a monumental public architecture there was no call; nor would the means have been available if there had been. Most of the public buildings of the English colonies in the seventeenth century had a decidedly domestic air; many were to all appearance simply bigger though not necessarily better houses and few had any features not to be found in houses too. This is no matter for surprise, for nearly all—the Anglican churches of the South are the chief exceptions— are descended from English domestic ancestors.

A building which, with its dual function, bridged the gap between the domestic and the public was the New England garrison house. This served as a private dwelling in times of peace and as a fort and place of refuge for as many of the community as it would hold during Indian attacks. Outwardly there was little to distinguish garrison houses from other houses. Some of them, however, were built of logs sawn square and dovetailed at the corners, a technique introduced by Scottish settlers; the McIntire Garrison House at Scotland, Maine, is a two-story example from about 1707 (7, 8). A rarer type of fortified dwelling, which resembles the bawn or "strong house" required by law in the English settlements in Ireland, is represented by the stone-built Henry Whitefield House at Guilford, Connecticut, of which the oldest part was built in 1639–40.

The essential public building in every New England community was the meeting house. The earliest New England meeting houses were outwardly indistinguishable from dwellings (9). However, a distinctive solution to the architectural problem, which was to provide for secular meetings as well as religious worship with a building that should be both the symbolic and the physical center of the town, came into use around the middle of the century: a square structure

7
McIntire Garrison House,
Scotland, Maine. Circa
1707. From west.

8
McIntire Garrison House,
Scotland, Maine. Plan of
first floor.

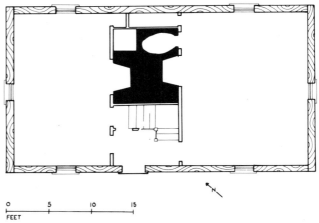

0   5   10   15
FEET

9
*Second Meeting House,
Sudbury, Massachusetts.
1653. Conjectural restora-
tion by Marian C.
Donnelly.*

10
*Old Ship Meeting House,
Hingham, Massachusetts.
1681. Conjectural restora-
tion by Marian C.
Donnelly.*

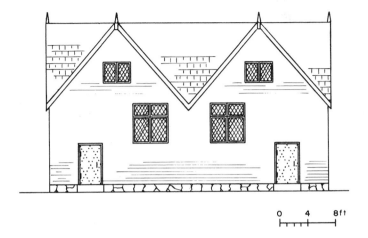

11
*Old Brick Church (St.
Luke's), Isle of Wight
County, Virginia. 1632
and (top stage of tower)
after 1657. View from
southwest.*

12
*Old Brick Church, Isle of
Wight County, Virginia.
Plan.*

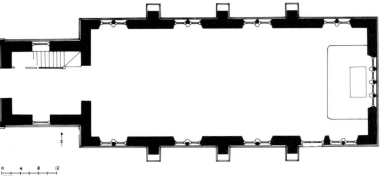

with a high hipped roof surmounted by a platform and belfry, its interior a single room with fixed benches and more often than not one or more galleries. The type was an adaptation of the English market hall—an adaptation, not an exact copy, for the English market hall was normally of two stories, with the ground story open on all four sides to the street or square to provide a covered space for the display and sale of produce and wares. (The first Boston Town House, built in 1657–58, was a substantial example on this side of the Atlantic.) In the meeting house there was no function for the open ground story and it was therefore omitted—much as in the Early Christian basilica of Western Christendom the galleries of the Roman civil basilica were omitted for want of a function. The English market hall was itself an adaptation of a type of house, built in England from Anglo-Saxon times to the fifteenth century in both town and country, with the living quarters on the second floor above a ground-floor storage cellar; in the market hall the walls of the cellar were omitted.

The only surviving seventeenth-century meeting house in New England is the Old Ship Meeting House at Hingham, Massachusetts, so called because its roof structure resembles an inverted ship's hull (10). It was built in 1681, enlarged in 1729 and again in 1755, when it also received a new belfry and porches; these additions, together with a restoration in 1930, have resulted in a building that cannot be regarded as typical. In the South, the architectural relics of the seventeenth-century Church of England are not much less rare; those still standing above ground amount to one church and a church tower in Virginia and one church in Maryland. All are of brick; not a single example of the churches of wooden frame construction, which constituted the great majority, has survived in the South from the entire colonial period. The most important is Newport Parish Church, or the Old Brick Church, near Smithfield, Virginia (11, 12).

The Old Brick Church is a remarkable building to have been begun a mere quarter of a century after the settlement of Jamestown, twenty miles upstream. It could easily be a parish church in an English county where brick was used for want of a suitable local stone. Here we have, in fact, the home-away-from-home ideal most completely realized in ecclesiastical terms. In England very few churches had been built since the Reformation; the country was amply provided with medieval churches and these were made over to accommodate the new liturgy. Gothic was therefore still the natural style for a church, and was to continue to be so in English eyes until Sir Christopher Wren invented classical paradigms for Anglican architecture in response to the need created by the Great Fire of

London in 1666. With its buttresses, pointed arches, and tracery, the Old Brick Church is essentially Gothic, an example of that survival which in England was to overlap the conscious revival of the medieval style. As for the crow-stepped gable, that was a feature which had reached England from Holland in the second half of the fifteenth century—well before the end of the Gothic era—and by this time was so thoroughly assimilated into English architecture that the builder of the church probably never thought of it as Dutch; in England a similar use of it is to be seen in the parish church of Woodham Walter, Essex, which was built in 1563. Yet the Old Brick Church is not without classical touches too: in the tower entrance with its round arch and triangular pediment, in the uppermost stage of the tower, which was built after 1657, and in the quoins that were added to the lower stages to the tower at the same time. An all-pervading naivety softens the contrast.

Buttresses, five a side, were also features of the first brick church of Bruton Parish, built at Middle Plantation (later Williamsburg) in 1683. A crude copy of a sketch made by a Swiss traveler in 1702 shows that it had a shaped gable of Anglo-Flemish type at the west end. In Dorchester County, Maryland, Trinity Church, probably of about the same date, has an apse, uncommon in English church architecture of its period. St. Mary's Chapel in St. Mary's City, built half a century earlier in 1634–38, was the first Roman Catholic church built by Englishmen in the New World. It had a Latin-cross plan and (as the finding of a mullion brick on the site has established) casement windows, but nothing is known of its general appearance. None of these churches had towers; besides the Old Brick Church, the only seventeenth-century churches in the South with towers were the first Chuckatuck church in Nansemond County, Virginia, and the first brick church at Jamestown, built in 1639–44, to which a tower was added in the very last year of the century. As for the frame churches, these were simple oblong buildings, about twice as long as they were broad, with the longer axis running east and west in conformity with Anglican practice.

Some of the most ambitious buildings of the colonial period served the needs of higher education. The first building for Harvard, the Old College, was built in 1638–42—but not very well, for in 1655 the then president described it as being "in a very ruinous condition" and it was demolished in 1678. It was wood-framed, with an E plan, and doubtless looked much like an English manor house of the later sixteenth century. Its replacement was the New College, or Harvard Hall, built in 1674–77. The external appearance of this is known from a print of 1726 by William Burgis. It was of brick and had a gambrel roof with dormers and cross gables; the doors were flanked by ball-topped pilasters in molded brick and there were some other would-be classical features. If it stood in England, one would assign it to the first rather than the second half of the seventeenth century. Of the appearance of the Indian College at Harvard, built in 1654–56 and demolished in 1698, nothing is known. That of Stoughton Hall, built in 1698–99 and demolished in 1781, is well recorded in the Burgis print. It was as classical as the Hutchinson House, but its fenestration with windows of two different widths (the narrower lighting the studies partitioned off from the keeping rooms) and three different widths of wall between them, gave its facade a quasi Mannerist variety.

The stylistic character of the only seventeenth-century collegiate building in the South, the first building of the College of William and Mary, is hard to determine, since the only record we have of its outward appearance is a copy of a sketch by the Swiss traveler who sketched the Bruton Parish Church of 1683. It was begun in 1695 at Middle Plantation, which in 1699 was renamed Williamsburg and became the capital of Virginia in succession to Jamestown, and finished in 1700. In 1705 it burned, though most of the walls survived the fire to be incorporated in the rebuilding, to Governor Alexander Spotswood's design, in 1710–16. It was to have been a square of 138 feet on plan, with a central court as in the colleges of Oxford and Cambridge but much smaller in proportion to the total area. Only the east range and the hall, which would have formed the center of the north range, were built. The east range was a full story higher than that of its Spotswood successor and had no central projection; it did have a second-floor balcony in the middle of the front. So much is certain.

What is not certain is that this first building of William and Mary was designed by Wren, despite the categorical statement in Hugh Jones's book of 1724 that it was "first modelled by Sir *Christopher Wren,* adapted to the Nature of the Country by the Gentlemen there." Telling against the attribution is the propagandist nature of Jones's book, on which he was working when Wren's great funeral in St. Paul's Cathedral could have suggested his name as one to conjure with, and the absence of any evidence that Thomas Hadley, who came from England to be "surveyor" of the building, had worked for Wren. For it, there are the considerations that the College was a royal foundation, for which Wren might have been asked to produce a design as Surveyor-General of the King's Works, and that Virginia was a part of the diocese of the Bishop of London, whose cathedral was even then being rebuilt to Wren's design.

Government buildings occupied little space in the seventeenth-century scene. Their character was thoroughly domestic. The first State House at Jamestown (ca. 1635), like many of the larger Elizabethan town houses in England, was a unit-house multiplied, in this case by three, with gables towards the street; the State House of 1676 at St. Mary's City had a cross-form plan with the porch balanced by a stair tower, like Bacon's Castle. State houses were, after all, simply houses for affairs of state. The first that could not have been taken for a house was in fact called by another name by the act of the Virginia Assembly that ordered its construction. This was the Capitol at Williamsburg, one of the only two buildings—the other was its successor of 1751–53—to be called capitols in the colonial period (13). The design was accepted in the last year of the century and the building went up in 1701–1705. It had two wings, one containing the House of Burgesses and clerk's office on the first floor with committee rooms above, the other the General Court and secretary's office with the Council Chamber and clerk's office above; the wings, which terminated to the south in semicircular tribunes, were linked by an arcaded loggia or "piazza" with a conference room above, and over the center rose a tall cupola of hexagonal plan.[2] It was an admirably functional design; the architect, whoever he was, had successfully freed himself from the house concept. Its sash windows were still quite a novelty even in England; the New York City Hall of 1699–1700, not dissimilar in many respects, still had casements. Yet the detail, the vocabulary of form, was domestic. And the classical orders, whose grandiloquence has so often in history been felt to be a sine qua non of governmental architecture, nowhere appeared. In fact they were not to appear as a major motif in the external design of any governmental building in the British colonies for another half-century.

Dutch Colonial

Both geography and the debt that English architecture owed to the Low Countries suggest that we turn to Dutch colonial architecture next. At once we meet a terminological inexactitude, for what we call Dutch colonial architecture has a much longer history than the Dutch colony of New Netherland, which was founded on paper with the chartering of the Dutch West India Company in Amsterdam in 1621 and practically with the building of a palisaded blockhouse and thirty bark-covered houses at New Amsterdam in 1626 and which ceased to exist when Peter Stuyvesant surrendered New Amsterdam to Colonel Richard Nicolls in 1664. Neither the change of rule under which New Netherland became New York and New Jersey nor the events that led to New York and New Jersey becoming independent states affected the development of the Dutch tradition of domestic architecture; nor was there any major change internal to that development such as occurred in British colonial architecture around 1700, and which in that case makes the separate treatment of the seventeenth and eighteenth centuries more than a matter of convenience.

14
Stadthuys (later City Tavern), New Amsterdam. 1641–42. From a lithograph by George Hayward after a sketch by Danckers.

After very simple beginnings—besides the bark-covered houses there were "hovels and holes"—the Dutch of New Amsterdam lost

little time building a town which must have seemed to its inhabitants as truly a home away from home as any in any colony anywhere. A lithograph from a sketch by Danckers shows how like its parent city New Amsterdam must have been (14). In 1679, when the sketch was made, the building in the center had for a quarter of a century served as the *Stadthuys* or townhouse; it was built in 1641–42 as the City Tavern, in which capacity it was much frequented by the British sailing between New England and Virginia. It had crow-stepped gables, like all the other buildings depicted except one, which had a hipped roof—another item in the invoice of Dutch contributions to English architecture. The *Stadthuys* was of stone; it may be assumed that the other buildings were of brick, which the Dutch preferred to all other materials and in the use of which their skill was unsurpassed.

Not one example of the standard Dutch town house, tall and narrow with the entrance in the gable end toward the street, has survived in New York or in Albany. Of the type of house represented by the *Stadthuys* the largest extant example—though owing to Dutch bourgeois carefulness not really a large building to be the manor house of the vast estate of Rensselaerswyck, formerly the patroonship of a director of the West India Company—is Crailo at Rensselaer, which was built about 1704. With its walls laid up in cross bond and its straight-sided gables finished with *muisetanden* (mouse-teeth), Crailo shows Dutch brickwork at its most characteristic. Other houses of the type are the Bries House at East Greenbush (1723) and the Leendert Bronck House at West Coxsackie (ca. 1738). The Dutch made less of chimneys than the English did and the end chimneys of such houses always go up inside the walls.

In northern New Jersey and southern New York, including Long Island, the preponderant type of house was quite different. Low and broad, of one or one and a half stories under a gently sloping roof which projected at least two feet beyond the walls to the front and rear, it was built of stone or wood or a combination of the two but never, apparently, of brick. The type is not found in Holland, and a theory once advanced that it was brought from Flanders by Flemish Protestant emigrants to New Netherland was not well founded. Whatever its origin, its development can be followed in existing or recorded examples. In the seventeenth century the roof was of two slopes only, with a flare given to the eaves by furring extra pieces to the rafters. Around 1700 a distinctive gambrel roof, with short upper slopes of about half the pitch of the lower, which retained their flared eaves, came into use. Then in the last quarter of the eighteenth century the *stoep* or raised platform before the front door

15
*Dyckman House, New
York City. Circa 1783.
Southwest view.*

16
*Dyckman House, New
York City. Plan of princi-
pal floor.*

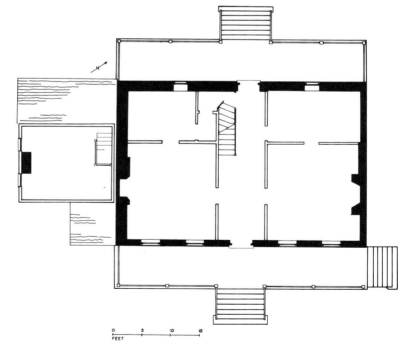

might be extended the full length of the house and posts added under the eaves, producing the equivalent of the English piazza or French *galerie* (15, 16).

Ecclesiastical architecture made a slow start in New Netherland. New Amsterdam itself had no regular church until 1642, when the need was filled by a building of stone, 72 feet by 52 feet on plan, paid for partly by subscription and partly with West India Company funds; the contractors were two Englishmen from Stamford, Connecticut. In the second half of the seventeenth century a number of octagonal churches were built; like John Wesley later, the Calvinists thought the octagon good for preaching. They were small, and were surrounded by tall candle-snuffer roofs. In the eighteenth century the Dutch in New Netherland reverted to the rectangular church plan. With its hipped roof and central cupola, the church built in 1715 at Albany looked much like a New England meeting house.

New Sweden and the Germans in Pennsylvania

Politically and economically, the colony of New Sweden on the Delaware River, which was chartered in 1636 and annexed by New Netherland seventeen years later, was the least successful of the attempts by European powers to stake their claims to a share of the American continent. And the only buildings of any size commissioned by Swedish communities that survive from the seventeenth century, the "Old Swedes" churches at Wilmington (1698–99) and Philadelphia (1698–1700), were both built by the same Philadelphia craftsmen, all born and trained in England. Yet the Swedes brought with them something that was to be of the greatest value as the course of empire took its way westward—the log cabin. In New England, garrison houses, as we have seen, were sometimes built of horizontal sawn logs, a Scottish technique. The construction of walls with round logs, notched at the corners and with projecting ends, was unknown in Britain, Holland, and France and never seen in America until the coming of the Swedes. On the frontier the log cabin so constructed was an ideal building, as it needed no nails and not much more skill with an axe than would normally be acquired in clearing a forest site. For two centuries, wherever wood was available, it was the frontiersman's first permanent dwelling.

The Germans, who settled in Pennsylvania in great number in the eighteenth century, were another people who had built with hewn logs in their homeland and continued to do so in America. Although concealed by clapboards, this is the method of construction of the *Saron* or Sister House, built in 1743 by a monastic community of the Seventh Day Baptists at Ephrata. The *Saron* and the adjoining *Saal* or Prayer House of 1740 are astonishing examples of the sur-

vival of medieval building forms into the mid-eighteenth century; the Cloister, as it is called, reminds one of the buildings in Dürer's engravings (17). Unlike the *Saron,* the *Saal* is a frame structure of oak with an infilling of stones and clay and a covering of clapboards. In other German buildings in Pennsylvania frame and infilling were left exposed to the weather as what in England would be called half-timber work—*fachwerkbau,* to give it its German name. Also a medieval technique, *fachwerkbau* was employed in German farm-houses in Wisconsin as late as the 1850s.

The French in the Mississippi Valley

The French in their earliest buildings in North America employed a kind of construction with logs set upright in the ground. This was called *en pieux* in New France and *poteaux en terre* in the Mississippi valley settlements. It differed from English palisade construction (rarely used for houses) in that the logs were hewn flat on two sides, to form the inner and outer surfaces of the wall, and set a few inches apart, the spaces between them being filled with a mixture of grass and clay (*bouzillage*) or stones and clay (*pierrotage*). An improvement was made when the logs were set on a sill instead of in the earth. This, *poteaux sur sole,* is the construction used in the oldest house surviving in the Midwest, now called Cahokia Courthouse, which was built about 1737 (18).

Whether *poteaux* construction was known in France is uncertain. The type of house represented by Cahokia Courthouse was not; it is a striking exception to the home-away-from-home rule. The dominant feature from which it derives its special character is the hipped roof (shingled at Cahokia, though originally it was probably thatched), which changes pitch to spread out over the veranda or *galerie* surrounding the whole house. Often the *galerie* had a raised floor and a railing, like the Dutch *stoep.* When the main floor is raised on a brick ground story and the *galerie* on brick piers, we have arrived at the Louisiana plantation house—though this should not be understood as an account of the actual historical development, for it is possible that the Cahokia type, so to call it, was a simplification of the plantation house. The oldest surviving plantation house in Louisiana is Parlange, at New Roads, built about 1750 (19, 20). Few buildings have ever been better adapted to the climate and physical conditions of a region than this, with the main rooms insulated by the capacious roof from the heat of the sun above and by the brick ground story from the damp of the earth below, the French windows providing maximum ventilation and the *galerie* an amplitude of cool and dry outdoor space.[3] No wonder such houses continued to be built, with only minor changes of stylistic detail, down to the middle of the nineteenth century.

In New Orleans (founded in 1718) the commonest kind of construction at first was *colombage sur sole.* Of medieval origin, this comprised massive posts with their lower ends tenoned into the sill

18
*Cahokia Courthouse,
Cahokia, Illinois. Circa
1737. General view.*

19
Parlange, Pointe Coupée Parish, Louisiana. Circa 1750. View from the south.

20
Parlange, Pointe Coupée Parish, Louisiana. Plan of principal floor.

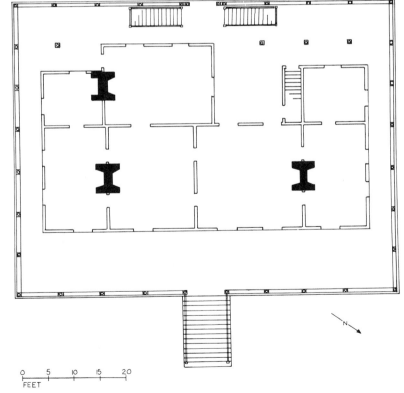

0   5   10   15   20
FEET

21
St. Louis Cathedral, New Orleans, Louisiana. Gilberto Guillemard, 1789–94. Measured drawing of facade by Benjamin Henry Latrobe.

(for the first story) or the girt (for the second) and their upper into the girt or plate, with diagonal braces, more often than not forming crosses, between them; the braces were also tenoned at both ends into the horizontal pieces and not, as in the English frame, at one end into posts. When there was an infilling of bricks, this was known as *briqueté entre poteaux* construction. Walls so built were faced with boards or plastered, or sometimes in New Orleans and its neighborhood left exposed to the weather (much to their detriment).

The first parish church of St. Louis was built to the design of the engineer-in-chief of Louisiana, Adrien de Pauger, in 1724–27. It was of cruciform plan, with a deep presbytery terminating in a half-octagon, and of *briqueté entre poteaux*, plastered on the exterior; its facade was pedimented, with panelled walls, rusticated quoins, and a circular window over the arched doorway.

De Pauger died before his church was finished and was succeeded as engineer-in-chief by Ignace François Broutin, who in 1727 designed the first building, of *briqueté entre poteaux* again, for the convent of Ursuline nuns who arrived in New Orleans that year. In 1729 Pierre Baron, a naturalist who had been sent to Louisiana by the French Academy, was appointed to the office. Baron completed the Ursuline Convent, with some changes in the design, and in 1730

22
Cabildo, New Orleans,
Louisiana. Gilberto
Guillemard, 1795–1801.
Front facing Jackson
Square.

built the first major brick building in New Orleans, the prison, which was a neat exercise in the Louis XV style. In 1732 he returned to France, and Broutin became engineer-in-chief again. In 1745 Broutin designed the second Ursuline Convent, to replace the building he had designed less than twenty years before, for whose timbers the humidity had already proved too much. Built of brick, the second Ursuline Convent is the only public building in New Orleans of the period of French rule to survive. The Ursulines were teachers; the order was founded in the sixteenth century to teach girls, whom the Jesuits, greatest of the teaching orders, did not teach. They were a poor order, and their buildings were plain. The Ursuline Convent at New Orleans has much in common with that at Bayeux, but even more with the Cistercian Abbey of Auberive, which had a three-bay pedimented center with the same curved roofs to the dormers as Broutin's original design.[4]

The cession of New Orleans and Louisiana west of the Mississippi to Spain in 1764 under the Treaty of San Ildefonso had little effect on the architecture of the region. The Spanish governor's house at Baton Rouge was a simple if spacious example of the Cahokia Court-house type, and the three buildings that went up on the northwest side of the Place d'Armes (now Jackson Square) in New Orleans at the end of the century were as French as the surname of their architect, Gilberto Guillemard, for all that he had spent nearly twenty years in the military service of Spain when he designed the first of them. The ground was cleared for this monumental group by two fires. The first, in 1788, destroyed De Pauger's church, the Casa Curial or Rectory, and the Cabildo or Council House (built in 1769–70 with a *galerie* across the street front), besides damaging other public buildings in the vicinity; the second, in 1794, destroyed buildings that had been repaired since the first but spared the new church for its dedication two weeks later.

The rebuilding of St. Louis began in 1789, the whole cost being borne by a commissioner of the Cabildo already famous for his benefactions to the city, Don Andres Almonester y Roxas. The new church had a broad two-story facade with a pedimented center and a tower, octagonal from the ground up, at either end. In 1820 Benjamin Henry Latrobe added a third tower immediately behind the center of the facade. It was the collapse of this in 1850 that led to the replacement of Guillemard's building, the best record of which is an elevation by Latrobe (21). Guillemard's other two buildings, the Cabildo and the Casa Curial (now the Presbytère), still stand (22). Both were begun in 1795; the Cabildo was finished in 1801, its twin not until 1815. Almonester, the donor of the cathedral, undertook the building of the Casa Curial at his own expense and also financed the construction of the Cabildo. Either building could be an *hôtel de ville* in the French provinces; the finest example of the type, which Guillemard conceivably had in mind, is the Hôtel de Ville at Nancy, designed by Héré de Corny in 1750.[5]

Old World Traditions and the Mercantile Impulse

For all their differences, the buildings of the English, Dutch, Swedish, German, and French colonists in North America had two things in common, one of which affected their character individually, while the other, by providing a milieu that favored certain building types over others, affected the architectural scene as a whole. First, they were built by and for people for whom home was Europe, so that to be fully understood they must be seen in relation to the European architectural traditions of their builders. Second, they were built in colonies which were founded—whatever personal motives may have impelled individual settlers—for mercantile purposes. Because of the different aims, methods, and history of Spanish colonization in the New World, neither statement would be true of the buildings to be considered in our next chapter.

A New World Tradition

Spanish colonial architecture had a history going back more than a century, to the founding, in 1496, of Santo Domingo on the island of Hispaniola, when the earliest Spanish colonial building still standing in the United States was begun—and more than eighty years in Mexico, whence the colonists who extended the dominion of Spain into the regions north of the present border came. At first, in the Caribbean, it had been an unmodified transplant from Europe, brought by designers and builders who came directly from the Peninsula. In Mexico, however, variants and transmutations of the Spanish styles appeared almost as soon as they were introduced. This was due not so much to the employment of Indian labor, although that was certainly a factor, as to the sheer volume of building, particularly church building, and the creation of the ethnically mixed *mestizo* class who "inevitably responded to a different range of aesthetic stimuli than did the Spanish-born or the *criollo.*"[1] An unsurpassed richness and inventiveness in sculptural decoration constituted the great strength of the architecture that resulted; an extreme conservatism (not to say timidity) in planning and construction was its general weakness.

In this chapter, then, we shall be concerned with buildings which with some important exceptions were the products of an architectural tradition that had already developed non-European characteristics, even though all the major changes of style that punctuated its history were due to waves of influence from the Old World. One of the most notable of the exceptions is a work of military architecture. Others of quite another kind are in New Mexico, where special conditions resulted in the creation of a distinctive regional style.

New Mexico

Nothing could be less like the first State House at Jamestown with its serried gables than the Palace of the Governors at Santa Fe, built in 1610–14 and still in great part surviving (23). Originally forming the side of the *presidio* or fortified enclosure, which measured more than 400 feet from east to west and more than 800 feet from north to south, it was built, as no British colonial building was, by Indian labor, and incorporates, as no British colonial building does, both European and Indian techniques. Adobe, of which the walls are constructed, was a material with which the Indians were thoroughly familiar; but before the Spaniards came they had used it in mass and never, as here, in bricks. (The sun-dried adobe bricks of Spanish New Mexico were very different from the burnt clay bricks of the British colonies, measuring about ten by five by eighteen inches and weighing fifty to sixty pounds each.) The flat roof, with its projecting beams or *vigas* and covering of earth, is of the type used by the

23
Palace of the Governors,
Santa Fe, New Mexico.
1610–14; portales *restored*
1909. Southwest view.

Indians in their own pueblos. The porch or *portal* facing the town square, on the other hand, is purely Spanish; the capitals of the wooden posts, resembling back-to-back brackets and therefore called bracket capitals (*zapatas* in Spanish), were a feature which the Moors took to Spain and which is found nowhere else in Europe.[2] Originally each end of the range toward the square was carried up to form a tower, the eastern one containing a chapel and the western a magazine.

This balancing of structures for the worship of God and the storage of gunpowder and weapons may be seen as symbolic of the aims and methods of Spain in America generally. In New Mexico, however, colonization was much more the work of missionaries, who were Friars of the Regular Observance of St. Francis, than of the military. The achievements of these Franciscans, who were nearly all Europeans by birth, are astonishing by any standards. As George Kubler has put it, "aside from the task of diverting a massive population from its ancient beliefs, these men executed ambitious building projects for which they themselves were the architects, contractors, foremen, and building-supply agents."

What was always one of the largest as well as the most dramatically sited of the New Mexico missions still stands structurally whole, though a victim of misguided "improvements" in recent years. This is the mission at Acoma, the pueblo on an isolated mesa, with its church dedicated to San Estevan (24, 25). The plan of the complex is unusual in that the *convento* or monastery lies to the north of the church, rather than the south, and the friar's house, which is surmounted by a covered *mirador* or viewing platform, forms one of the outer corners of the *convento* instead of standing next to the church.[3] In front of the church a walled enclosure, the *atrio*, served

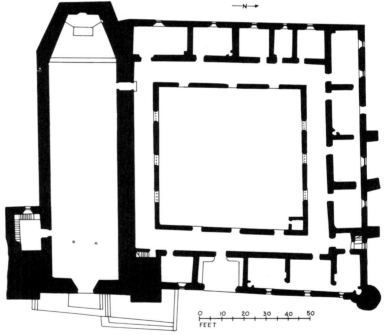

24
San Estevan, Acoma,
New Mexico. Between
1629 and 1642. Southeast
view.

25
San Estevan, Acoma,
New Mexico. Plan of
church and convento.

as a burial ground and could also be used for outdoor worship. The *atrio* is an ubiquitous feature of religious architecture in Spanish America. But unlike any outside New Mexico, the *atrio* at Acoma lies to the east of the church, for the church is entered through the east facade and has a western sanctuary.

This reverse orientation, or occidentation, is a matter to which we shall return. The facade of San Estevan is of the two-towered type whose history in Europe goes back to the end of the first millennium; some have seen its origins in a type of church facade with an arched central entrance flanked by vertical features, which may by courtesy be called towers, that appeared five centuries earlier in the East, where the motif was familiar as that of the palace gateway and thus symbolic of royalty. The facade of San Estevan with its battered walls and bare surfaces and rectangular openings is quite unlike any medieval two-towered facade in Europe; if one seems to see in it some resemblance to the pylon of an Egyptian temple the fancy is not an altogether empty one, for the pylon was also a royal palace symbol and the batter of its walls is due to the imitation in stone of an adobe prototype.

To enter the church at Acoma is to receive an impression of spaciousness greater than what might be expected from its actual dimensions: 128 feet by 30 feet on plan and 30 feet in height, so that the volume is practically a quadruple cube. How miraculous such a space must have seemed to the Indians, who had never known anything larger than a *kiva*! And their wonder would have been increased by a special lighting effect. Today San Estevan has only three windows, two in the south wall and one above the choir loft in the east.[4] In the bright light of New Mexico they are enough for all practical purposes. However, the church originally had another window between the roof of the nave and that of the sanctuary, which was two or three feet higher than the nave. The effect of this transverse clerestory was to flood the sanctuary and the altar with light—natural light, but to the Indian worshipper in the nave, who could not see its source and who was not accustomed to windows, surely supernatural.[5]

The use of the transverse clerestory accounts for the occidentation of San Estevan and for the extreme rarity of eastern sanctuaries in New Mexico.[6] Services were usually held in the morning; churches were therefore planned with the sanctuary to the west or north to give the altar maximum illumination from the morning sun through the transverse clerestory. As for its origin, the feature was apparently peculiar to New Mexico. Whoever invented it—presumably one of the missionary friars—had a real understanding of the principles of

26
Santo Tomás, Trampas,
New Mexico. Circa 1760.
Southwest view before
addition of wooden bell
turrets in 1967.

the Baroque—and a precocious one, seeing that Bernini's S. Andrea al Quirinale, the first Roman church in which the high altar was illuminated from a hidden source, was not begun until 1658. In comparison with the Old Brick Church at Smithfield, built in the same decade, San Estevan may seem unsophisticated in structure and crude in finish. Yet it is a building that is of its age in a sense in which the still Gothic church in Virginia is not.

Two plan types were employed in the colonial churches of New Mexico. Of the single–cell type extant examples include, beside Acoma, San Miguel, Santa Fe (after 1640), San José, Laguna (ca. 1700), Santa Ana in the pueblo of the same name (1734), and the Santuario of Chimayo (early nineteenth century). The other type has a transept between the sanctuary and the nave. Examples of this standing in good condition are Santo Tomás, Trampas (ca. 1760), and San Francisco, Ranchos de Taos (ca. 1780) (26, 27, 28). These are both of the second half of the eighteenth century, but the plan appeared early in the seventeenth, as is evidenced by the remains of Nuestra Señora de los Angeles de Porciuncula, Pecos (before 1625), and the substantial ruins of the stone-built churches of San Gregorio, Abó (ca. 1630), and La Concepcion, Quarai (before 1633). It derived from the Gesù in Rome, built as the head church of the Jesuit order between 1568 and 1577, to which the architect Vignola gave a new kind of plan, especially suitable for preaching, by compressing the transept arms to serve as large side chapels, lit, like the sanctuary, by windows in the drum of the dome over the crossing. In the

27
*San Francisco, Ranchos de
Taos, New Mexico. Circa
1780. East view.*

28
*San Francisco, Ranchos de
Taos, New Mexico. Plan.*

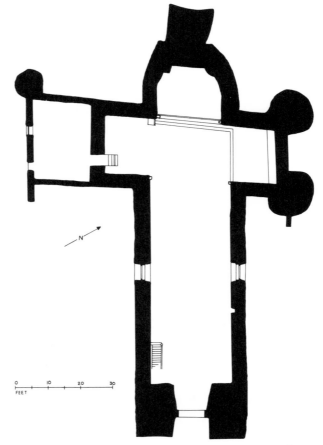

29
San José, Laguna, New Mexico. Circa 1700. Facade with espadaña.

30
San José, Laguna, New Mexico. Interior, looking west.

seventeenth and eighteenth centuries the Gesù was the most influential church in the Catholic world. In Mexico many hundreds of parish churches are versions of it, simplified as a rule by omitting the side chapels but retaining the dome over the transept crossing. In New Mexico it was simplified further by omitting the dome and substituting a transverse clerestory for the windows in its drum.

A variant of the two-towered facade as seen at Acoma and Ranchos de Taos (and formerly at Santa Cruz and in the parish church of Santa Fe) has a balcony stretching from one tower to the other at the level of the choir loft. The balcony may have been used in conjunction with the *atrio* for outdoor worship. If a sketch of the abandoned church at Pecos made in 1846 shows the original facade, as it probably does, the balconied facade was introduced before 1625; an example from the late seventeenth century is at Zuni, where the church, now in ruins, was built about 1660, while eighteenth-century examples include San Felipe (ca. 1706) and Trampas (ca. 1760). The simplest and commonest type of facade has neither towers nor balcony; it consists of a plain wall pierced by the doorway and the choir-loft window and carried up above the roof as an *espadaña*. Such is the facade of San José, Laguna, built about 1700 (29). The interior of this church is notable for the Indian murals—Indian in style and iconography as well as execution—in the nave, contrasting with, and yet as an expression of pueblo culture complementing, the purely Spanish *retablo* and decorations in the sanctuary (30).[7]

The church architecture of New Mexico changed hardly at all during the two and a half centuries of Spanish and Mexican rule, and when a flood destroyed the church of Santo Domingo Pueblo in 1886 it was rebuilt without a single feature it might not have had in the seventeenth century. The early friars set out to build churches which should be functional liturgically and Christian and Catholic in their symbolism, employing only structural principles and techniques already known to their Indian converts or easily learnt by them. The results often possess certain qualities, attractive to a century that values primitivism in art, which it would be an act of unnecessary self-denial not to enjoy because they are due to accident rather than intention.

Florida

There is nothing regional about the design of the Castillo de San Marcos at St. Augustine, the most important architectural relic of Spanish rule in Florida (31, 32). Here, in contrast to the mission churches of New Mexico, is a building which is not only purely European but also international in style—international as only military architecture was when it was begun in 1672. Substantially

31
Castillo de San Marcos
(Fort Marion), St. Augus-
tine, Florida. Ignazio
Daza, 1672–87. Curtain,
bastion, and cavalier.

32
Castillo de San Marcos,
St. Augustine, Florida.
Plan.

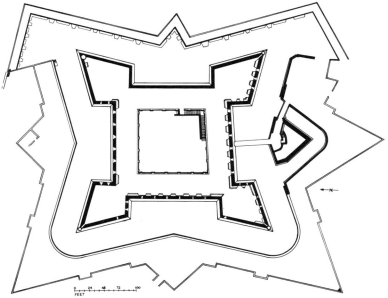

finished by 1687, the Castillo de San Marcos represents a type of fort whose prototype was built at Nettuno in Italy in 1501–1502 to the design of the brothers Antonio and Giuliano da Sangallo. Military architects had been confronted with the problems presented by cannon fire since the second quarter of the fourteenth century; the great innovation of the Sangalli in what has been called "the military equivalent of Bramante's Tempietto in Rome"[8] was the substitution of triangular bastions, no higher than the outer walls or curtains, for the round towers of traditional fortress design.

On plan the Castillo de San Marcos is a square of about 200 feet, with bastions projecting about 90 feet from each corner. Its parapet is pierced for sixty-four guns, which were hauled from the inner court of parade to the firing platform or *terreplein* up a ramp (now converted to stairs). Entrance was by drawbridge over the moat and a doorway with a portcullis in the south curtain; on the outermost corner of the northeast bastion stands a round viewing tower, or cavalier.

The designer of the Castillo de San Marcos was Ignacio Daza of Havana. His greatest contemporary in the field of military architecture was the Frenchman Sebastien le Prestre de Vauban, and Vauban's influence is paramount at St. Augustine. However, the design of the bastions, which have acute outer angles and their shorter walls, or flanks, at right angles to the curtains, does not follow Vauban's practice, which was to make the outer angles of the bastions obtuse and return their flanks at right angles to the faces, as their longer walls were called. The batter or slope of the face of the ramparts, with the 25-foot-high walls thinning from 12 feet at the base to 7 feet at the top, is close enough to the batter of one-sixth of the total height employed by Vauban.

Daza's fort withstood three British sieges, in 1702, 1728, and 1740. Its success was due in large part to the material of which it is built, the *coquina* or shell-limestone quarried on Anastasia Island nearby. In forts of stone or brick, casualties among the defenders were often caused by flying pieces of masonry shattered by cannon balls, and by the seventeenth century this had led to the building of ramparts of solid earth, with stone or brick used only for their outer facing and for parapets and buttresses. But *coquina* was no ordinary stone. Nathaniel Johnson, governor of South Carolina, bore witness to its special qualities in a report to the British Board of Trade in 1720. The castle, he wrote, was built of a stone which looked like free stone but was much better for fortifications. "It will not splinter," he explained, "but gives way to cannon balls as though you would stick a knife into cheese."

Although built later, in 1736, the Fuerte de Matanzas, the ruins of which stand in the marshes fifteen miles south of St. Augustine, was essentially medieval in plan, with a keep. A third example of Spanish military architecture in Florida is the Fuerte de San Carlos in Pensacola, rebuilt in its present semi-circular form, of brick, in 1783, the year in which Florida was returned to Spain after twenty years of British rule. As for ecclesiastical architecture in Florida, the facade of the Cathedral of San Agustin, built in 1793–98 to the design of the engineer Diaz Berrio, with a correctly detailed Doric doorway and a tall gable wall or *espadaña,* pierced for bells, was retained and restored when the church was rebuilt and enlarged after a fire in 1887. Of the forty or so missions founded in Florida by the Franciscans beginning in 1593 the architectural remains are negligible.

Texas and Arizona

In Texas the Franciscans founded their first mission, near Nacogdoches, in 1690. It was followed by five more in east Texas, but trouble with the Indians and the French soon led to their abandonment. Activity was renewed under the leadership of the dynamic Fray Antonio Margil in 1716. By 1731 a dozen missions had been established. Today there are three eighteenth-century mission churches standing in Texas, all in or near San Antonio, while ninety miles to the southeast, at Goliad, stands the chapel of the Presidio la Bahia, which was established in 1749 to protect the mission of Espiritu Santo de Zuñiga.[9]

These four buildings must be seen in the context of Mexican eighteenth-century church architecture. The earliest, Nuestra Señora de la Purisima Concepcion de Acuna, was begun by 1743 and dedicated by 1755 (33, 34). With its Gesù-derived Latin-cross plan, barrel-vaulted nave, and two-towered facade, this church could have been built almost anywhere in Mexico in the early eighteenth or, for that matter, the seventeenth century; the merlon-like features on the parapets, at the corners of the towers and around the drum under the dome, are reminiscent of the sixteenth. The drum is circular in plan—unexpectedly, for octagonal drums were the rule all over Mexico between the sixteenth century and the advent of Neo-classicism, even when the domes resting on them were circular. In northern Mexico arches and windows were often polygonal rather than circular; the most influential model in this respect was the Basilica of Guadalupe north of Mexico City, built between 1695 and 1709. The main doorway of the Concepcion, with its half-octagon arch, is an example of the fashion, as is also the octagonal window

33
Nuestra Señora de la Purisima Concepcion de Acuna, San Antonio, Texas. 1743–55. Facade and towers.

34
Nuestra Señora de la Purisima Concepcion de Acuna, San Antonio, Texas. Plan.

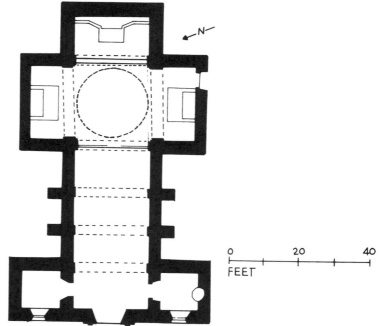

in the facade of the Presidio la Bahia chapel, which was built sometime after 1765.

The church of the mission of San Antonio de Valero, better known
as the Alamo, was begun in 1744 and still under construction in
1777. Here it is the centerpiece of the facade, the *portada,* that claims
attention (35). It was never finished; clearly a second order with
columns flanking the upper niches was intended. It represents a
regional style of Baroque that flourished in the far north of Mexico
in the second quarter of the eighteenth century, for it is modelled
on the lateral *portada* of Durango, the cathedral of the diocese that
included Texas. The imitation is not too skillful; the square blocks
between the columns and the entablature are a solecism, resulting
no doubt from a misreading of the architrave in the prototype, and
the raising of the heads of the niches above the level of the crown
of the central arch is another questionable departure.

In San José y San Miguel de Aguayo we encounter something
altogether different (36). The mission, founded by Margil in 1720,
was established on its present site about 1739. The present church
was built in 1768–77; it is of limestone with sandstone trim and has
an octagonal dome between the groin-vaulted nave and the sanctuary, which is barrel-vaulted, but no transept. The facade is flanked
by two square towers; only one of them received its belfry stage,
which has something of the clumsiness of the Alamo *portada.* There
is nothing clumsy about the *portada* of San José. This and the
window of the baptistery on the south side of the church are said to
have been carved by one Pedro Huizar. The designer of these two
features, whether Huizar or another, was fluent in the idiom of the
last, near-Rococo phase of the Mexican Ultra-Baroque. Characteristic
motifs of the style are the shell-like ornament or *rocaille,* the mixtilinear arch and window, and the niche pilaster. All are employed
in San José with a skill that invites comparison with the masterpieces
of the style in central Mexico.[10]

Niche-pilasters such as flank the doorway of San José, which are
the result of a desire to turn the seemingly if not actually structural
pilaster into a purely decorative feature, are essentially Rococo, even
though they were never used in France, where the style originated.
In Mexico they first appeared in conjunction with a distortion of the
classical column which was used by the architects of the Ultra-
Baroque so much that it has been suggested that the period from
about 1730 to about 1770 might be called the *estípite* age. The *estípite*
may be roughly but adequately defined as a stack of square balusters
with a capital on top. Like so many features of Spanish Baroque it
is of sixteenth-century, Mannerist origin; its lineage may be traced

35
San Antonio de Valero
(The Alamo), San Anto-
nio, Texas. 1744–after
1777. Facade.

36
San José y San Miguel de
Aguayo, San Antonio,
Texas. Pedro Huizar,
1768–77. Facade.

back to the downward-tapering pilasters of Michelangelo's Lauren-
tian Library in Florence through the fantastic elaborations of that
theme in the engravings of the German Wendel Dieterling. After
1770 the *estípite* yielded to the niche-pilaster as the dominant motif
in Mexican facades and *retablos*.

That the *estípite* should be absent from San José yet still be the
main decorative motif of the later San Xavier del Bac, near Tucson,
Arizona, shows how remoteness could delay stylistic change (37, 38,
39). (Tucson is about a thousand miles further than San Antonio
from Mexico City.) This church was begun in 1775 and the main
fabric was completed by 1783; the facade and the elaborate interior,
with three *retablos* and much painting and other carved plasterwork,
were not completed until 1797. The facade would hardly have passed
muster in central Mexico even in 1775. The meager *estípites* are
deployed across it at wide intervals, as if Lorenzo Rodriguez had
never demonstrated in the *sagrario* of Mexico Cathedral the special
rhythm that the combination of *estípites* and niche-pilasters could
impart to a facade. Inside the church the iconographically comprehensive *retablos* are more sophisticated, while the structure itself is
both logically developed as a design and notably well built of brick.
The plan once again is of the modified Gesù type. A hemispherical
dome is set on an octagonal drum over the crossing and there are
oval saucer domes over the sanctuary, transept chapels, and nave;
a round-domed sacristy is neatly fitted into the angle between the
right transept and the sanctuary. The design is attributed to Ignacio
Gaona, who is said to have been a Spaniard and to have had a brother
who was his assistant.

Bac was one of the northernmost of the twenty-four missions
founded by the Jesuit Eusebio Kino between 1687 and about 1700 in
Sonora and Arizona—Pimeria Alta, as the whole area was then
called. After 1767, when the Jesuits were expelled from Mexico,
these missions were placed in the charge of the Franciscans, who
rebuilt most of their churches before Mexican independence ended
government support. San Xavier is a more ambitious building than
any erected by the Franciscans in Sonora and, despite its shortcom-
ings, much more literate in design than the only other mission
church in Arizona of which there are more than slight remains, San
José de Tumacácori. This was begun in 1806. Its facade, with a
portada of a two-story type going back to the sixteenth century,
shows that whoever was responsible for it knew that the Baroque
was over, while in breaking so many of the rules of classical design
it suggests that he knew little else.

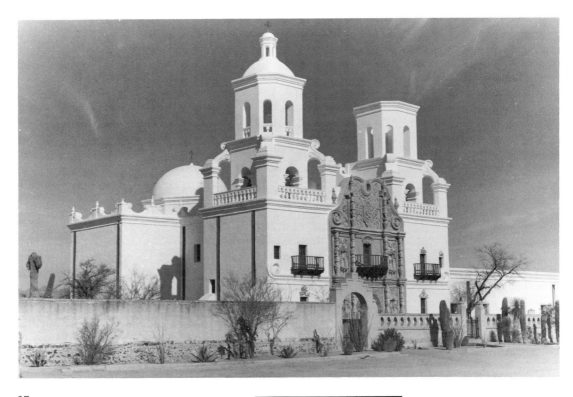

37
San Xavier del Bac, near
Tucson, Arizona. Ignacio
Gaona, 1775–97. South-
west view.

38
San Xavier del Bac, near
Tucson, Arizona. Plan.

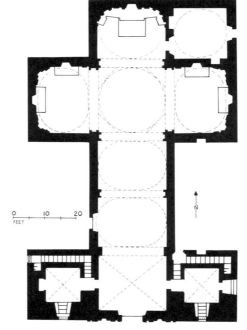

39
*San Xavier del Bac, near
Tucson, Arizona. Interior,
looking north.*

California

The colonization of California—Alta California, as it was called to distinguish it from the peninsula to the south—was motivated by the fear of Russia expanding her American territory southward from Alaska. It began in 1769, with the establishment of the first *presidio* and the first mission at San Diego. The *padre presidente* to whom the religious side of colonization was entrusted was the heroic Franciscan Fray Junipero Serra. By his death in 1784 he had founded nine missions; his successor Fray Fermin de Lasuén founded nine more by 1803, and by 1823 there was a chain of twenty-one missions and two *asistencias* stretching from San Diego to Sonoma. Three more *presidios* were established, at Monterey, San Francisco, and Santa Barbara.

Of the Californian *presidios* practically nothing remains. Of the missions the remains are substantial and extensive, the more extensive because—in contrast to the New Mexico missions, where the mission buildings consisted of the church and the *convento,* which housed one or rarely two friars and their domestics—they had to house the great numbers of Indian converts who worked on the agricultural and stock-raising estates of which they were the centers.

As in all the mission fields, the first buildings were simple in the extreme. The chapel of San Juan Capistrano, completed in 1777 and the only church of Serra's time still standing, was typical. Ninety feet long but only seventeen feet wide, it has a sanctuary raised three steps above the nave floor and a choir loft at the opposite end; it is built of adobe with a wooden roof which was originally thatched. (Manufacture of the red roofing tiles that became a regional feature began in 1786). All the other extant churches date from the 1790s or later.

There are no *estípites* in California; this is a Neo-Classical architecture in its flat wall surfaces and clarity of form, albeit that in only one major structure, the facade of the church of the mission of Santa Barbara, is an ancient classical motif employed at full scale. A spirit of compromise is apparent even in the ornate facade of the Capilla Real at Monterey—not a mission church but the chapel of the *presidio*—which dates from 1794. There are still some touches of the Baroque, in the shell heads of the niches, the shell above the relief of the Virgin of Guadalupe, and the breaking of the curved and scrolled gable to embrace the Virgin's aedicule. The total effect, however, is dry and linear, with none of the plasticity of the Ultra-Baroque.

The earliest of the major mission churches standing today is San Carlos Borromeo at Carmel, begun in 1793 (40). The master mason, who was in all probability the designer too, was Manuel Estevan

Ruiz. It would seem that Ruiz, if he was the designer, knew the work of Francisco Antonio Guerrero y Torres, who (in Kubler's phrase) ''broke the spell'' of the *estípite* in Mexico City. In the facade the combination of classical doorway and stellar *claraboya* is reminiscent of Guerrero's Pocito Chapel of 1779; the extraordinary interior, with a barrel vault of boards supported by parabolic arches of stone and the upper part of the walls and the Doric pilaster order bent inwards to meet the curve of the arches, shows—even though the forms are quite different—the same experimental approach to stone-cutting, daring indeed when the labor force was Indian and had to be trained on the job, as the *patio* of Guerrero's Valparaíso House (now the Banco de Mexico) of 1769. The ovoid dome crowning the south tower is of Muslim derivation; the ogee molding above the south door and the doorway to the mortuary chapel, with its mixtilinear arch flanked by composite piers supporting a Doric entablature, recall the Gothic Plateresque of Spain. The Muslim, Gothic, and Plateresque traditions all made their contributions to Spanish Baroque architecture in the Old World and the New; here they have survived the Baroque age to mitigate the austerities of Neo-classicism.

In 1812 an earthquake damaged the vault of San Carlos Borromeo and in the following year it was taken down; what one sees today is the result of a rebuilding in the 1930s.[11] The same earthquake brought down a large part of the second church of the mission of San Juan Capistrano, killing forty Indian worshippers. This church was begun in 1797, the year in which the main structure of San Carlos was finished, and dedicated in 1806; the architect was Isidoro Aguilar of Culiacán. The sanctuary still stands, with enough of the walls, arches, and internal order to permit a paper restoration of the

41
*San Luis Rey de Francia,
near Oceanside, Califor-
nia. Antonio Peyri, 1811–
15. Church from south.*

42
*San Luis Rey de Francia,
near Oceanside, Califor-
nia. Plan.*

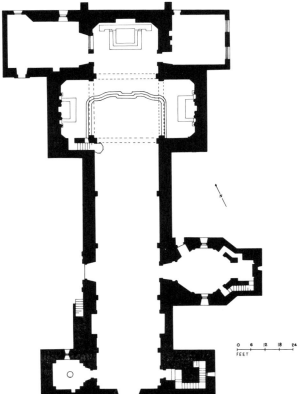

43
Santa Barbara, Santa Barbara, California. Antonio Ripoll, 1815–20. Facade.

body of the church, although the exact form of the tower must remain in doubt. It was the largest of the Spanish churches in California—180 feet long, with a nave 30 feet wide and 60 feet high—and the first of cruciform plan. The nave and crossing were vaulted with domes, and the transept arms, like the sanctuary, with groin vaults. The entire structure was of sandstone, quarried six miles away.

After the earthquake of 1812 no more high vaults were built in California, and masonry domes were confined to towers, baptisteries, and mortuary chapels. Thus the dome over the crossing of San Luis Rey de Francia, built to the design of Fray Antonio Peyrí in 1811–15 as the second cruciform church in the colony (and the last, as it turned out), is of wood, while the octagonal mortuary chapel is covered with an octagonal dome of brick (41, 42); the nave is wooden-roofed, though clearly designed for a vault. The facade of San Luis Rey is carried up above the roof of the church as an *espadaña* of mixtilinear profile. The resemblance of this feature to the shaped gables of Bacon's Castle may not be purely coincidental; that is, it may have reached Spain from the Low Countries. Yet it is unnecessary to suppose that it travelled to California from anywhere but Mexico. Many Baroque facades in Mexico have *espadañas* of similar outline, which tend to go unnoticed behind the incrustation of ornament and decorative features. In San Luis Rey, as also in San Diego de Alcalá (1808–13), with the stripping away of all Baroque ornament and the centering of the facades on *portadas* of Neo-Classical severity, the *espadañas* themselves have become the only decorative feature

The rebuilding of the church of Santa Barbara in 1815–20 was made necessary by the complete destruction of its predecessor by the 1812 earthquake (43). The architect was Padre Antonio Ripoll, who in designing the facade consulted a Spanish edition of Vitruvius in a copy still preserved in the mission library. One of the plates shows a tetrastyle temple portico with a fret interlace on the frieze, and this Ripoll took as his model, increasing the number of columns to six, attenuating their shafts, and standing them on high pedestals. The result is hardly Vitruvian; the splitting of the columns into two groups of three to accommodate the doorway is naive, and Ionic capitals were beyond the technical skill of the Indian stonemasons. On aesthetic grounds one may well prefer the masculine and unaffected towers. But Ripoll's temple-form facade brought the story of ecclesiastical architecture in Spanish California to an end with a brave Neo-Classical gesture.

Within a year of the completion of Santa Barbara the Mexican revolution set in motion forces that led to increased activity in domestic building in Alta California, resulting in the single-storied but spacious *casas de campo* and *casas de pueblo* of the later twenties and the thirties. In 1835–37 the Bostonian Thomas Larkin, United State consul in Monterey, built the first two-story house, initiating a peaceful pentration by American architectural fashions a decade before the transfer of rule. Not only did the second story catch on; so did the two-storied porches, which were perhaps suggested to Larkin by his experience of the piazzas of houses in North Carolina during ten years he spent in that state. The result was what has come to be called the Monterey Style, the products of whose revival in the 1930s far outnumber the nineteenth-century examples.

A Time of Change

In British America the period 1700–76 saw many times as much building as the seventeenth century did. And architecture underwent a fundamental change. At the opening of the period the form and appearance of buildings were determined by that complex of practices and predilections, transmitted from one generation to the next by personal example and word of mouth, which we call tradition; by its end tradition had yielded to taste, which as the eighteenth century understood the term was the product of the combination of cultivated sensibility and special knowledge. In America the special knowledge could be acquired only from books, and it was the stream of books on architecture which began to issue from the London booksellers' shops soon after the accession of George I and reached flood force in the 1730s that did more than anything else to bring the change about.[1] It took time; the new books were rarely used—probably rarely seen—before 1730, and the dominance of taste, evidenced by the taking of designs for whole buildings from them, was not absolute until mid-century. Nonetheless, there were three important developments in the first thirty years of the century: the establishment of the double pile as the standard type for houses of any pretension, a change in the treatment of domestic interiors, and the introduction of a new type of church.

The Double-Pile House

The earliest known use of the term double pile occurs in the notebooks of the amateur architect Sir Roger Pratt, which were compiled in the third quarter of the seventeenth century. The earliest known double-pile house was Coleshill, Berkshire, built to Pratt's design circa 1650; the next seems to have been Thorpe Hall, Northamptonshire, which was built in 1654–56 to the design of Peter Mills, a London bricklayer. Like the Foster-Hutchinson House in Boston, Thorpe Hall shows the influence of the published designs of Philip Vingboons, and the type generally owed much to Holland. Certainly there was more than a little that was Dutch about the first double pile in Virginia, the Governor's Palace at Williamsburg, with its tall proportions, cantilevered balcony, steep hipped roof, and two-story cupola (44). The act of the Assembly that authorized its construction in 1706 made no mention of a plan but specified the internal length and breadth, the number of stories, the materials (brick, with slate for the roof), and the use of sash windows. It also provided "that in all other respects the said house be built and finished according to the discretion of the overseer"—or the supervising architect, as we would say today—and went on to appoint to that position Henry Cary, who until its completion a few months before had been overseer of the capitol in which the Assembly sat. Cary completed the main structure within three years, but the house was not fully finished for another twelve, during six of which the work was under the direct supervision of Alexander Spotswood, lieutenant governor of Virginia from 1710 to 1722. Spotswood was responsible for "many alterations and decorations," as an early writer puts it. The most significant of the alterations was the creation of a parlor out of the upper end of what had been built as a great hall of medieval pattern. This gave the entrance side of the house a classical symmetry of plan corresponding with the symmetry of the facade. The decorations included a formal garden laid out in the Anglo-Dutch style which was still current in England, though soon to make way for something quite different.

The stairs of the Governor's Palace at Williamsburg occupied one of the rear corners of the building. In what came to be the commonest double-pile plan, they were in a central passage. This is the arrangement in the McPhedris-Warner House at Portsmouth, New Hampshire, built in 1718–23, which is the grandest double pile surviving from the early eighteenth century in New England (45). The same arrangement is found in Brafferton Hall, which was built in 1723 as the Indian school of the College of William and Mary and would appear to be the second double pile in Virginia, and in the matching President's House of 1732 (46, 47). With nothing more than transom windows to admit daylight at first-floor level, poor lighting of the passage was a built-in problem. One solution was to widen the passage to accommodate a full-size window to one side of the door. This was done in two large Virginian houses, Westover and Nomini Hall, both begun about 1730 (48). The result was a plan whose asymmetry was not very classical but which may have been well suited to the habits and customs of those living in the house, since it was in effect simply a doubling of the hall-passage-parlor plan Virginians knew so well.

Externally these houses and the many others like them are rectangular blocks of a basic simplicity, with proportions that were often determined geometrically. By their time, jetties, cross gables, and projecting porches were things of the past. Ornament is confined to variations in the color and texture of the brickwork, as when glazed bricks are used for headers and rubbed bricks for quoins, window arches, and string courses. Nor is there really very much classical detail—an eaves cornice certainly, perhaps a pediment over the front door, or more rarely a tabernacle frame, complete with pilasters, to give consequence to it. In contrast to this external plainness the interior of the house was much more elaborately finished than before. In seventeenth-century rooms the walls were plastered and white-

44
*Governor's Palace, Wil-
liamsburg, Virginia.
1706–20. View from
south. From the Bodleian
Plate.*

45
*McPhedris-Warner
House, Portsmouth, New
Hampshire. 1718–23.
Street front.*

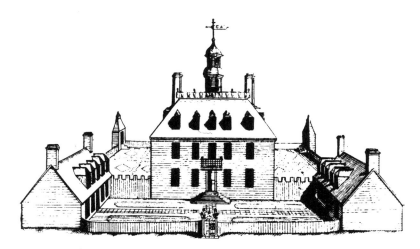

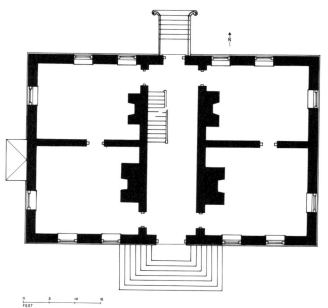

46
College of William and Mary, Williamsburg, Virginia. Left, Brafferton Hall, 1723; center, Main Building, Alexander Spotswood, 1709–15; right, President's House, 1732. View from east. From the Bodleian Plate.

47
President's House, College of William and Mary, Williamsburg, Virginia. Plan of first floor.

48
Westover, Charles City County, Virginia. Circa 1730–35. View from northwest.

washed, beams and joists and the massive lintels over fireplaces were left exposed, doors and wainscot were of vertical boarding. Around 1700 wood panelling—no novelty in England, of course—came into use. At first—in the Samuel Wentworth House at Portsmouth, New Hampshire, for instance, and in Morattico, Richmond County, Virginia—it was used as a means of articulating the wall surfaces, with little or no suggestion of structure or strictly architectural effect. Later the full architectural treatment with pilasters and a complete entablature made its appearance; Stratford, in Westmoreland County, Virginia, begun in 1725, contains one of the earliest examples. Of an intermediate sort of treatment that became popular—without pilasters but with pedimented doorcases and an entablature scaled as if there were pilasters rising from the dado—an early example is to be seen in the drawing room of Graeme Park at Horsham, Pennsylvania, begun in 1721. Panelling was usually of pine, and pine was always painted; in the eighteenth century only walnut and mahogany, used mostly for doors, stairs, and stairrails, were not painted.

If one had to single out one feature that immediately distinguished eighteenth-century buildings from their seventeenth-century predecessors, it would be the sash window. As we have seen, the first building of the College of William and Mary at Williamsburg, completed in 1700, and the Virginia capitol there, completed in 1705, had sash windows. That they were already being used in houses in the colonies is attested by a letter written in 1701 by a Boston merchant to his London agent, in which they are called "the newest fashion." They were, it seems, an English invention to which the Dutch contributed the weight-and-pulley device to hold the sash at the required height as an improvement over the notch and catch that performed the function in the earliest examples. The importance of the sash window as an element of design was that the grid of sash bars provided a new and easily read measure of scale. (It was one that could be employed to produce illusionistic effects—as in Westover, where the slightly smaller size of the second-story windows, which are identical in design with those below them, increases the apparent height of the house.) To the end of the colonial period window frames and sashes were set close to the outer face of the wall, in contrast to the practice in London, where an Act of Parliament of 1709 required that all window and door frames be set back at least four inches behind it.

Sash windows, eaves cornices, dormers, these were the three leading features common to houses and public buildings in the early eighteenth century. The second Town House at Boston, built in 1712–13 to replace the wooden building which burned in 1711, had all three; so did the second building of the College of William and Mary, built after the burning of the first in 1705 (46). Not much is known about the former, but of the second building of William and Mary there were enough records of various kinds, including a plan by Thomas Jefferson, to ensure an accurate restoration in 1928–31. It was built in 1709–15 to the design of Governor Spotswood, who reused the walls of the original building but reduced the height of the east front from three full stories above the half-basement to two and added a pedimented entrance pavilion. This last feature made the building, for all its domesticity of detail, rather more monumental in character than either of the two other major college buildings of the decade in which it was completed. These were the first buildings of Yale College, built of wood in 1717–18, and Harvard's Massachusetts Hall, built of brick in 1718–20. The Yale building, like the William and Mary building, contained a hall, chapel, and library as well as students' chambers and studies; Massachusetts Hall contained chambers and studies only. Both were elongated double piles of three full stories; Yale had three doorways in each front and a central cupola, while Massachusetts Hall, which followed the example of Stoughton Hall and formed an open-sided quadrangle with it and Harvard Hall, has two doorways in each front with no central feature of any kind. Both had sash windows, eaves cornices, and dormers.

Dormers were not called for in houses of worship, but eaves cornices and sash windows were soon adopted by the Congregationalists of New England. The Old Brick Meeting House in Boston, built in 1713, had both, as well as round windows, like those in the tribunes of the Williamsburg capitol, and classical pilasters applied to its two-story porch. With a squarish plan, the entrance in the middle of one of the long sides, and a hipped roof with central cupola, this was a meeting house of seventeenth-century form in eighteenth-century dress. As time went on, Congregational meeting houses grew more churchlike. But rectangular sash windows were the rule until after the end of the colonial period; Congregationalists generally eschewed the type of window that came into use in Anglican churches in the colonies early in the eighteenth century and may be regarded as the ecclesiastical counterpart of the secular sash, the round-arched, or compass window, as it was called. Its use was due to the example of Sir Christopher Wren, who, in the fifty-one churches that he designed to replace those destroyed in the Great Fire of London in 1666, established a new style, an Anglican Baroque, for Church of England architecture.

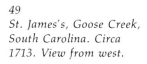
The Influence of Wren

The Wren church did not cross the Atlantic at once. The first Trinity Church in New York City was begun in 1698, when all Wren's London churches had been in use for twelve years or more and all but a handful had received their steeples, but it still had traceried windows and a Gothic spire. A quarter of a century was to pass before the first American church with a steeple of the Wren type was completed— in the year of Wren's death. In the meantime, however, the basic vocabulary of forms employed by Wren in his churches, including the compass window, had reached the colonies with the English-trained carpenters and bricklayers who contracted to build churches (as other buildings) according to simple specifications of size and materials, which might or might not be accompanied by rudimentary plans. Some of the results are still to be seen, though often obscured by later additions and alterations, in about thirty country churches scattered through the South from Maryland to South Carolina, with more than twice as many in Virginia as in all the rest of the area. To keep to examples begun before 1730, St. James's, Goose Creek, near Charleston, South Carolina, built about 1713, is notable for its West Indian character[2] and the completeness of its furnishings, which include a pompous reredos of painted stucco with composite pilasters and the royal arms in the pediment (49); Merchants' Hope Church in Prince George County and Ware Church in Gloucester County, both built about 1715, are Virginian representatives of the oblong **A**-roofed type at its smallest and simplest

49
St. James's, Goose Creek, South Carolina. Circa 1713. View from west.

60

50
Christ Church, Lancaster County, Virginia. 1732. View from northwest.

and at its most spacious and highly finished respectively; Old Wye Church at Wye Mills, dating from 1717, in which the compass windows are flanked by residual buttresses of medieval form, may stand for the same type in Maryland; Vauter's Church in Essex County, Virginia, was built in 1719 and given a T plan (common in Virginia, where it was possibly due to Scottish precedent) by the addition of a "wing" twelve years later. These were all, one may be sure, the work of builder-architects.

The second brick church of Bruton Parish at Williamsburg, built in 1711–15 to replace the building of 1683, was designed by Governor Spotswood at the request of the Assembly of the colony, which was to share its cost with the parish. Spotswood, like Wren, was a mathematician. He produced a Latin-cross plan with dimensions derived from an equilateral triangle with sides of 75 feet, which was to be the total length of the building; the altitude of such a triangle is 66 feet, which, most conveniently for the staking out of the building before construction, is the length of a surveyor's chain. As for the Latin-cross plan, that was convenient because the parish was to pay for the nave and sanctuary and the colony for the transept or wings. The church of the capital, Bruton fathered no less than seven Virginian churches with cruciform plans (very rarely used in England since the Reformation). The handsomest of its progeny, and one of the handsomest of all colonial churches, is Christ Church, Lancaster County, built in 1732 (50); those with the strongest resemblance to their parent are St. John's, Hampton (1728), Mattapony (ca. 1732), and St. Paul's, Norfolk (1739).

None of the foregoing churches in the South had steeples originally, though one was added to Bruton Parish Church in 1769–70. Wren's London churches had to have steeples, and this faced him with the problem of how to translate a feature which in the phrase of another architect of Anglican churches, James Gibbs, was "of Gothic extraction" into the form-language of classical architecture

51
*St. Philip's, Charleston,
South Carolina. 1711–23.
View from north. Draw-
ing by Thomas Birch.*

without diminishing its symbolically charged verticality. He solved it in a fascinating variety of ways, with the result that every parish had its own distinctive landmark, visible and recognizable from the Thames or from the heights to the north of the city. In designing his steeples Wren drew on many sources, Baroque and ancient, but in only one did he follow a particular continental model; the steeple of St. Magnus the Martyr, near London Bridge, is a restrained, Anglican version of that of St. Charles Borromeo in Antwerp (built about 1620.)

The first eighteenth-century colonial church to have a steeple, the second St. Philip's, Charleston, was also, according to a well-informed traveller, the Rev. Charles Woodmason, writing in 1766, "built on the Model of the Jesuit Church at Antwerp", though it is easier to see its steeple as a stubby version of the steeple of St. Magnus's (51). St. Philip's was begun in 1711 but not opened for service until 1723; it was destroyed by fire in 1835. In the eighteenth century it was enormously admired; Woodmason wrote that it was "allowed to be the most elegant Religious Edifice in British America." Built of brick and plastered, it had a nave of five bays, 100 feet long and 60 feet broad, with a single tier of round-arched windows alternating with pilasters. The interior was galleried, with Corinthian pilasters, applied to the piers of the arcades, carrying a full entablature which ran unbroken from end to end. From the entablature a plaster barrel vault rose over the central space, while the ceilings over the aisles were flat. The octagonal tower rose out of a sixth bay, to which were attached three tetrastyle Tuscan porticoes, facing north, west, and south—the first porticoes with free-standing columns in the English colonies. None of Wren's churches (except St. Paul's) had porticoes. But Wren had recommended their use in a letter written when he was consulted in connection with plans to build more churches in London, authorized by an Act of Parliament in the very year in which St. Philip's was begun. His views would

52
Old North Church (Christ Church), Boston, Massachusetts. William Price, 1723; spire, 1741, rebuilt 1807. Steeple from west.

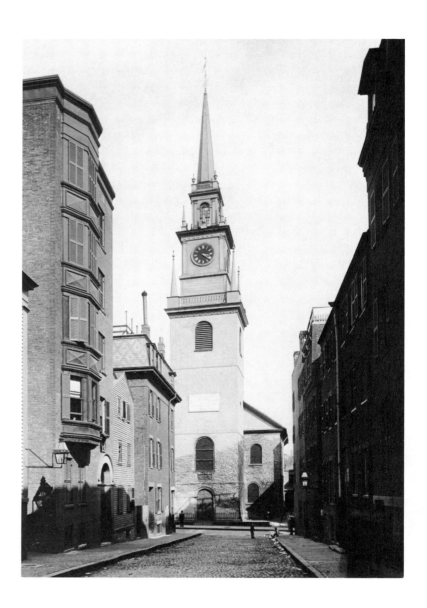

*Old North Church, Bos-
ton, Massachusetts. Inte-
rior, looking east.*

almost certainly have been known to the Society for the Propagation of the Gospel, which helped to raise funds for St. Philip's, if not to its unidentified designer, and the church represented an application of Wren's principles even if it was not an imitation of any one of his churches.

Such an imitation was begun in the year in which St. Philip's was opened for worship: Christ Church, or Old North Church, in Boston (52, 53). In the letter referred to, Wren expressed doubt as to the possibility of building a church "so capacious . . . as to hold above 2,000 persons, and all to hear the service and both to hear distinctly and see the preacher," and then went on to name St. James's, Westminster, known today as St. James's, Piccadilly, as the building in which he had come closest to realizing this ideal. "In this church I mention," he writes, "though very broad, and the middle nave arched up, yet there are no walls of a second order, but the whole roof rests upon pillars, as do also the galleries; I think it may be found beautiful and convenient, and as such, the cheapest of any form I could invent." Was there any connection between Wren's recommendation of St. James's, Piccadilly, and its adoption as the model for Old North Church, Boston? If there was, it may well have been through the Society for the Propagation of the Gospel, which raised funds for Old North too. Perhaps the Society even supplied information and visual materials for the use of the cabinetmaker and dealer in books and engravings, William Price, who made the design. In any case, although the "middle nave" is less "arched up," while square pillars take the place of the columns rising from the gallery fronts in Wren's church and a semicircular apse has been added, in all essentials the interior of Old North is an imitation of St. James's. The tower also follows St. James's very closely, with stringcourses dividing it into the same four stories and the same combination of arched and round windows; the wooden spire, which was not built until 1741, is a taller version of that of another Wren church, St. Lawrence Jewry.

Old North was scarcely finished when another copy of St. James's, Piccadilly, was built in Rhode Island, this time of wood. Trinity Church, Newport, was designed and built by Richard Munday, a carpenter, in 1725–26; its spire is a duplicate of the Boston one, and like it was built in 1741. But the sincerest flattery of Old North came from the Congregationalists of Boston, when the Old South Meeting House was built in 1729–30 to the design of Robert Twelves (54). Although Old South has the traditional nearly square meeting house plan, its external treatment, to the top of its brick tower, is virtually identical with that of the Anglican building. The spire, which was

54
Old South Meeting
House, Boston, Massa-
chusetts. Robert Twelves,
1729–30. From a photo-
graph of circa 1890.

often imitated in New England later in the century, is different but nonetheless of Wren type; its lowest stage and its silhouette are reminiscent of the spire of St. Mary-le-Bow.

Neither St. James's, Piccadilly, nor St. Lawrence Jewry was to be found in any book. The direction of a new movement in English architectural publishing was set in 1715 by two books: the first volume of *Vitruvius Britannicus,* a collection of all that seemed best in British classical architecture to its Scottish architect compiler, Colen Campbell, and *The Architecture of A. Palladio* by the Venetian architect Giacomo Leoni, which purported to be an English edition of Andrea Palladio's *Quattro Libri dell' Architettura,* first published in Venice in 1570. Both in their different ways were designed to promote what we now call Anglo-Palladianism, which was soon to gain a dominance in the English architectural scene that lasted some forty years and to whose adherents Wren's Anglican Baroque was something to be left behind as quickly as possible.

As we have already noted, in America designs for whole buildings were not taken from books until the middle of the century. Before that, books were resorted to for plans on the one hand and for ornamental features and detail on the other. Not all were English; the plan of Stratford—a house which was altogether exceptional in the colonies for the suggestion in the treatment of its chimneys of the Baroque style of Sir John Vanbrugh—looks as if it came from a plate in Sebastiano Serlio's *Architettura,* which architects in Britain began to find useful soon after its publication in the sixteenth century (55, 56). The coeval Rosewell, in Gloucester County, Virginia, appears to have been the first American building whose plan was derived from *Vitruvius Britannicus,* combining features of Buckingham House, London (John Talman, 1705), and Roehampton House, Surrey (Thomas Archer, 1710–11).

Neither Stratford nor Rosewell was Palladian in any real sense. The Ionic doorcase of Whitehall, the house near Newport, Rhode Island, which George Berkeley (then Dean of Derry, later Bishop of Cloyne) remodelled and enlarged and occupied in 1728–31, was perhaps the first Anglo-Palladian feature in America (57). Anglo-Palladian rather than Palladian, for Berkeley took the design not from the *Quattro Libri* or Leoni's edition of it but from *The Designs of Inigo Jones* by William Kent, published in 1727 (the year before he came to Rhode Island). Inigo Jones was revered by the English Palladians no less than Palladio himself, and imitated nearly as often. By working in a style that owed a great deal to Palladio in the early seventeenth century he had given their movement an English ances-

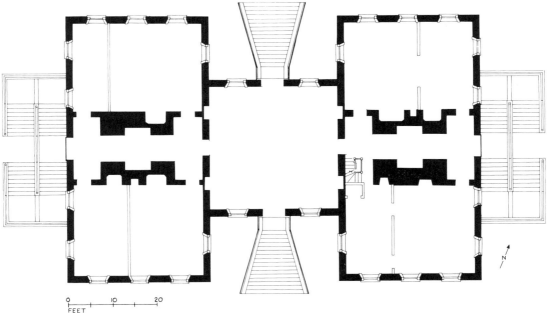

55
Stratford Hall, West-
moreland County, Vir-
ginia. Circa 1725–30.
View from south.

56
Stratford Hall, West-
moreland County, Vir-
ginia. Plan of principal
floor.

try. This was a matter of much consequence because the Anglo-Palladian program was strongly nationalist; England was to have a national architecture, free from the associations with popery and absolute monarchy that tainted the Baroque of continental Europe. One may be sure that it was not simply the requirements of scansion that caused Alexander Pope to name the British architect first in his exhortation to the leader of the movement, Lord Burlington:

"Jones and Palladio to themselves restore,
And be whate'er Vitruvius was before."

All three of the names in Pope's couplet, it will be noted, appeared in the titles of the three books by members of the Anglo-Palladian movement mentioned above. But Palladio's name on a title page was no guarantee that the contents would have met with the master's approval. Leoni had deliberately altered Palladio's designs to suit his own taste, and his "corrected" versions were republished in the mid-thirties by Edward Hoppus and Benjamin Cole in a volume shamelessly entitled *Andrea Palladio's Architecture . . . Carefully Revis'd and Redelineated.*[3] The fact of the matter was that Palladio's name sold books. Among those who recognized this was the author of *Palladio Londinensis: or, The London Art of Building,* the Colchester carpenter William Salmon. *Palladio Londinensis* was first published in 1734 and reached its seventh edition in 1759. It was of all the many books of its class—the builder's handbook—the one most used in America. Its contents comprise some geometry and instructions for drawing the classical orders, together with much useful information about business and structural matters, based on contemporary London practice, and a few designs for doorways and windows and chimneypieces. There is really nothing Palladian about the latter; Salmon was publishing stock designs—"corrected," to be sure—of the sort that had been common property in the masons' yards for twenty or thirty years. Two of his doorway designs, executed (presumably in London) in Portland stone, were used at Westover (58). Their builders' Baroque, so to call it, contrasts tellingly with the Palladianism (or Jonesianism) of Berkeley's doorway in Rhode Island.

Two buildings which illustrate the coexistence in the 1730s of the old and the new, respectively, are the Hancock House, Boston, built in 1737–40, and Drayton Hall, in South Carolina near Charleston, which was built in 1738–42. Each represented the ultimate in domestic magnificence for its time and place. The Hancock House was built by Joshua Blanchard, who had been the mason of Old South Meeting House. Of granite with sandstone dressings, it had a standard double-pile plan with four rooms to a floor, the main stairs in

57
*Whitehall, Newport,
Rhode Island. George
Berkeley, 1728. Doorway.*

58
*Westover, Charles City
County, Virginia. Circa
1730–35. Doorway in
south front.*

a wide central passage, and a service stair between the rooms on one side of it. The exterior, with an elaborate pedimented frontispiece of two orders against a rusticated background, was exceptionally rich in effect for the colonies but would not have been surprising in England thirty years earlier; the balcony over the front door, with the massive brackets supporting it, was a product of the old Anglo-Dutch architectural alliance.

In South Carolina domestic architecture had been less homogeneous than in the other southern colonies. The oldest existing house, Medway, which is now buried under later accretions, was built in 1686 by a Dutch settler with the stepped gables of his native land; Middleburg, built in 1699 for a Huguenot settler and now the oldest surviving wooden house in South Carolina, showed the Barbadian influence already noted at Goose Creek; Mulberry, built in 1714, has the odd conceit of four all but detached corner pavilions capped with curvilinear roofs and may have been some Huguenot builder's interpretation of a French château, though the first owner was an Englishman and the body of the house is a double pile with a great hall of English descent (59); the Brick House on Edisto Island, built about 1725, was another double pile with a great hall, its exterior enriched with stucco quoins and other ornamental features reminiscent of French work of the early seventeenth century. Exeter, begun in 1726 or soon after, had an **H** plan closely resembling one published by Stephen Primatt in *The City and Country Purchaser and Builder*

59
*Mulberry, St. John's Par-
ish, South Carolina.
1714. General view.*

60
*Drayton Hall, Charleston,
South Carolina. 1738–42.
View from southeast.*

61
*Drayton Hall, Charleston,
South Carolina. Hall.*

62
*Drayton Hall, Charleston,
South Carolina. Plan of
principal floor.*

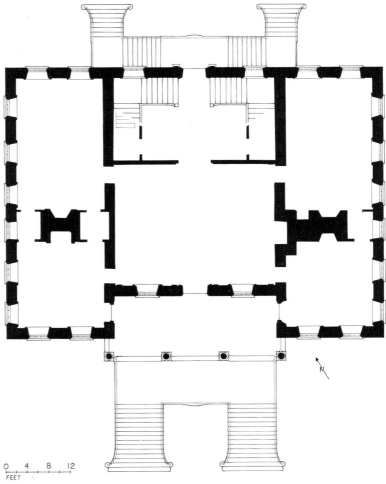

O 4   8   12
FEET

in 1667; Crowfield and Fenwick Hall, built in 1730, were hip-roofed double piles of the usual Southern kind, both with great halls. Yet in all this variety there was nothing that could be regarded as an anticipation of Drayton Hall (60, 61, 62).

Drayton Hall was the first Anglo-Palladian house in America. Until research turns up the name of an architect or builder that can be attached to it, the credit for this must go to John Drayton, the member of the King's Council for whom it was built. Its most Palladian and least English feature is the portico on the entrance front—least English because two-story porticoes were rarely built in England, where the climate prevented any kind of portico from being more than a showpiece. It is modelled on the portico on the garden front of Palladio's Villa Pisani at Montagnana; the columns, more widely spaced than Palladio would have allowed, are of Portland stone and were imported from England. The English side of Anglo-Palladianism is represented in the entrance hall, which is panelled in wood with pilasters and a full Doric entablature, by a chimneypiece based on a plate in Kent's *Designs of Inigo Jones* and also—in a most striking and indeed unique manner—by the double stairs that occupy their own hall behind the garden front. These are modelled on the stairs of Coleshill, which in the eighteenth century was believed to be a work of Inigo Jones, although the architect was actually Sir Roger Pratt.[4] They are the least Palladian feature of the house. Palladio had never, in his country houses, placed a grand staircase on the main axis, and Pratt owed the idea to the Dutch.

No public building completed before 1750 is comparable to Drayton Hall. The style of the Pennsylvania State House, now Independence Hall, which was built (except for the tower, to which we shall come later) in 1731–36, has been described by Sir John Summerson as "a Palladianism totally lacking in scholarship and virtuous only by a combination of chance and instinct." One of the two master builders who contracted for its construction, the carpenter Edward Woolley, supplied the design; he was paid five pounds for drawing the plans and elevations. Another carpenter-architect, Richard Munday, whom we met in connection with Trinity Church in Newport, Rhode Island, designed and built the state house (Old Colony House) there, in 1739–41 (63). It is a jolly affair in its Dutch way, with a balconied frontispiece more than a little like that of the Hancock House in Boston. Faneuil Hall, the market house presented to Boston by Peter Faneuil and built in 1740–42 to the design of the painter John Smibert, who had come to America with Berkeley, was more up-to-date. In what Summerson has called a "somewhat naively learned design," Smibert applied a Doric pilaster order to both stories of his

63
Old Colony House, New-
port, Rhode Island. Rich-
ard Munday, 1739–41.
View from southeast.

64
Christ Church, Philadelphia, Pennsylvania. Begun 1727; spire, Robert Smith, 1750–54. View from south.

65
Christ Church, Philadelphia, Pennsylvania. Interior, looking east.

building, and this would appear to be the first time that a full-scale order was used externally for any public building except a church in the colonies.

The first colonial church to have an applied order was, as we saw, St. Philip's, Charleston. The second was Christ Church, Philadelphia, which has Doric pilasters framing two tiers of windows on either side of the nave (64). Christ Church was begun in 1727, but work proceeded slowly enough through the 1730s for someone concerned to get hold of a copy of *A Book of Architecture* (1728) by James Gibbs, as the interior order, with the entablature reduced to a square block over each column, and the Palladian or Venetian window at the east end show (65). In the second half of the century *A Book of Architecture* was to be the most influential work of its kind, which was a very different kind from Salmon's *Palladio Londinensis*, in America—so far as church architecture was concerned, in the whole English-speaking world. It is not known for certain who was responsible for this first American use of it in Philadelphia. A physician, John Kearsley, used to be named as the architect of Christ Church. He certainly superintended its erection on behalf of the parish, and when he died a newspaper said that he was "well acquainted with the principles of architecture, a monument of which we have in *Christ Church.*" He was also one of the committee of three which superintended the building of the State House. Yet it is more likely that the design of Christ Church was the work of some member of the powerful Carpenters' Company of Philadelphia, which had been founded in the 1720s—tradition says 1724—and dominated the building scene in that city.

Taste Triumphant

In 1760 James Bridges, architect, offered to rebuild St. Nicholas's Church, Bristol, for the modest sum of £1,250, in accordance with what he described as "a plan I saw executed, when on my travels through the Province of Pensilvania, in America." Had his offer been accepted—in the event, St. Nicholas's was rebuilt to another, less economical, design by him—Bristol would have had the only eighteenth-century building of any consequence in England modelled on an American prototype. Which Pennsylvanian church Bridges had in mind is not a matter of importance; what is remarkable is that in 1760 an architect as sophisticated as he was could propose to imitate any American building in Bristol, then in point of size the second city in England and in point of architectural sophistication the third (after London and Bath). Fifteen years before it could not have happened; in 1760 it could because around the turn of the century taste had succeeded tradition as the main shaping force in colonial architecture.

Drayton Hall was not without its naiveties. The first American building that could have earned unqualified approval from the English *cognoscenti* of the age was the templelike Redwood Library at Newport, Rhode Island, built in 1749–50 (66). Here for the first time in the colonies appeared that ingredient in Anglo-Palladianism which was the special contribution of Lord Burlington, the Neo-Classical. A plate in Edward Hoppus' edition of Palladio (1736), inspired by a building in Burlington's own garden, was the main source of the design. The wooden siding of the walls was worked to give the illusion of chamfered stone rustication. This contrivance, however distasteful it may be to those brought up to believe that design should express the nature of materials, would have seemed a happy one to those who had read Burlington's protegé Isaac Ware on boarded walls: "These are of a very inferior kind, and only fit for meaner purposes," and who agreed with him that it was "the honour of the architect that the form triumph over the materials."

Peter Harrison

The Redwood Library was designed by Peter Harrison, the most talented colonial architect of whom we have any real knowledge. Born in York in 1716, Harrison landed in Newport for the first time in 1739, as a member of the crew of a merchant vessel commanded by his brother Joseph; before the end of the year he was given a command of his own. His seagoing career lasted for nine years, after which he settled down near Newport to farm his wife's land and help manage the affairs of his business partnership with his brother, trading in luxury goods with England, South Carolina, and the West Indies. In 1766 he was appointed Collector of Customs at New

66
Redwood Library, Newport, Rhode Island. Peter Harrison, 1749–50. Portico.

Haven, where he lived until his death of a stroke, after suffering much persecution as a loyalist and a government official, in 1775.

With occasional exceptions—he was paid forty-five pounds for "drawing the plan" of Christ Church, Cambridge—Harrison's designs were supplied gratis, while he had no financial interest in the construction of the buildings he designed. The only other amateur architect we have met with more than one building to his name has been Alexander Spotswood, and it is interesting to compare the qualifications of the two men for the practice of architectural design. Spotswood's rested, in the view of his contemporaries, on his mathematical ability, Harrison's on his skill as a draftsman (which he employed in cartography some years before he turned to architecture) and on his book-learned familiarity with what was admired and to be imitated; at his death he owned the largest collection of books on architecture recorded in the colonies, numbering twenty-seven titles. The degree of control exercised by Spotswood and Harrison over the detail of their buildings differed too. Spotswood's "platt or draught" that was laid before the vestry of Bruton Parish in 1711 is unlikely to have been more than a plan with a single elevation; matters of detail would be left to the master craftsmen. The set of six drawings that Harrison sent to the building committee for King's Chapel, Boston, in 1749 included plans, elevations, and a section, while for Christ Church, Cambridge, in 1760 he supplied designs for the pulpit and organ loft as well as plans and elevations for the building itself.

King's Chapel must be accounted Harrison's masterpiece, even though the steeple was never completed and its granite-walled exterior is bleaker than it would have been had the building committee been able to afford the shipping and working of the Bath stone offered by Ralph Allen for the columns and other classical features and ornaments. The interior is modelled on St. Martin-in-the-Fields, the church with which the Roman Catholic (and Roman-trained) Gibbs had set a new standard for Anglican architecture (67). As in St. Martin's, there is a Venetian window at the east end and Corinthian columns carry isolated blocks of entablature. Here, however, the blocks of entablature are not square but oblong, and each is carried by two columns instead of a single one. It is a change which shows that Harrison had a feeling for the structural origins of the classical elements of design. For an entablature is a stylized representation of a beam spanning the space between free-standing supports and the visible parts of a roof above it; when reduced, as Gibbs (and Brunelleschi before him) reduced it, to a square block with four identical faces, it loses all structural meaning.

In the exterior design of King's Chapel Harrison solved a problem that had proved too much for Gibbs: how to combine a steeple and a portico. In St. Martin-in-the-Fields the tower rises out of the body of the church behind the portico, with the result that it seems to be riding the roof. Harrison brought his tower forward so that it shares only its east wall with the nave, and he emphasized the separateness of tower and nave by giving the latter a hipped roof instead of the gabled roof usual in churches of the time. Instead of a pediment, which would have conflicted with the hipped roof, he gave the portico a balustrade—and with it a resemblance, certainly intentional, to Inigo Jones's west portico of St. Paul's, destroyed in the Great Fire of 1666, which he knew from his copy of Kent's book. Thus even in imitating a work of Gibbs that was in no sense Palladian, Harrison paid a tribute to the great seventeenth-century forerunner of Anglo-Palladianism.[1]

Harrison's other public buildings were the Synagogue (1759–63) and the Brick Market (1761–72) in Newport and Christ Church, Cambridge (1760–61). The Touro Synagogue, as it is now called, was the first public synagogue in colonial America. Here Harrison turned for detail to Gibbs—this time, to his *Rules for Drawing the Several Parts of Architecture* (1732)—and to Kent's *Designs of Inigo Jones*. But the model for the building as a whole was the Bevis Marks Synagogue of the Spanish and Portuguese Jews in London, dedicated in 1701, whose builders had worked for Wren and adopted the plan of James's, Piccadilly.

67
King's Chapel, Boston, Massachusetts. Peter Harrison, 1749–54. Interior looking east.

68
Brick Market, Newport, Rhode Island. Peter Harrison, 1761–72. View from northwest.

69
Christ Church, Cambridge, Massachusetts. Peter Harrison, 1760–61. Interior, looking west.

For the Brick Market Harrison adopted, and adapted, the elevation of the New Gallery of Somerset House, London, as shown in *Vitruvius Britannicus*, where Campbell notes that it was "taken from a Design of Inigo Jones, but conducted by another hand"—that is, Jones's pupil, John Webb (68). Besides omitting the rustication of the arcaded ground story and the balustrades under the second-floor windows and changing the order from Corinthian to Ionic—modifications justifiable on grounds of economy—he substituted corner pilasters, with two faces, for the single-faced end pilasters of his model. This change, called for by the wrapping of the Somerset House facade around a freestanding building, gives a sense of structure to the pilasters and is analogous to the coupling of the columns in King's Chapel. The Brick Market stands near the foot of the street of which Munday's Colony House forms the head. Nowhere can the difference between the architecture of tradition and the architecture of taste be better seen.

Christ Church, Cambridge, like the Redwood Library, is of wood simulating stone, although funds ran out before the walls could be rough-cast to complete the illusion. The building is Doric outside, with a full entablature under the eaves, and Ionic within; details are from Gibbs (69). For the supports of the coved ceiling over the nave Harrison abandoned the logic of his coupled columns in King's Chapel and employed single columns with square entablature blocks. The result justifies him, for not only do the repeated units of the order define the nave and aisles when seen in series but each tells individually as a decorative yet stately object in the luminous interior.

*Church Design
and James Gibbs*

In Anglican church architecture in the colonies the third quarter of
the eighteenth century was the age of Gibbs, for all that Gibbs
himself died near the beginning of it, in 1754. In 1750–54 a steeple
with a spire modelled on St. Martin-in-the-Fields was added to the
already Gibbsian nave of Christ Church, Philadelphia (64); the
builder, and designer too in all probability, was the carpenter Robert
Smith, the most successful of all the Philadelphia builder-architects
of the time. In 1752–61 St. Michael's, Charleston, was built with a
Doric portico and a disproportionately tall steeple—fifty-six feet taller
than the church is long—which is unmistakably Gibbsian even
though it does not follow any particular one of Gibbs's designs; of
masonry to the top of the second octagon, this steeple is one of the
most daring structures of the colonial period (70, 71). The interior
is not Gibbsian at all; a galleried hall with a tray ceiling unsupported
by columns, it most resembles St. Alphege's, Greenwich, of which
Nicholas Hawksmoor was the architect. The designer of St. Michael's
has not been identified; he may well have been its builder, Samuel
Cardy. In 1764–66 St. Paul's Chapel, New York City, was built to
the design of Thomas McBean with an interior which was the closest
to St. Martin's to date; the steeple—St. Martin's with an extra
octagonal stage—was added thirty years later.

   Country churches still showed regional characteristics, usually in
conjunction with academic or at least bookish features that distinguished them from similar buildings of the first half of the century.
Thus in Virginia cruciform plans were adopted for Abingdon Church,
Gloucester County, and Aquia Church in Stafford County, both
begun in 1751, while Abingdon (a Latin cross) has pedimental gables
and Aquia (a Greek cross) a rusticated doorway of a type much used
by Gibbs. In South Carolina, Pompion Hill Chapel was built in 1763
to the same plan as St. James's, Goose Creek, with entrances in the
middle of the north and south sides and the same roof, hipped above
the wind beams, but with the addition of an apsidal chancel (outwardly rectangular) and a Venetian east window; St. Stephen's,
Santee, was built in 1767 to the same plan with a ceiling imitating
St. Michael's, Charleston. However, the South Carolinian partiality
for porticoes did produce two country churches that were quite out
of the ordinary. The earlier, Prince William's Church at Sheldon,
was built in 1751 in the form of a Roman temple, with a tetrastyle
portico to the west and half-columns around the nave, all of brick.
Nothing as classical had been built for Anglican worship since Inigo
Jones's St. Paul's, Covent Garden. Woodmason thought it "far more
elegant than St. Michael's" and noted that it was "by many esteem'd
a more beautiful building than St. Philip's." The other porticoed

82

70
St. Michael's, Charleston, South Carolina. Samuel Cardy (?), 1752–61. View from north.

71
St. Michael's, Charleston, South Carolina. Plan.

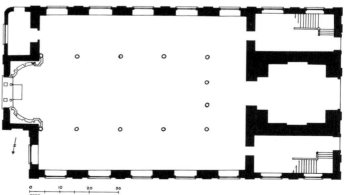

country church in South Carolina, St. James's, Santee, was built in 1768; it has matching Tuscan porticoes to north and south.

In New England, where Anglican churches were few and far between, the frame building of Old Trinity at Brooklyn, Connecticut, built in 1770–71, merits a mention. It was designed and in large part paid for by Godfrey Malbone, who had moved to Brooklyn from Newport in 1766 to manage his father's estate there and who objected to the prospect of being taxed for a new Congregational church. His models were the Synagogue and Trinity Church in Newport, the former for the general design of the interior, the latter for its detail. The hipped roof and compass windows of Old Trinity contrast with the gable roof and square-headed windows of the Brooklyn meeting house, in competition with which it was built. The latter differs from it also in having a steeple modelled on the steeple of Old South in Boston, which was a favorite model with the Congregationalists when they built steeples (which in the colonial period was seldom); the most elegant version is the steeple of the Farmington meeting house, built in 1771. Early in the previous decade the other Boston steeple, that of Old North, had been imitated at Wethersfield, Connecticut, whose brick meeting house, built in 1761–64, was considered the finest in New England outside Boston.

The Congregationalists had no use for Gibbs. Whether this was because they were conservative in architectural matters—as they certainly were—or because they regarded Gibbs's style as specifically Anglican is an open question. Surprisingly enough, the most thoroughly and uncritically Gibbsian of all the churches in the British colonies was built, on the eve of the Revolution, for the Baptists. This is the First Baptist Meeting House at Providence, Rhode Island, which went up to the design of Joseph Brown in 1774–75 (72). Brown was another amateur architect—like Harrison a merchant, like Spotswood a student of mathematics. However, mathematics was not to serve Brown in designing the First Baptist Meeting House as it served Spotswood in designing Bruton Parish Church. What did serve him, from beginning to end, was *A Book of Architecture*. The interior, originally square, follows St. Peter's, Vere Street; the porch is a more open version of the porch of the same church. For the steeple Brown turned to plate 30 in Gibbs's book, where he found three alternative designs for the steeple of St. Martin-in-the-Fields. He chose the middle one, which was executed line for line by the master carpenter James Sumner of Boston. That the steeple of a Baptist meeting house should follow a design made for an Anglican church by a Catholic architect is clear proof that considerations of

72
*First Baptist Meeting
House, Providence, Rhode
Island. Joseph Brown,
1774–75. View from
southwest.*

taste took precedence over all others by this time. The whole building is of wood; the spire, white today, was originally painted to simulate various marbles.

Public Buildings
1750–1776

Among secular public buildings of the third quarter of the century Harrison's Brick Market at Newport was exceptional in representing the academic side of Anglo-Palladianism; the style of most of them was that carpenter's classic, Palladian only by courtesy, of which Independence Hall was an extensive earlier example. Nor was Dutch influence a thing of the past, at least at the opening of the period; the cupola crowning the tower added to Independence Hall by Edmund Woolley in 1750–53 bore a marked resemblance to a design by Pieter Post.[2] The capitol at Williamsburg as rebuilt in 1751–53 after a fire in 1747 had a two-story portico, Doric below and Ionic above, which essayed Palladian propriety—without much success, according to Thomas Jefferson.[3] The South Carolina State House, built in 1752–56 and burnt in 1788, seems to have been a much more literate design; the general scheme of its facade—it had a pedimented center, with Ionic pilasters above and arches below (a common Palladian formula), flanked by Venetian windows—was repeated in the Exchange and Custom House of 1767–72. Both of these Charleston buildings have been attributed to William Rigby Naylor, who was the son-in-law of Samuel Cardy, the builder of St. Michael's. The Maryland State House as rebuilt in the seventies had the special distinction of being the first domed state house in America. It was designed in 1772 by Joseph Horatio Anderson, who claimed to have been "regularly bread to those Sciences architectural design and construction & the only one upon the Continant." Yet in 1784 his dome, which was of octagonal plan and pointed contour, was found to have been built "contrary to all rules of architecture," and in the next three years Joseph Clark, a rich merchant and occasional architect, replaced it with the existing much taller structure.

Anderson made his claim to architectural expertise in a letter written in 1770 from Philadelphia to the corporation of Rhode Island College (now Brown University); he had read in the papers that the college was about to build and tendered his services "as Architect & Superintendant for that purpose." Although there is no positive evidence that his offer was accepted, University Hall at Brown, built in 1770–71, may be attributed to him. An elongated double pile of four stories, with three entrances a side, a pedimented pavilion in the center, and a cupola, it represents one of the two main types of college building in the eighteenth century, the other colonial examples being Spotswood's William and Mary, Nassau Hall at Princeton (1754–56), and Hollis Hall at Harvard (1762–63), while the original building of Dartmouth College (1784–91) was a post-Revolution one. The alternative type, which lacks any emphatic central feature, reappeared early in the second half of the century in Connecticut Hall at Yale (1750–52), which is virtually a duplicate of Harvard's Massachusetts Hall built thirty years earlier. The first building of King's College (Columbia University), erected in 1760, was a hybrid, with no less than four pedimented pavilions—one for each entrance—but no central feature below the cupola. New Harvard Hall, built in 1764–66 to replace the burnt building of 1677, had a pediment on each front and a very large cupola; the chapel, which occupied the western part of the first floor, was distinguished by compass windows. As Morrison has said, it was the first major Harvard building to attempt a nondomestic effect.

Before 1750 public buildings in the colonies were ecclesiastical, governmental, or educational; the third quarter of the century saw the beginning of that multiplication of building types which is one of the developments that make its last quarter the beginning of the modern era in architecture as in so much else. The first hospital in the colonies, the Pennsylvania Hospital, was founded in 1751 and, thanks to Benjamin Franklin's interest and his invention of the device of matching funds, opened its doors in 1755. The building was designed, and its erection supervised, by Samuel Rhoads, carpenter, member of the American Philosophical Society, and one of the managers of the hospital. The five-part design was a translation of Bethlem Hospital (Bedlam), London, designed by Robert Hooke in 1674, into carpenter's classic. Only the east wing was completed in 1755; the west wing followed in 1786, while the center was not completed (in another style) until 1805. The long wards accommodated men on the first floor and women on the second; in the basement were cells for the insane, who could be observed by the public outside the building across a small moat like those in modern zoos.

The insane were to have been relegated to the basement again in the New York Hospital, built in 1773–75, but the building burned before any could be admitted. By then, the first American hospital built exclusively for the insane was already in use. This was the Public Hospital at Williamsburg, Virginia, built in 1770–73 "for the Reception of Persons who are so unhappy as to be deprived of their reason." It was a plain two-story affair, with a pedimented pavilion in the middle of each front; access to the cells (twelve to a floor) was from central corridors. The designer, but not in this case the builder, was Robert Smith of Philadelphia, whom we know as the builder of

the spire of Christ Church in that city and who followed that up with
designing and supervising the construction of Nassau Hall at Princeton. In addition to these, Smith had designed a building for Pennsylvania College and churches in Philadelphia for the Presbyterians
and the Lutherans. He was also, it is said, master carpenter for the
Philadelphia Bettering House, a building of curious plan which combined the functions of an almshouse and a workhouse. In 1768 he
designed the Hall of the Carpenters' Company of Philadelphia, a
cruciform structure with four pediments and a central cupola, which
was built in 1770–73. Historical associations have made Carpenters'
Hall the best known of all Smith's buildings, but his biggest commission was Walnut Street Prison in Philadelphia, which he designed
and built in 1773–74. This had a street range 184 feet long and 32
feet wide, with a tall cupola and the pedimented center of which
Smith was so fond, and two wings of the same width running back
90 feet to form a squat U on plan. Technically, it was notable for its
fireproof construction, with the floors supported by groined brick
vaults. It would doubtless have had a more important place in the
history of prison design if it had not been planned six years before
John Howard's Act of Parliament of 1779 recommended the "separate
system," or solitary confinement, as a means of prison reform.[4]

*The Golden Age of the
Colonial House*

The hallmark of Palladianism in domestic architecture is the temple
portico with a single giant order employed as the central feature of
a facade. In the American colonies it made its first appearance in the
Pinckney House, Charleston, which was begun in 1746. With the
portico flattened against the front and having pilasters instead of
columns, this house was reminiscent of that pre-Burlingtonian Palladianism of Dutch origin which had arrived in England in the 1660s.
By all accounts one of the grandest houses in the colonies, the
Pinckney House was a casualty of the Civil War.

The finest New England house of the later 1740s was Shirley Place
at Roxbury, Massachusetts (73). It was built for Governor William
Shirley soon after his purchase of the land on which it stood in 1746.
Unlike the Pinckney House, which was of brick, Shirley Place was
a frame structure, faced with rusticated boards. The latter have
suggested to some the hand of Peter Harrison, and the possibility
that he was the architect is strengthened by the fact that Mrs.
Harrison and Mrs. Shirley were related. Certainly the design was as
bookish as any of Harrison's. The plan followed closely that of
Wilbury House in Wiltshire, which was designed and built for himself between 1710 and 1725 by William Benson (Sir Christopher
Wren's successor as Surveyor-General of the King's Works), as

published by Colen Campbell in the first volume of *Vitruvius Bri-tannicus* (74). The Wilbury plan was itself based on Palladio's Villa Poiana at Poiana Maggiore, and so far as its plan went Shirley Place was without question the most purely Palladian house in America to its date. Baroque rather than Palladian, though, were the giant Doric pilasters supporting isolated sections of entablature on each elevation. (An Ionic version of this motif was already to be seen in New England in the Foster-Hutchinson House.) It is the coupling of eight of the ten pilasters on the east or entrance front—on the west front, which had a large Venetian window in the center, there were only four pilasters—that perhaps affords a clue to the specific source of inspi-ration. For the entrance front of Castle Howard in Yorkshire, Sir John Vanbrugh's first masterpiece, has coupled Doric pilasters with a discontinuous entablature, while behind it rises a cupola which may well have been the model for Shirley Place's "ornate and some-what gargantuan cupola," as Morrison has called it. These resem-blances constitute additional circumstantial evidence in favor of the attribution of Shirley Place to the Yorkshireman Harrison, who must have seen Castle Howard in his youth and may even have renewed an admiration for it on his last visit to England in 1747.

The use of architectural books increased greatly after the mid-century, as did also the number of books available. Eighteen titles appear in colonial records up to the end of 1750; by the end of 1760 the total had nearly tripled, to fifty-one. The impact of books on domestic design in the 1750s is well seen in three Virginian houses: Carter's Grove, Gunston Hall, and Mount Airy. Carter's Grove, near Williamsburg, was built in 1750–53. As a plantation account book shows, Carter Burwell, the owner, contracted separately with local craftsmen for the building of his house, while for the finishing of the interior he brought a joiner and woodcarver, Richard Bayliss, from England, paying his and his family's passage money. Exter-nally, Carter's Grove is a typical double pile, not unlike Westover. Its plan, however, is perfectly symmetrical and is set out according to a geometrical system of squares and root-two rectangles (75). Instead of Westover's off-center passage, there is an oblong entrance hall with its longer axis parallel to the front of the house and a square stair hall centered behind it. The design of the woodwork in the hall, with its Ionic pilasters, and in the west parlor, where the order is Doric, came from Salmon's *Palladio Londinensis*, a copy of which Carter Burwell purchased from a Williamsburg bookseller while his house was going up (76).

Gunston Hall, in Fairfax County, is another house of traditional form with elaborate woodwork by a craftsman brought from England

73
Shirley Place, Roxbury,
Massachusetts. 1746. Ele-
vation of entrance front,
restored by W. W.
Cordingley.

74
Shirley Place, Roxbury,
Massachusetts. Plan of
first floor by W. W.
Cordingley.

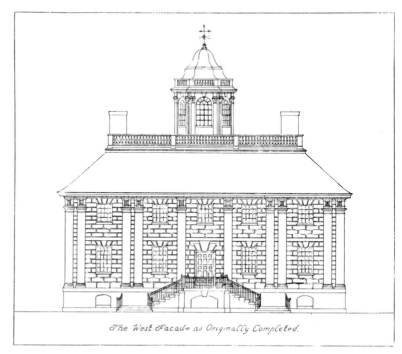

The West Facade as Originally Completed.

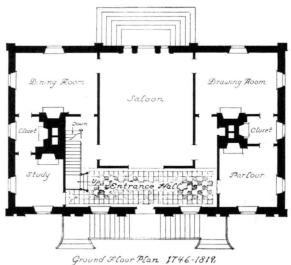

Ground Floor Plan 1746-1819.

75
Carter's Grove, James
City County, Virginia.
1750–53. Plan of first
floor.

76
Carter's Grove, James
City County, Virginia.
Entrance hall and stairs.

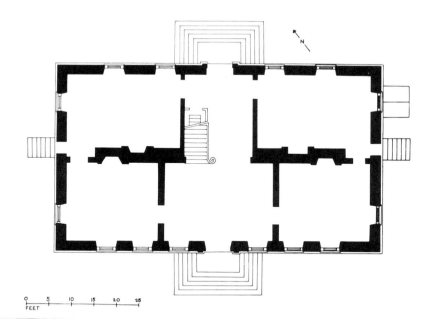

to execute it. Built in 1755–59 for George Mason, author of the Virginia Bill of Rights, Gunston Hall is a story-and-a-half double pile. The two porches, as well as the interior woodwork, are the work of William Buckland. Born at Oxford in 1734, Buckland was apprenticed at the age of fourteen to an uncle, a London joiner; in 1755, having served his articles, he bound himself as an indentured servant to George Mason's brother Thomson, then in London on a visit, convenanting to "well and truly serve the said Thomson Mason, his Executors or Assigns in the Plantation of Virginia beyond the Seas, for the Space of Four Years, next ensuing his Arrival in the said Plantation, in the Employment of a Carpenter & Joiner." His assignment to George Mason for the finishing of Gunston Hall gave the young joiner a chance to demonstrate his taste and skill of which he availed himself to the full. The landward porch is a novel adaptation of the so-called Palladian motif, while the porch toward the gardens and the Potomac River is of the half-octagon plan that architects in England were beginning to adopt as a relief from Palladian rectangularity and combines a Doric order with a touch of Gothic—or Gothic Rococo—in its ogee arches. Nothing like either of them had been seen in the colonies before, and the same may be said of the dining room, where the doors, windows, and overmantel have frames with scalloped cresting on the cornice which made it the first colonial example of "the Chinese taste," or Chinoiserie. The drawing room, on the other hand, is purely classical. It has a modillion ceiling cornice, and its door, windows, and two niches for the display of china are set in tabernacle frames with fluted pilasters and moulding enrichments of great delicacy (77). The books used here were *The British Architect* and *A Collection of Designs in Architecture* by Abraham Swan, *The Builder's Companion* by William Pain, and *A Collection of Ornamental Designs, Applicable to Furniture Frames, and the Decoration of Rooms* by Thomas Chippendale. The first and last of these Buckland could have brought with him from London—Chippendale's book appeared the year before he left—but the other two were not published until 1757 and 1758, respectively. Evidently Mason was determined that his house should be finished in the very latest taste. For the drawing room he imported from England a marble mantel in the Neo-Classical Style that took its name from the Scottish architect Robert Adam and was to dominate the architectural scene in America after the Revolution.

Buckland also had a hand in the interiors of Mount Airy, Richmond County (78).[5] This house, together with several others in Virginia, has been attributed to John Ariss, who in 1751 advertised in the *Maryland Gazette* that he would undertake "Buildings of all

77
Gunston Hall, Fairfax County, Virginia. William Buckland, 1755–59. Drawing room.

78
Mount Airy, Richmond County, Virginia. 1758–62. South front.

Sorts and Dimensions . . . either of the Ancient or Modern Order of Gibbs' Architect," giving an address in Westmoreland County, Virginia. But there is no reason to suppose that Ariss was the only builder in Virginia to own a copy of *A Book of Architecture*, from which the plan and elevations of Mount Airy, which was begun in 1758, were taken—the plan from a design that Gibbs had made for the poet Matthew Prior, and the elevations from "A Design for a Gentleman in Dorsetshire" (three plates further on). Gibbs's shade must have been gratified. In his introduction he had stated that it was the opinion of "several Persons of Quality and others" that "such a Work as this would be of use to such Gentlemen as might be concerned in Building, especially in the remote parts of the Country, where little or no assistance for Design can be procured."

The Dutch Palladian type of house, with pilasters applied to a pedimented central pavilion, continued to be built in the late colonial decades. The Vassall-Longfellow House at Cambridge, Massachusetts (79), and Nanzatico in King George County, Virginia, are examples in New England and the South, respectively. In the mid-sixties the only two colonial houses to have giant porticoes with free-standing columns went up, in Maryland and New York City. The former, Whitehall, in Anne Arundel County, was begun in 1764 for Governor Horatio Sharpe, and the three-room central block was completed the next year. After Sharpe's retirement in 1769 wings were added to convert what had been built as a pavilion for the entertainment of boating parties from Annapolis into a house for year-round occupation. The central room is admirable equally for its stately proportions and its exquisite woodwork, which includes Baroque masks in the ceiling cove of a virtuosity unsurpassed in colonial America; it is likely, though not proved, that the carver was William Buckland again (80). The New York house with a prostyle portico is the Roger Morris Mansion, built in 1765. Whereas Whitehall was thoroughly Palladian, the portico of the Roger Morris Mansion showed, with its slender and widely spaced columns, the new freedom from the rules of proportion claimed by Robert Adam and his followers. But the finest house of the colonial period in New York was the stone-built Apthorpe House of circa 1767. This had a deeply recessed porch with engaged Ionic columns and a pediment; the full entablature was carried around the house and there were four pilasters at each end, where the roof was of pedimental form; there were pediments over the first-floor windows, while the doorway within the porch followed the Palladian motif. No other house in the colonies made such a display of confident Latinity.

79
*Vassall-Longfellow
House, Cambridge, Mas-
sachusetts. 1759. Entrance
front.*

80
*Whitehall, Anne Arundel
County, Maryland. 1764–
65. Central hall.*

The Miles Brewton House at Charleston, South Carolina, built in
1765–69 (81), and Shirley in Charles City County, Virginia, circa
1769, have two-storied porticoes. At Shirley the present columns
and steps are early nineteenth-century replacements; in all probability the original upper columns were Ionic, as in Drayton Hall, the
Miles Brewton House, and the Palladian prototypes. Both the Miles
Brewton House and Shirley have rich interiors. The Miles Brewton
House was finished by Ezra Waite, "civil architect, Housebuilder in
general and Carver from London." The drawing room, with its coved
ceiling, tabernacle frames, and pedimented chimneypiece, reminded
Fiske Kimball of Inigo Jones's Double Cube Room at Wilton; the
gallery of Colen Campbell's Mereworth Castle, itself inspired by
Jones, affords even closer parallels. Inside Shirley the grand feature
is the flying stair, which rises in a hall taking up more than a quarter
of the ground floor.

The Wentworth-Gardner House at Portsmouth, New Hampshire,
shows that much skilled craftsmanship could still be lavished on the
straight-fronted, hip-roofed double pile in the sixties. But houses of
any consequence more commonly had a pedimented pavilion projecting from the center of the front. Mount Airy seems to have been
the first colonial example; it was closely followed—in design, as well
as in time—by Mannsfield (ca. 1760), near Fredericksburg. Both
houses had flanking buildings, "dependencies" in Southern parlance,
connected to the main block by quadrant passages with solid walls;
at New Bern, North Carolina, quadrant colonnades reached out to
embrace Governor William Tryon's guests. (The conceit is Palladio's,
used by him of his design for the Villa Trissino at Meledo.) Tryon

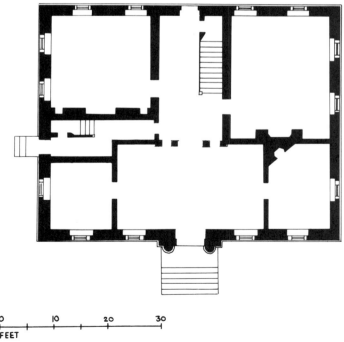

```
0          10        20         30
├───┬───┼───┬───┼───┬───┼───┬───┤
FEET
```

82
*Cliveden, Germantown,
Pennsylvania. Benjamin
Chew, 1763–64. Entrance
front.*

83
*Cliveden, Germantown,
Pennsylvania. Plan of
first floor.*

brought his architect, John Hawks, from England; Hawks had worked
under Stiff Leadbetter on Lord Harcourt's house in Oxfordshire,
Nuneham Park (1760), with which the New Bern Palace had points
in common. Blandfield, in Essex County, Virginia, built circa 1770,
differs from Mount Airy and Mannsfield in being of brick instead of
stone and in having the dependencies connected with the main block
by straight passages.

In their Virginian plainness the elevations of Blandfield are very
different from those of the two finest Pennsylvanian examples of the
pedimented-center type of house, Mount Pleasant and Cliveden, with
their livelier, more Baroque effect and display of pattern-book features. Mount Pleasant, in Fairmount Park, Philadelphia, was begun
in 1761 for an immigrant sea captain, John MacPherson; the name
of its architect is not known. Cliveden, in Germantown, was begun
two years later for Benjamin Chew, attorney general of Pennsylvania
(82). Chew was his own architect. Surviving drawings from his hand
show that he toyed with the idea of a three-story house modelled on
Kew Palace, which had been built for Frederick Prince of Wales to
William Kent's designs in the 1730s; the plan of Cliveden as built
surely must have been suggested by Colen Campbell's "New Design
for Tobiah Jenkyns Esq." in the second volume of *Vitruvius Britannicus* (83). The columnar screen between the entrance hall and stair
is an unusual and stately feature which was employed also by William Buckland in the Chase-Lloyd House at Annapolis, Maryland,
in 1771; Buckland combined it with the stateliest of all types of stair,
the Imperial stair, in which a central flight ascends to a landing at
half-story level and parallel side flights return on either side to reach
the upper floor (84).

The Chase-Lloyd House is of three stories and distinctly urban
character. The Hammond-Harwood House, Annapolis, completed to
Buckland's design in 1774, is a country house in town (85). A five-
part composition with half-octagon fronts to the outer pavilions or
dependencies, this house has a good claim to be considered the
culminating work of domestic architecture in the colonies as well as
the crowning achievement of Buckland's career. Gibbs was the principal source, and in this it differs from the last group of houses, also
cinquepartite, that remains to be mentioned in this chapter. All are
in Virginia; the earliest, Belle Isle, Lancaster County, was built
about 1760, while Battersea, Dinwiddie County, and Brandon, in
Prince George County, went up between 1765 and 1770 (86). Robert
Morris's *Select Architecture*, published in 1757, was clearly the book
referred to in each case. (It was a book much used by Thomas
Jefferson—to whom Brandon has been attributed.) While the

84
Chase-Lloyd House,
Annapolis, Maryland.
William Buckland, 1771.
Stairs.

85
Hammond-Harwood
House, Annapolis, Mary-
land. William Buckland,
1773–74. Street front.

86
Brandon, Prince George
County, Virginia. 1765–
70. View from south.

The Domestic Interior

Hammond-Harwood House is strongly centripetal, owing to the pediment spanning three of the five bays of the central block, these Virginian houses show in an extreme degree what Vincent Scully has seen as an "American instinct . . . toward horizontal expansion and dispersion."

In interior design the general tendency was toward lightness and delicacy. Rooms were sometimes given the full classical treatment, with floor-to-ceiling panelling, tabernacle frames and complete entablatures, down to the end of the colonial period—at Shirley, for example, in the early seventies. But a simpler treatment, encouraged by the introduction of wallpaper, was becoming common; in this, panelling was confined to a dado, the entablature beneath the ceiling was reduced to a cornice, and doors were framed by architraves supporting a frieze and cornice at most. In both kinds of room the richest feature was the chimneypiece, in the ornamentation of which two main styles may be distinguished. Kent's *Designs of Inigo Jones* was the source for the chimneypiece in Governor Wentworth's council chamber in the Wentworth-Gardner House circa 1760, as it had been for that in the entrance hall of John Drayton's house near Charleston twenty years before; the result, as Kimball recognized, is the most elaborate of all the chimneypieces carved in the colonies. But the Baroque massiveness of Jones-Kent ornament was by then beginning to look a little old-fashioned, and designs for chimneypieces of the same type enlivened and lightened with Rococo ornament had already crossed the Atlantic in copies of *The British Architect* by Abraham Swan. Buckland, as we have seen, used Swan's book (which in 1775 became the first book on architecture to be

87
Mount Vernon, Fairfax County, Virginia. 1757–87. Dining room, with chimneypiece and ceiling of 1775.

published in America) in the later fifties at Gunston Hall. There he eschewed any hint of *rocaille*, but in the Hammond-Harwood and Brice houses in Annapolis he used it, albeit in a restrained manner, in chimneypieces derived from plates in the same book. Two other notable chimneypieces taken from Swan, in both cases almost line for line, are in the "mahogany room" of the Lee House at Marblehead, Massachusetts, dating from 1768, and in the dining room of Washington's Mount Vernon, from 1775 (87).

In 1776 the imported mantel in the drawing room at Gunston was still the only Adam Style chimneypiece in America. Of plaster ceilings in the style there was a small handful. Kenmore, at Fredericksburg, Virginia, had three, put up in the early seventies; two of them are knowledgeable translations of designs in *The City and Country Builder's and Workman's Treasury* by Batty Langley, which was first published in 1740, into the more delicate forms popularized by the great Scottish architect. At Mount Vernon there was the west parlor ceiling of circa 1770, a timid and underscaled affair, and there was the fine one of 1775 in the dining room. In England it would have been unimaginable that a room should have been given an Adamesque ceiling and a Rococo chimneypiece in the same year. The Mount Vernon dining room shows how dependent the colonial building owner was on the sources and resources, books and craftsmen, that chance made available.[6]

An Architectural Revolution

In the long run the most important developments in European architecture in the second and third quarters of the eighteenth century were those which led to the overthrow of the Renaissance-Baroque tradition by Neo-Classicism. Three epoch-making structures were the Assembly Room at York (1730–32), in which Lord Burlington recreated, with minimal concessions to contemporary needs, what the Romans called an Egyptian hall, the facade of St.-Sulpice, Paris (begun in 1733), in which G. N. Servandoni "broke with all the accepted rules of church design" to follow principles of composition that were to be those of Neo-Classicism, and the church of Ste.-Geneviève, Paris (begun in 1756, secularized as Le Panthéon in 1791), in which J.-G. Soufflot restored to the column, defined by Alberti as "the principal *ornament* in all architecture," its primal structural function.

In many respects Ste.-Geneviève was a practical demonstration of the rationalist theory of the abbé M.-A. Laugier as set forth in his *Essai sur l'architecture*, which, first published in 1753, was the most influential theoretical work of the age. The other books that did most to forward the Neo-Classical cause were the products of the great flowering of classical archaeology in the 1750s and 1760s, depicting ancient Greek architecture and the architecture of the Eastern Roman Empire. It soon became evident that the rules that had controlled classical design since the Renaissance had been derived from too few buildings within a too limited geographical range. Even those prescribing the proportions of the orders were called in doubt. "The great masters of antiquity," wrote Robert Adam, "were not so rigidly scrupulous, they varied the proportions as the general spirit of their composition required, clearly perceiving, that however necessary these rules may be to form the taste and correct the licentiousness of the scholar [that is, student] they often cramp the genius and circumscribe the ideas of the master." By 1773, when these words appeared in the preface to *Works in Architecture of Robert and James Adam*, Palladianism in Britain had made way for the Adam Style, which was the first nationally accepted Neo-Classical Style in Europe.

In America, political revolution delayed the architectural one, and the first complete building in the Adam Style was not begun until 1788. Three years before that a building with a claim to notice in any history of Western architecture was designed, in Paris, by a former governor of Virginia for that (his native) state. The building was the Virginia State Capitol, Thomas Jefferson its designer. Jefferson was born twenty years before the leading American practi-

Thomas Jefferson

tioner of the Adam Style, and it is proper to consider his work before we turn to the latter, from which it differs in intention and character.

Jefferson's very first building was the south outchamber, the "honeymoon cottage," of his own Monticello. It was built in 1769; he designed the house proper, in the form in which it was finished in 1780, in 1771–72. Monticello I (so to distinguish it from the much enlarged and altered building that stands today) had a Palladian *parti*, modified by the introduction of octagonal elements suggested by Robert Morris's *Select Architecture*, with a two-storied portico on either front (88). So described it sounds ordinary enough; what made it extraordinary was the reversal of the normal Palladian scheme, in which the service wings flank an entrance court, so that the wings flanked a lawn on the other side of the house, while the slopes of the site were utilized to turn their flat roofs into terrace walks, reached from the lawn by short flights of steps; underground passages linked the wings with the main block. Such underground passages, as Jefferson knew from his reading of Pliny the Elder, were features of the ancient Roman villa, and the hilltop site which he chose for the house, to the surprise of his contemporaries, was of precisely the kind favored by the Romans for their country retreats in the Alban Hills.[1]

Two other pre-capitol designs by Jefferson must be noticed, though neither was executed. The earlier, made while Jefferson was working on the design of Monticello I, was for an octagonal chapel, presumably at Williamsburg. *Select Architecture* contained a plan for a chapel of this form which Jefferson developed in classical terms with

88
Monticello, Albemarle County, Virginia, as first built. Thomas Jefferson, 1771–80. Plan of principal floor.

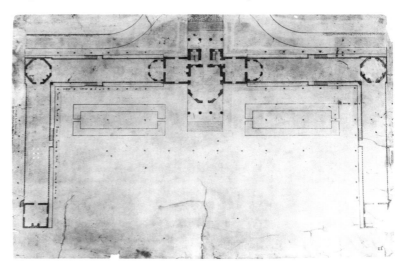

a peristyle of twenty-four Tuscan columns and a hemispherical Roman dome, complete with oculus. The other design, one of several for remodelling the Governor's Palace at Williamsburg, was made between Jefferson's sponsorship of a bill to move the Virginian capital to Richmond in 1779 and the destruction of the Palace by fire late in the following year; it was evidently conceived as a scheme for converting the building, of which Jefferson wrote in his *Notes on the State of Virginia* that it was "capable of being made an elegant seat," into a private dwelling. The hall is enlarged into an octagon with a projecting bay. But the features without precedent in domestic architecture in America or Europe are the two porticoes, octastyle, pedimented, and of the full width and height of the building. Had the design been executed, the old Palace would have become the first temple-form house in the history of Neo-Classicism.

The Virginia State Capitol was the first public building of temple form (89). An early design, made about 1780, resembled the design for the remodelling of the Williamsburg Palace in being amphiprostyle and octastyle. In 1785, however, when the state's Directors of Public Buildings wrote to Jefferson in Paris asking him "to consult an able Architect on a plan fit for a Capitol" and he complied by obtaining the collaboration of C.-L. Clérisseau, the simpler form of a Roman temple with a hexastyle portico at one end only was adopted. "We took as our model" Jefferson explained, "the Maison Carrée at Nîmes." The shade of the abbé Laugier must have approved of the choice. In his *Essai sur l'architecture,* after deducing from his ideal of the "cabane rustique" or primitive hut that the only essentials in any kind of architecture are the column, the entablature and the pediment, Laugier went on to praise the Maison Carrée "because everything in it is according to the true principles of architecture." And the probability that Jefferson had the *Essai* in mind is turned into a virtual certainty by his statement to the Directors of Public Buildings that his design was inspired by "the most perfect and precious remains of antiquity"—a phrase whose similarity to Laugier's characterization of the Maison Carrée as "un des plus précieux restes de la bonne antiquité" can hardly be coincidental.[2]

The final drawings for the capitol were sent to Richmond early in 1786; they were followed nearly a year later by a plaster model. Inevitably there were a number of departures from the Roman prototype. Jefferson himself explained the reason for one: the order was changed from Corinthian to Ionic "because of the difficulty of the Corinthian capitals"—an allusion to the scarcity of stonecarvers in Virginia, or anywhere in the United States, at the time. Some, such as the windows and the two-storied interior, were necessary concessions to the functional requirements of the program. Another, the omission of the half-columns along the sides of the Roman temple, may have been due to Jefferson's reading of Laugier, who thought that engaged columns should be used only as a "licence authorized by necessity" and should then be three-quarter columns at least. In execution, however, pilasters, to which Laugier objected even more strongly as "only a bad representation of columns," were added. Samuel Dobie, who supervised the completion of the building, was presumably responsible for this, for no other building by Jefferson has external pilasters.

During his four years in Europe Jefferson conceived a great admiration for French architecture, and this showed in most of the designs he made after his return to America in 1789. The remodelling of Monticello carried out in 1796–1809, giving it the appearance of a single-story house, made it both more French (for houses with only one full story were the fashion in France) and more Roman (for Roman villas were generally of one story) (90). It did not, however, destroy its overall Palladian character. The octagonal dome and drum with which it was crowned resembles the same feature on Burlington's villa at Chiswick and designs in Gibbs's and Morris's books far more closely than it resembles the dome of Pierre Rousseau's Hôtel de Salm in Paris, with which Jefferson, by his own account, was so "violently smitten" that he "used to go to the Tuileries almost daily to look at it." Moreover, while inventing his own version of the

French window, with triple-hung sash instead of casements, and adopting other French practical conveniences, Jefferson remained faithful to English books for architectural detail and to Palladio for the proportions of the orders. Monticello II is a very eclectic work of architecture which lacks the unity and consistency of Monticello I. Yet while the critic may regret what Jefferson did to his house, the historian will recognize Monticello II as standing proof of Frank Lloyd Wright's contention that designing a house is like painting a portrait—and as one of the most fascinating self-portraits in the history of architecture. From its site to its gadgetry—wind-dial, geared double doors, dumb waiter—it is all Jefferson.

Jefferson's admiration for Palladio, already old-fashioned by European standards when he designed Monticello I, makes even his later work different from other varieties of Neo-Classicism. For the Governor's House in Richmond around 1780 and for the President's House in Washington in 1792 he produced versions of La Rotonda, Palladio's four-porticoed villa outside Vicenza. Neither ever came near to being built. Edgemont, although it lacks the central domed room that earned the Villa Capra its local name, has a portico on each of its four sides. Designed in 1797, square on plan with a part-octagonal bay projecting into the covered space of the portico on the garden front, Edgemont is one of Jefferson's most fetching works even if its wooden construction contravened his principles. As at Monticello, he made skillful use of a sloping site—here not only to provide underground passages to the flanking pavilions but also to conceal the basement story on the entrance side. The garden-front portico, unlike the other three, is without steps and raised on a triple-arched loggia (a Palladian feature), and thus becomes an outdoor room. The same functional distinction is made, again with the aid of a sloping site, between the two porticoes of Jefferson's own

"occasional retreat," Poplar Forest. The plan of Poplar Forest, which
was begun in 1806, was probably suggested by one in Kent's *Designs
of Inigo Jones.* It is a transformation of the Villa Capra plan in which
all the rectangles, including the square of the outer walls, are turned
into octagons, while the central rotunda is turned into a square
dining room, expressed externally by a platform surmounting the
hipped roof; Jefferson's addiction to the octagon was never more
ingeniously indulged. Jefferson's last two houses, Farmington near
Louisville (the only building by him outside Virginia, begun in 1808)
and Barboursville (1817), had three octagonal rooms between them—
Farmington two, back to back with a hall between. Barboursville was
much like Monticello II. The dome designed for it was never built,
however, so that despite the high value he set on the feature Jefferson
saw only two domes rise to his design, one at Monticello and the
other five miles away at the University of Virginia.

In designing the University of Virginia Jefferson was creating a
physical environment for a public institution of which he was the
begetter, a situation in which few architects have found themselves
(91, 92, 93). The revolutionary idea of building a university as an
"academical village" came to him in 1804 or 1805. In 1810 he already
saw it in the form of "lodges" for the professors, with classrooms

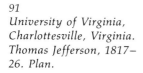

91
*University of Virginia,
Charlottesville, Virginia.
Thomas Jefferson, 1817–
26. Plan.*

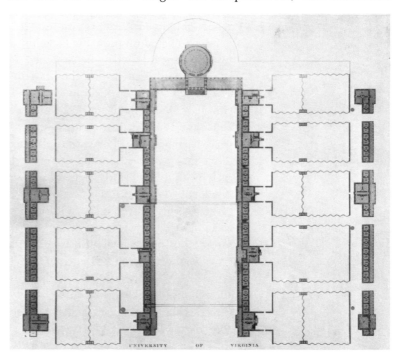

92
University of Virginia,
Charlottesville, Virginia.
Rotunda, from south.

93
University of Virginia,
Charlottesville, Virginia.
Pavilions on east side of
lawn.

on the ground floor, joined by "barracks" for students, "opening into a covered way to give dry communication between all the schools," the whole "arranged around an open square of grass or trees." In 1817, as soon as construction of the first lodge—or pavilion, as they came to be called—was authorized, he wrote for suggestions to William Thornton and Henry Latrobe. The latter responded with a design showing a domed central building, much higher than the pavilions, intended for an auditorium. Jefferson accepted the suggestion but made it a library. Another change from the original design, in which the green of the academical village, seven or eight hundred feet across, became something more like a grassy street two hundred feet wide (the "lawn"), was due to the exigencies of the site, which also necessitated terracing. And behind the ten pavilions, separated from them by gardens in which the professors were to grow their vegetables, were added more dormitories and six dining halls, or "hotels."

Just as Jefferson had taken the best preserved Roman temple of rectangular plan as his model for the Virginia State Capitol, so for the library of the University of Virginia he took the best preserved and greatest circular one, Hadrian's Pantheon. In his own terminology, one was an exemplar of cubic, the other of spherical architecture. His imitation of the Pantheon is half the height and width of the prototype. Externally, the design is verticalized by the building being raised on a terrace and by the number of columns across the front of the portico being reduced from eight to six, while the portico and the rotunda proper are tied together, as they are not in the prototype, by the entablature of the portico being continued around the rotunda. Internally, the building is of three stories, including the basement, so that the sphere is only a proportional device without any spatial reality. Jefferson had never seen the Pantheon; a more recent building which he had seen and admired, the house in the form of a broken column in the Désert de Retz near Paris, was evidently in his mind when he planned the first floor of the library with its three oval rooms and dumbbell-shaped stairhall. To each of the pavilions he gave a different form and a different order, carrying out his intention, as he described it to Thornton, that they should be "models of good taste and good architecture, and of a variety of appearance, no two alike, so as to serve as specimens for the Architectural lecturer." Today's architectural lecturer with a taste for source-hunting can have a field day at the University of Virginia, beginning with the overall layout. (Palaestra, Roman villa, or French academicism?) But in the balance of the human scaled and the monumental, of uniformity and variety, in the clarity with which the hierarchy of functions is given physical expression, and in the rightness of the relationship between the buildings and the spaces between them, Jefferson's last work of architecture has qualities that transcend such considerations.

The Virginia capitol was the forerunner of the countless temple-form buildings that sprang up all over the United States in the second quarter of the nineteenth century. During Jefferson's lifetime the influence of his architecture was limited; Jeffersonian Classicism, most typically represented by a four-square kind of house with one or more Tuscan porticoes, was in the main a Southern style. Among its practitioners were builders who had worked for Jefferson at the University of Virginia or elsewhere, and one of them, John Neilson, in collaboration with the building owner, John Hartwell Cocke (who had rejected a design by Jefferson), was responsible for the remarkable house called Bremo, in Fluvanna County, Virginia (94). Here four porticoes, three projecting and one recessed, create a spatial counterpoint around the main block, while lateral pavilions echo the pedimented portico on the entrance front, behind which is a hall in the exact form of a cube.

94
Bremo, Fluvanna County, Virginia. John Hartwell Cocke and John Neilson, 1820. Park front.

Monumental public buildings, Jefferson believed, were among the first needs of the new nation. They were slow in appearing. The most important of all, the United States Capitol, was the subject of an architectural competition instigated by Jefferson in 1792 but was not finished until 1830. The next two legislative buildings after the Virginia capitol to be completed were the Connecticut and Massachusetts state houses. Both were designed by Charles Bulfinch.

Like Jefferson, whom he visited in Paris while on his Grand Tour of Europe in 1785–87, Bulfinch was a gentleman-architect, an amateur in the sense of being self-taught, though after bankruptcy in 1796 he turned professional in the sense of taking fees. There any resemblance between them ends. For Jefferson architectural design was an exercise of the intellect, for Bulfinch of sensibility. Jefferson hoped, through the example of his works, to establish a better, more classical taste among his countrymen, perhaps even to help implant in them those qualities of "Roman virtue and greatness" of which (as he had read in Leoni's translation of Palladio) ancient architecture gave "a certain knowledge." Bulfinch, it is safe to assume, was never greatly concerned with any moral purpose in architecture; he was content to cater to the taste of his New England clients, which was, as in colonial times, for the latest (or what they took to be the latest) from England—where Jefferson found architecture "in the most wretched style [he] ever saw, not meaning to except America . . . nor even Virginia."

The latest in England when Bulfinch was there in the mid 1780s were the Adam Style and the works of Sir William Chambers; the innovations of Soane and the last works of Soane's master, the younger Dance, were still in the future. The Adam Style had been taken up and modified since the sixties, when the Adams' practice was at its height, by other architects, of whom one of the most talented was James Wyatt. In London there were two buildings, one by Wyatt and the other by Chambers, that no visitor could miss. Wyatt's was the Pantheon, on Oxford Street, with an interior modelled on Santa Sophia, which had been an enormously popular rendezvous for masquerades from its completion in 1772 until 1784, when it became a concert hall. Chambers's was Somerset House, the great Thames-side building for government departments and learned societies begun in 1776 and finished, but for much later wings, in 1786. It was these two buildings which Bulfinch took as his models for the Massachusetts State House, designed in the year of his return from Europe though not built until 1795–97 (95, 96). Its main front is a lightened or Adamized version of the center of the south front of Somerset House, which in a letter to the legislative committee

95
*Massachusetts State
House, Boston, Massa-
chusetts. Charles Bul-
finch, 1795–97. View
from southwest.*

96
*Massachusetts State
House, Boston, Massa-
chusetts. Old Representa-
tives Hall.*

Bulfinch referred to as "a building celebrated all over Europe," while its largest interior, the Representatives Hall, follows in all essentials the Great Room in Wyatt's Pantheon, a fact not mentioned by Bulfinch to the committee, which probably would have considered the model a frivolous one. The Massachusetts State House was much admired from the first, and the fact that a central dome became an almost universal feature of American state houses and capitols is due at least as much to its example as to that of the national capitol.

The state house at Hartford, designed in 1792 and built in 1793–96, was Palladian rather than Adamesque. Externally it was a much simplified version of Liverpool Town Hall, which was built to the design of the John Woods, father and son, in 1748–55. More original, and of considerable historical importance as "the first professionally designed American theater by a native architect," was The Theatre on Federal Street, Boston, built to Bulfinch's design in 1793–94. Its facade was based on a plate in a book by one of Adam's most talented English followers, John Crunden; a tetrastyle portico of the Corinthian order projected from the front on a high basement story which formed a *porte-cochère*. The interior departed radically from English practice with a domed auditorium of three-quarter-circle plan and cantilevered boxes. The model was the Grand Théâtre at Bordeaux by Victor Louis, which Bulfinch had seen on his travels and called "the most superb in France."

Earlier than any of these buildings, and in fact Bulfinch's first executed design, was the Hollis Street Church in Boston, built in 1787–88. For its plan Bulfinch went back to Wren's St. Stephen Walbrook. It was the first church in what had been British America to have a central dome, while its entrance front, with a Doric portico flanked by two towers with cupolas, was without precedent in American or in English architecture, though soon to be imitated in the First Presbyterian Church, Baltimore (1789–95). Bulfinch was the architect of eight churches and meeting houses in all. In planning his first two meeting houses (at Pittsfield and Taunton, both designed in 1789) he took the biggest step toward the abolition of all architectural distinctions between the two building types by placing the main entrances at the end instead of in the middle of the long sides. His finest buildings for worship were New South Church, Boston (1814), and the First Church of Lancaster (1816) (97, 98). New South, built of Chelmsford granite, had a tall steeple and a tetrastyle Doric portico attached to, and dominating, an octagonal nave. The marked difference in style between the spire and the body of the church was due to the conservatism of the building committee, which preferred this purely Gibbsian design to a Neo-Classical version of

*97
New South Church, Bos-
ton, Massachusetts.
Charles Bulfinch, 1814.
Portico and steeple.*

98
Meeting House, Lancaster, Massachusetts.
Charles Bulfinch, 1816.
View from southwest.

the spire of Old North also submitted by the architect.[3] No such disharmony mars the Lancaster meeting house, with its delicately detailed Adam Style cupola. Architectural quality, even more than the red brick of which it is constructed, sets this building apart from the contemporary carpenter-built New England meeting house, often pretty enough in its way, of which the Unitarian Church at Wayland, designed in 1814 by Andrews Palmer, is a good example (99). It is no less different from the many churches that still followed in the tradition of St. Martin-in-the-Fields, such as the Center Church at New Haven (1812–14) by Asher Benjamin and the Independent Presbyterian Church at Savannah (1817–19) by John Holden Greene.

Early in 1818 Bulfinch was appointed architect of the Capitol in Washington. New England was much the loser by his departure, seeing only two more buildings of any importance, one in Massachusetts and the other in Maine, go up to his design. The first was Massachusetts General Hospital, built in 1818–23. In 1816 Bulfinch visited the middle states to study hospital design, and the central section of the Pennsylvania Hospital, designed by David Evans, Jr., and added to Samuel Rhoads's building in 1794–1809, supplied the prototype of the clinical amphitheatre, the Ether Dome,[4] of Massachusetts General. Stylistically the two buildings are utterly different; Evans's is the Adam Style at its showiest, while Bulfinch's has all the simplicity of his later manner.

Bulfinch's last building was the Maine State House at Augusta, built in 1829–32. From several designs the legislators chose one "representing the Boston state house reduced." In a letter to the governor, Bulfinch wrote that while he had preserved the general outline of his earlier building he had tried to prevent the design being "a servile copy" and had "aimed at giving it an air of simplicity, which, while I hope it will appear reconcilable to good taste, will render it easy to execute in your material"—which was again granite. Among the changes was the substitution of a Tuscan portico, complete with pediment, for the Corinthian colonnade of the Massachusetts State House, and of a circular cupola with an Ionic peristyle for the Wren-like lantern on the dome of the latter. That Bulfinch should have described the cupola to the Governor as "a copy of the Temple of Vesta at Rome" shows his awareness of the spirit of the times which by 1829 set much store by the close imitation of specific ancient buildings; that it should have borne only a vague resemblance to the nominal model shows how his approach to antiquity differed from that of the architects who in the near future were to respond to the need for towers with molding-for-molding reproductions of the Monument of Lysicrates.

99
Unitarian Church, Way-
land, Massachusetts.
Andrews Palmer, 1814.
View from west.

The Adam Style House

In domestic architecture the Adam Style brought in a new kind of plan, with rooms of different and contrasted shapes instead of the squares and rectangles of Palladianism. (Adam himself described the change as "a remarkable improvement in the form, convenience, arrangement, and relief of apartments.") It was a kind of plan that was Neo-Classical programmatically in its derivation from the Roman *thermae* or public baths and aesthetically in the clarity of definition of the individual spaces, to which respect for the integrity of the wall-plane (however richly ornamented that might be) made an indispensable contribution.

The first American house with this kind of a plan, and the first complete building in the Adam Style in America, was The Woodlands in West Philadelphia (100, 101). Its owner, William Hamilton, had recently returned from England when in 1788 he set about re-modelling a house built by his father some thirty-five years before. Perhaps he brought the plan with him; in any case it is remarkable in incorporating a specimen of almost every room form in the Adam repertory: square, oblong, circular, octagonal, oblong with semicircular apses at either end, and oval. The last of these, the oval, was virtually unknown in domestic architecture in Britain before Adam. In France, however, it had been established as an admired form for a grand room by the example of Le Vau's château of Vaux-le-Vicomte in the seventeenth century, and one thing Adam had in common with Jefferson was an admiration for French domestic architecture.

Externally, too, The Woodlands is a remarkably comprehensive Adam Style design. On the entrance front six Ionic pilasters, with the outer pairs coupled, support a pediment with paterae on the frieze. The cornice is continued around the house to join the full entablature of the portico on the other front, which has six widely spaced Doric columns attenuated to Ionic proportions. The door on this front has a semi-elliptical fanlight, and on either side of the portico is a Venetian window recessed within an arch; semicircular windows light the basement.

Within months at most of Hamilton's beginning work on The Woodlands, the banker William Bingham was building the first American town house in the style, in Philadelphia. Modelled on Manchester House in London, it was by all accounts of a sumptuousness never before seen in the city of brotherly love; Bulfinch, after visiting it in 1789, wrote that it was "in a stile which would be esteemed splendid even in the most luxurious parts of Europe," and six years later he copied its street front in his first house for Harrison Gray Otis in Boston. Adamesque features in the Otis House that do not appear in The Woodlands were delicate wrought-iron balconies,

100
The Woodlands, Philadelphia, Pennsylvania. 1788–89. Entrance front.

101
The Woodlands, Philadelphia, Pennsylvania. Plan of first floor.

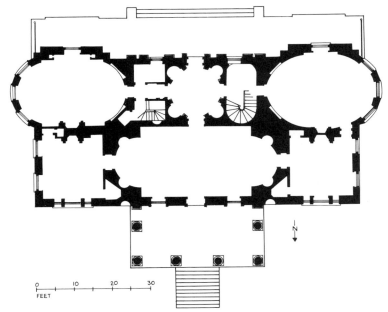

spiderweblike leading in the semicircular window on the top floor, and small panels bearing reliefs set into the wall above the second-floor windows. Neither The Woodlands nor the Bingham House had a roof balustrade, as many of the later houses in the style did—including the President's House in Philadelphia, whose construction with public funds was authorized by the Pennsylvania legislature in the hope of attracting the federal government to the city in 1791.

It was in the year 1791 that Bulfinch designed his first three houses. The most innovative was the house for the Boston merchant Joseph Barrell at Somerville. On the garden front of Pleasant Hill, as it was called, a central pavilion, formed by the projection of an oval salon on the ground floor and a loggia with Corinthian columns above it, rose half a story above the rest of the house. The bowed center became a common feature in domestic architecture. Within the decade Bulfinch used the projecting oval again in the Knox Mansion at Thomaston, Maine (1794), and the Mason House, Boston (1799); Samuel McIntire used it in the Lyman House at Waltham, Massachusetts (1793), and the Derby Mansion at Salem (1795), and unidentified architects in Gore Place, Waltham (1797), Lemon Hill, Philadelphia, and Montebello, Baltimore (1799) (102, 103). In 1796 Bulfinch substituted the circle for the oval in the Swan House at Dorchester, Massachusetts, and David Manigault made the same substitution in his own house at Charleston, South Carolina, completed in 1797. Whether based on the oval or the circle—or the octagon, as in the Nathaniel Russell House at Charleston, finished to the design of Russell Warren by 1809—the bowed center resulted in what Adam had called "a greater movement . . . in the outside composition."

In porticoes the wide spacing and attenuation of the columns noted in The Woodlands were typical of the American Adamesque; in *The American Builder's Companion* (1806) Asher Benjamin showed columns with shafts lengthened two diameters beyond normal practice, and builder-architects sometimes carried the process to the point of caricature. The next domestic portico after The Woodlands which can be dated with certainty was that of the more-than-half-Palladian presidential mansion in New York (from 1791 to 1797 the official residence of the governors of New York State), which was completed to the design of John McComb, Jr., in 1790. In 1791 Hampton Plantation House at McClellanville, South Carolina, received the addition of a portico copied from the one added to David Garrick's villa at Hampton on the Thames, to Adam's design, fifteen or twenty years before. Homewood, Baltimore, designed by its owner, Charles Carroll, Jr., in 1801, was the earliest of a group of porticoed houses

102
Gore Place, Waltham,
Massachusetts. 1797.
South front.

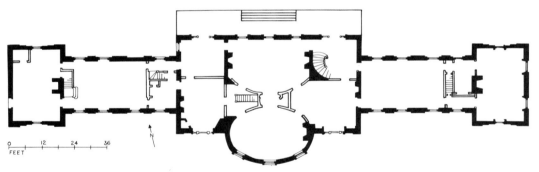

103
Gore Place, Waltham,
Massachusetts. Plan of
first floor.

104
Homewood, Baltimore, Maryland. Charles Carroll, Jr., 1801–03. Entrance front.

105
Gardner-Pingree House (Essex Institute), Salem, Massachusetts. Samuel McIntire, 1804–05. Street front.

of which it would be hard to find the like in Britain—long and low, composed of three of five parts of only one full story, with the central block rising slightly higher than the rest (104). Others are Ridgeway at St. Matthews, Kentucky (ca. 1805), Rose Hill in Lexington (1818), and the Baum-Taft House in Cincinnati (ca. 1820).

Columnar porches, as distinct from porticoes, were much used. Often they were semicircular on plan, like that of the Gardner House (now the Essex Institute) in Salem, Massachusetts, which was built in 1804–05 to the design of Samuel McIntire (105). For facade orders pilasters were the rule, and Ionic and Corinthian about equally used. All the main facade treatments employing a pilaster order were used by Bulfinch. The Morton House at Roxbury, Massachusetts (1796), had two pairs of coupled pilasters rising through its two stories to support a pediment. The Mason House had very slender pilasters rising through three stories at each end of its bowed front; a design for the Elias Hasket Derby Mansion at Salem shows a two-story front with an astylar ground story and pilasters deployed across the second. Commonest of all was the combination of an astylar ground story and two upper stories with a pilaster order, as in Bulfinch's own house in Boston (1793), the houses by him in Franklin Place, Boston (1794), the Ezekiel Hersey Derby House at Salem (ca. 1800), and his second house for Harrison Gray Otis in Boston (1800–02). This had been the standard treatment of the London house front, when an order was used, since the middle of the seventeenth century; in the Adamesque variations on the theme the pilasters were often, as in all the examples named except the Franklin Place houses, omitted from the central bays.

Another feature of the London scene that was naturalized in the early years of independence was the row of contiguous houses sharing party walls; the economics of building succeeded where in the seventeenth century government fiat had failed. The most ambitious project of the kind was begun in 1793 in Boston, to Bulfinch's design. Tontine Crescent, as it was called from the method by which the architect hoped to finance it, was doubtless inspired by the Adelphi, the great Thames-side development of the Adam brothers next to Somerset House. It was planned as two segmental rows of sixteen houses facing each other to form an ellipse; only one row was built. The houses were of the standard London plan, three bays wide with front and back rooms and a side passage for entry and stairs; the row was given a monumental treatment with a pedimented building in the middle and a pilaster order applied to the last two houses at either end, which stood slightly forward from the rest. The central building was pierced by a carriageway. Its upper stories with their Ionic columns were reminiscent of the Society of Arts building in the Adelphi and, housing as they did a library and the office of the Massachusetts Historical Society, not dissimilar in function.

"The Decoration of the Inside"

"The massive entablature, the ponderous compartment ceiling, the tabernacle frame, almost the only species of ornament hitherto known, in this country, are now universally exploded, and in their place, we have adopted a beautiful variety of light mouldings, gracefully formed, delicately enriched and arranged with propriety and skill." Thus Robert Adam on the "almost total change" in "the decoration of the inside" that his example brought about in domestic architecture in Britain in the 1760s. In general terms the change can be described as the substitution of decorative forms derived from Roman domestic architecture for architectonic forms derived from the Roman temple. There were precedents: grotesques, as one common kind of Roman decoration was called, had been employed by Raphael and others in Italy in the sixteenth century and more recently in England by William Kent. What was new was that Adam used them and other Roman motifs consistently in the service of a philosophy of design that placed sensibility and visual effect above "the rules."

By the time it was established in America the style of decoration introduced by Adam had itself undergone a change. In 1785 Horace Walpole, after a visit to the future king George IV's Carlton House, which had just been completed to the design of Henry Holland, wrote: "How sick one will be of Mr. Adam's gingerbread and sippets of embroidery after this chaste palace!" Holland's style owed more to the publications of certain mid-eighteenth-century French architects than to Adam, but the new taste for chastity affected the Adam Style and there was a general reaction against what came to be regarded as excesses in the work of its originator. The Adamesque interior in America is apt to be almost overwhelmingly chaste; typically the decoration is sparse and walls and ceiling are an unrelieved bridal white. Nor is the detail often such as to invite or hold close attention; there were enough craftsmen who could follow or adapt designs from the builders' guides (most often those by the English William Pain and the American Asher Benjamin), but only the carver-architect Samuel McIntire, in whose houses at Salem the inevitable paterae and chains of husks are combined with naturalistic ornaments, stands out as an interior designer with any real artistic personality.

106
Nathaniel Russell House,
Charleston, South Caro-
lina. Russell Warren, be-
fore 1809. Entrance hall.

    In nothing did the Adam Style house differ more from its colonial predecessor than in the design of the stair. Colonial stairs rise in straight flights; corners are turned with landings; balusters and rails are full-bodied if not massive. The Adam stair is much lighter in appearance, with the balusters attenuated or reduced to plain sticks; and on plan it is nearly always partly, and sometimes wholly, curvilinear. Both circle and oval were employed. Among the earlier examples, the main stair in the David Manigault House at Charleston is fully circular, while in Bulfinch's Thomas Russell House at Charlestown, Massachusetts (1793–96) it was a complete oval on plan; in the Ezekiel Derby House at Salem it was semicircular; in the Nathaniel Russell House, at Charleston, Warren combined circle and oval at different levels (106). Whatever their geometrical form, such stairs, which are as ingenious in construction as they are graceful in effect, were the chief means of imparting movement to the interior of the house. They are also the feature of the Adam Style with the strongest appeal to twentieth-century taste.

Enter the Professional Architect

With the possible but unproved exceptions of The Woodlands and Gore Place, all the American buildings mentioned in the last chapter were designed by native Americans who had had nothing that could be called professional training in architecture for the good reason that in their youth there had been no professional architects in America to train them. We come now to the work of the immigrants active during the same period, most of whom had had some technical training—in engineering if not in architecture—and some of whom had already practiced architecture on the other side of the Atlantic, and to the early designs of the first Americans to be professionally trained, by one of those immigrants, as architects.

The immigrants' work was not always up-to-date. James Hoban, who arrived from Ireland in 1785, remained faithful to the Irish Palladianism of the third quarter of the century in both the President's House in Washington and the First Bank of the United States in Philadelphia; the latter, designed in 1795, is closely modelled on the Royal Exchange in Dublin (Thomas Cooley, architect) on which Hoban had worked. Nor is their work always distinguishable from that of the American-born; in his Park Street Church in Boston, designed in 1809, Peter Banner, an Englishman whose name first appeared in the New York city directory in 1795, adopted the attenuated manner of the New England builder-architects so wholeheartedly that he may fairly be said to have gone native. Yet without the immigrants' contribution American architecture of the Federal period, for all Jefferson's originality, would be little more than an interesting backwater outside the main stream of architectural history.

The first of them to arrive was the engineer Pierre Charles L'Enfant, who came from France to join Washington's army in 1777. Eleven years later it fell to him to remodel the old New York City Hall to serve, as Federal Hall, for Washington's inauguration and the first session of Congress. In the Louis XVI style with a liberal application of American and republican emblems, Federal Hall was an architectural declaration of independence that was admired enough by both the public and the president to ensure L'Enfant's appointment as planner of the new capital city on the Potomac. His only other architectural work of note was a large and strange house in Philadelphia for Robert Morris, begun in 1794 and demolished while still a shell in 1800; also Louis XVI in style, it had a French mansard roof—the earliest in America outside New Orleans by some sixty-five years.

Of the immigrants who left their mark on American architecture in the Federal period the most gifted—in the order of their arrival—

were Etienne Sulpice Hallet (ca. 1782), William Thornton (1787), Joseph François Mangin (1794), George Hadfield (1795), Benjamin Henry Latrobe (1796), Maximilien Godefroy (1805), Joseph Jacques Ramée (1811), and William Jay (1817). Four of them were involved in the central public work of the age, the building of the national Capitol.

The United States Capitol

The competition, suggested by Jefferson, for designs for a Capitol and a President's House "to be erected in the city of Washington & territory of Columbia" was announced in the newspapers in March 1792. When the designs came in, Hoban's for the President's House was quickly approved, being preferred to one submitted anonymously by Jefferson. For the Capitol, ten designs were received, most of them from builder-architects who, however competent they may have been in domestic work, were clearly out of their depth when it came to a monumental building which should symbolize the achievements and aspirations of the new nation. Among the more accomplished was Samuel McIntire's, with elevations put together from two plates in Gibbs's *Book of Architecture*; it would have made a fine English country house, but America had been ruled from English country houses long enough. Less domestic, in spite of the model that inspired it, was the Gargantuan version of Palladio's Villa Capra with which Samuel Dobie, who had supervised the completion of the Virginia Capitol, weighed in.

The Commissioners for Federal Buildings found none of the designs entirely satisfactory, but favored the one by Etienne Hallet. They showed it to the president, whose approval of it, tempered by financial prudence—"if it were not too expensive, it would, in my judgment, be a noble and desirable structure"—seemed to Hallet to have settled the question, and he proceeded to revise it to meet the commissioners' requirements in the matter of "the distribution of parts." Then in October, three months after the competition had closed, Dr. William Thornton, the winner in 1789 of the first American architectural competition, for a building for the Philadelphia Library Company, asked to be allowed to submit drawings in accordance with the terms of the original advertisement. The request was granted, and early in 1793 Thornton submitted a design which, in Jefferson's words, "captivated the eyes and the judgment of all." Most importantly, it captivated the eyes and judgment of Jefferson himself and of Washington, with the result that in March the commissioners adopted it.

The choice of Thornton's design was attended by a major practical disadvantage. Hallet, who had come from France in connection with an abortive scheme to found an academy of the arts on French lines, was an experienced architect and presumably would have been capable of supervising the execution of his own design. Thornton, born in the West Indies and educated in Europe, was the complete amateur without technical knowledge of construction or experience in the supervision of building operations. Many of the troubles that were to plague the long building history of the Capitol were due to the necessity of appointing other architects to supervise the execution of a design to which they were officially but not personally committed.

First Hoban was appointed superintendent of the Capitol and the President's House while Hallet, who had been retained by the commissioners to revise Thornton's plan, was made assistant superintendent for architectural matters. This arrangement was terminated in less than a year, when Hallet was dismissed for exceeding his authority. Next, in the fall of 1794, the young English architect George Hadfield was made superintendent on the recommendation of the painter John Trumbull, who was then secretary to the American minister in England; he held the position until the spring of 1798. James Hoban, still busy with the President's House, was then put in charge as Surveyor of the Public Buildings, an office abolished in 1802 and revived in 1803 to be given by Jefferson to Benjamin Henry Latrobe, who held it until the end of Jefferson's second term in 1811. Between 1811 and 1814 little was done; in 1814 British troops burned the Capitol, which then consisted of two wings without a center, and also the President's House, which owes its soubriquet to the white paint applied to conceal the effects of the fire. In 1815 Latrobe was recalled for the work of repair and reconstruction; he resigned in 1817 and was succeeded by Bulfinch, under whom the center and dome were built by the end of 1822 and the building was completed in 1827 (107, 108). Bulfinch followed Latrobe's design for the most part. The biggest changes he made were due to Congress's insistance on more committee rooms and on a higher dome. One member of the cabinet wanted a dome of Gothic form.

Thornton had no specific model for the Capitol. A design made by William Kent in the 1730s for new Houses of Parliament in London has a circular dome of Pantheon type rising behind an octastyle portico on a rusticated basement, like Thornton's earliest known design for the east front, but it is unlikely that he knew Kent's drawings. In any case his elevations are less Anglo-Palladian than Louis XVI, while his plan also showed French influence if, as is probable, the semicircular Senate Chamber was suggested by the School of Medicine in Paris (designed in 1771 by Jacques Gondouin). His Hall of Representatives was elliptical; one of Latrobe's first

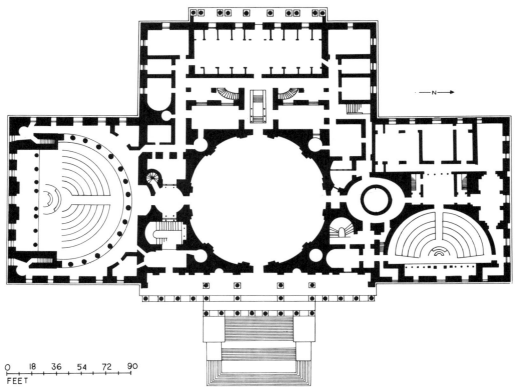

0   18   36   54   72   90
FEET

107
*United States Capitol,
Washington, District of
Columbia. William
Thornton, Benjamin
Henry Latrobe, and
Charles Bulfinch, 1793–
1830. View from east in
1847. From a daguerreo-
type by John Plumbe, Jr.*

108
*United States Capitol,
Washington, District of
Columbia. Plan of princi-
pal floor.*

109
*United States Capitol,
Washington, District of
Columbia, Senate Ro-
tunda, with columns of
tobacco order.*

proposals in 1803—by then there was another French precedent in the Room of the Five Hundred (later the Chamber of Deputies), built to the design of J. P. Gisors in 1795–97—was to change it into a semicircle, as he actually did in the rebuilding after 1814.

In a letter to Jefferson, Latrobe wrote: "My principles of good taste are rigid in Grecian architecture. I am a bigoted Greek in the condemnation of the Roman architecture of Baalbec, Palmyra, and Spalatro." He was never able to express his admiration for Greek architecture on the outside of the Capitol, although he made a design for the west front in which the entrance was through a propylaeum with a Greek Doric portico. Inside he was able to give his Grecianism full play and used a wide range of Greek orders: in the basement under the Supreme Court and in the central Crypt versions of Paestum Doric, in the Senate Chamber and Lobby a fifth-century Ionic, in the Hall of Representatives the Corinthian of the Monument of Lysicrates, in its vestibule and at the entrance to the Library that of the Tower of the Winds. For the vestibule and stairs and small rotunda in the north wing he invented two new orders representing two staples of agrarian America, the capitals of the one being carved with ears of corn, of the other with flowers and leaves of the tobacco (109). Members admired the corn cob capitals, as they were inaccurately but alliteratively called, more than anything else Latrobe ever did for them.

While the interior of the United States Capitol as completed in 1827 was Latrobe's, the exterior was the work of three architects. The elevations with pilasters were by Thornton; the east portico was by Latrobe (who was responsible for moving the main entrance, which was in the west front in Thornton's original design); the dome and the west terrace and colonnade were by Bulfinch. As major public buildings not infrequently do, the Capitol looked old-fashioned by the time it was finished. Not only were Thornton's elevations of Louis XVI character, but in the grouping of the columns on the west front Bulfinch went back to his model for the Massachusetts State House, Somerset House. Yet the intrinsic quality of the building considered as a whole was such that it would be a severe critic who did not concede that history proved Jefferson right in at least the first part of his prediction in a letter to Latrobe: "I think the work when finished will be a durable and honorable monument of our infant republic, and will bear favorable comparisons with the remains of the same kind of the ancient republics of Greece and Rome."

William Thornton and
Benjamin Henry Latrobe

After his connection with the Capitol was severed, Hallet disappeared from the architectural scene, although he was still in America when he died in 1825. Nor are the later works of Thornton, who died in 1826, numerous. They include, however, two of the finest houses of the Federal period, the Octagon House in Washington and Tudor Place in Georgetown (110, 111). The Octagon, built in 1799–1800, is fitted into its corner site with a plan in which circular, triangular, and oblong components are ingeniously combined; the half-cylinder swelling out from the front and the splayed side walls impart movement, in the Adam sense of the term, to the house as seen from the street, while its detail, outside and in, is also Adamesque. Tudor Place, completed in 1816, is reminiscent of Wyatt rather than Adam. The first-floor windows on the south front resemble those used by Wyatt in Bowden, Wiltshire (1786), and like them echo in two dimensions a columnar central feature crowned by a low dome. But whereas in Bowden the wall behind the columns is convex, in Tudor Place it curves back to complete the circle under the dome.

Hadfield, who also died in 1826, had a disappointing career for one who in youth had shown much promise.[1] The two buildings for which he is best remembered fall within the scope of the next chapter. And so we may now turn to the extra-Capitoline work, so to call it, of his exact contemporary—they were both born in 1764—Latrobe.

Benjamin Henry Latrobe was the son of the head of a Moravian school in Yorkshire; his mother was American. After receiving most of his general education in Germany and his architectural training in the office of Samuel Pepys Cockerell, he set up in private practice

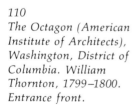

110
The Octagon (American Institute of Architects), Washington, District of Columbia. William Thornton, 1799–1800. Entrance front.

111
Tudor Place, Georgetown,
District of Columbia.
William Thornton, 1816.
Garden front.

in London in 1791. In 1795 he went bankrupt and decided to emigrate; he landed at Norfolk, Virginia, early in 1796. He came with good introductions and was soon visiting Mount Vernon as Washington's guest.

In the course of his American career Latrobe had dealings with many of the famous (and some of the infamous) of the early days of the republic, while canals and waterworks, dockyards and steamboats, as well as buildings of all kinds, engaged his powers of invention. As a professional architect in a country in which professionalism was a new and somewhat suspect concept, he suffered frustration at every turn. Yet in the sixty or so buildings which he designed between his arrival in America and his death in 1820 (in New Orleans, from yellow fever), he set new standards for American architecture. Only fifteen of those buildings stand today.

Latrobe's first public commission in America was the Virginia Penitentiary at Richmond. In 1785 Jefferson, in Paris, came across a plan for an octagonal prison published by the architect P. G. Bugniet in the *Mercure de France* twenty years before, and sent the engraving home to Virginia together with a design of his own based upon it. Twelve years later, in 1797, the idea thus implanted came to fruition when the state of Virginia decided to build a new prison. A competition was held, and won by Latrobe. In the quarter-century since Robert Smith had built the Walnut Street Prison in Philadelphia, two major events affecting prison design had occurred. The first had been the passage of the British Act of Parliament of 1779 which initiated the "separate system"—miscalled solitary confinement—recommended by the prison reformer John Howard; in the Richmond prison Latrobe provided solitary cells for men and for women but modified the Howard system by also providing communal cells for from three to seven "reformed prisoners." The other event affecting prison design had been the publication in 1791 of Jeremy Bentham's *Panopticon, or the Inspection House*, which recommended the building of circular prisons in which all the prisoners' activities could be supervised both visually and audially (through speaking tubes) by guards in the center; at Richmond Latrobe placed the men's cells and workrooms in a semicircular range of building, commanded by the governor's house, behind a rectangular section comprising three courtyards, the women's cells and workroom, the infirmary, certain service rooms, and the reception building. The elevations, of random masonry on the entrance front and brick elsewhere, were of a severity consonant with the building's function (112).

The Virginia Penitentiary may fairly be called the first modern prison in America. By the end of the century Latrobe had two more firsts to his credit: in Sedgeley, Philadelphia, built in 1799, the first

112
Virginia Penitentiary, Richmond, Virginia. Benjamin Henry Latrobe, 1797. Entrance front, from a sketch by the architect.

Gothic Revival house in America, and in the Bank of Pennsylvania in the same city, built in 1798–1800, the first use of a Greek order in America. The Bank of Pennsylvania was by far the more important building (113, 114). Built of Schuylkill marble, in general form it resembled a temple with a portico at each end, like Jefferson's early design for the Virginia Capitol, and a rotunda in the center. But there was no attempt to create the illusion of a temple; Latrobe expressed the rotunda externally with a lantern of a type borrowed from Soane's Bank of England set on a forty-five foot dome, stepped on the outside, emerging from a square block which not only rose above the main cornice but also projected slightly on either flank of the building. All the external detail was Greek, the Ionic columns of the porticoes being a simplified version of those of the north portico of the Erechtheum at Athens. Inside, for the first time in the history of what had been British America, masonry vaulting was employed for architectural effect, as well as for practical reasons.[2]

Philadelphians did not have to wait long to see the first Greek Ionic columns in America joined by the first Greek Doric ones. These stood in the porches of the Pump House in Central Square, which was built (like the bank, of Schuylkill marble) to Latrobe's design in 1799–1801 to house the steam pump of the Philadelphia waterworks. Some have seen in this building the influence of one of the customs houses or barrières by Ledoux which were built at the gates of Paris in 1784–89. But the Pump House was crowned with a low dome while the cylindrical tower of the Barrière de la Villette is flat-roofed, and this difference, together with the wall arches in which its windows were recessed, suggests that a belvedere tower in Soane's *Sketches in Architecture* (1793) gave Latrobe his first idea. In any case the final result had neither the calculated heaviness of Ledoux's design nor the mannered elegance of Soane's.

Latrobe has been called the American Soane. Certainly their roles in history were quite similar. They were the greatest architects of their generation in their respective countries, and each did more than any of his compatriots for the recognition and advancement of architecture as a profession. (It was Latrobe who introduced in America the practice by which an architect's fee is established as a percentage of the cost of the building—not without much difficulty, and rarely obtaining the five percent then customary in Europe.) But their personal styles were as different as their personalities. This comes out very clearly when one examines Latrobe's surviving masterpiece, St. Mary's Roman Catholic Cathedral in Baltimore (115, 116, 117).

113
Bank of Pennsylvania,
Philadelphia, Pennsylva-
nia. Benjamin Henry
Latrobe, 1798–1800. From
a drawing by the
architect.

114
Bank of Pennsylvania,
Philadelphia, Pennsylva-
nia. Plan.

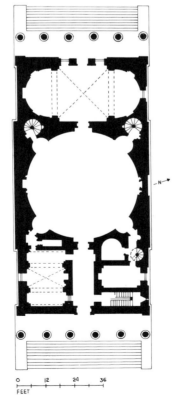

115
St. Mary's Cathedral,
Baltimore, Maryland.
Benjamin Henry Latrobe,
1814–18; belfry domes,
1832; portico, John H. B.
Latrobe, 1863. View from
southwest.

116
St. Mary's Cathedral,
Baltimore, Maryland.
Plan. The choir was added
in 1890 in conformity
with Latrobe's original
design.

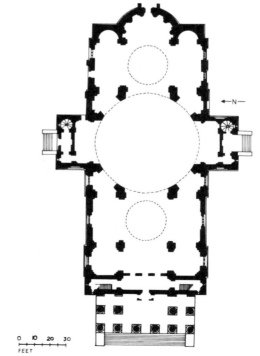

117
*St. Mary's Cathedral,
Baltimore, Maryland. In-
terior, looking southeast
across rotunda.*

For Baltimore Cathedral Latrobe submitted two designs, one classical and one Gothic; the bishop and diocese chose the classical.
Construction began in 1806, but the design eventually executed (the
seventh, according to the architect) was not made until 1808.³ The
first design is reminiscent of Soufflot's Panthéon. In making the
seventh Latrobe looked further back in time. It was hardly possible
that any English-trained architect designing a cathedral on a Latin-
cross plan with a dome spanning the full width of the nave and aisles
(a requirement of the client) should forget St. Paul's Cathedral.
Latrobe did more than remember it; Baltimore Cathedral is a con-
densed translation of St. Paul's into Neo-Classical terms, with quo-
tations from Wren's rejected Great Model design for the same
building. The most important of the latter is the ring of eight piers
with segmental inner faces and straight outer ones, forming a circle,
from which the dome can rise without the aid of (un-Roman) pendentives, inside an octagon, which is expressed externally in a plinth
beneath the dome. As in both the Great Model and St. Paul's as
built, there are two different intervals between the piers. In the
Great Model Wren used semicircular arches for both spans, with the
result that their crowns are at different heights; in St. Paul's as built
he used two segmental arches across the narrower spans, extending
the face-moldings of the upper ones into semicircles to match the
arches across the wider spans. Latrobe used both semicircular and
segmental arches but reversed Wren's arrangement, making the
wider arches segmental and the narrower ones semicircular, with
only one arch spanning each of the narrower intervals between the
piers. This combination of wide segmental arches flanked by narrower and lower segmental ones is a leitmotiv of Soane's Bank of
England. Yet Baltimore Cathedral is no more Soanesque than the
Philadelphia Pump House was. Above all, it is quite without that
"sense of deflation, as if all *mass* had been exhausted from the
design" which (in Summerson's words) characterizes Soane's personal style.

The difference between Baltimore Cathedral and the churches of
the colonial period is one of kind. Their interiors, whether their
architect's inspiration was from Wren or Gibbs, are essentially—
however they may be subdivided horizontally by colonnades or ver-
tically by galleries—single volumes of space, comprehended at a
glance. At Baltimore the visitor passes through a succession of spatial
units, each defined by the surfaces, flat or concave, of the actual
masonry structure, until he reaches the circular space under the
dome, the full extent of which cannot be seen from the entrance.
There physical movement is succeeded by ocular, the eye circling

with the cornice or leaping with the arches from pier to pier. The dome above is low and sheltering, as may be thought appropriate in a dome covering a church's main congregational space.

After Baltimore Cathedral Latrobe's finest church was the much smaller St. John's, Washington, which he designed in 1815. In its original Greek-cross form, this was as lucid an exercise in Neo-Classical geometry as could be found. A cupola here gives the worshipers beneath the domical ceiling of the central square a sense of vertical release as well as light—a potentiality of domed structures which Latrobe exploited to the full in the same year in designing the Baltimore Exchange, a work in which he was associated with Maximilien Godefroy. The central hall of the Exchange was 53 feet square on plan; two of its sides opened into barrel-vaulted spaces crossed at second-floor level by balconies, supported by Greek Ionic columns, while the other two had wall arches matching the face arches of the vaults; between the four arches pendentives carried a circular gallery, level with the roof of the rest of the building, offering views not only down to the floor of the hall 50 feet below but also out over the city through huge arched windows in a high drum (cylindrical inside, octagonal without), which was surmounted by a hemispherical dome; the crown of the dome, built like the rest of the structure of brick, was 115 feet above the floor. Nothing like it had been seen in America before, and Latrobe's management of the statics, with the weight of the drum distributed in such a way as to provide maximum abutment where it was needed for the gallery pendentives, was impeccable.

Latrobe's inventiveness was nowhere more evident than in his houses. Varied though they were in plan, compactness was a quality of them all, while they showed a concern for privacy—in the invariable presence of discreetly placed service stairs, for example—which is documented in the architect's letters. Nor were mechanical aids to domestic convenience overlooked. Both Adena at Chilicothe (1805) and the Van Ness House in Washington (Latrobe's largest house, built in 1814–17) had rotating servers in their dining room walls; as early as 1799 a design for John Tayloe (who built Thornton's Octagon instead) included a water closet on the second floor, and by placing tub and toilet in the same room in the Markoe House, Philadelphia (1808), Latrobe initiated a practice which was to give the term *bathroom* its special American meaning. Outside, Latrobe's houses were plain to the point of severity, being designed entirely in terms of the architectural basics of circle and square, cube and cylinder, mass and void. Inside, he employed all the room shapes that were the legacy of Robert Adam to Neo-Classicism, though in Adena (where the impossibility of supervision due to remoteness may have been a reason) and in the Van Ness House (where it could not have been) he used rectangles almost exclusively—the stair well of the Van Ness House is the exception—in *partis* much resembling the colonial double-pile house. There was always a high space rising through the upper floor. In the Pennock House, Norfolk (1796), this takes the form of a stair hall entered directly by the front door and lit by windows in both stories. But more often than not the two-story space is top-lit through a glazed lantern, as in Clifton, near Richmond (1808) and in the Tayloe House design, in which a domed rotunda with a gallery at upper floor level affords direct access to all the rooms on both floors. Top-lit domed rotundas without galleries were the central features of the Pope House, Lexington (1811), and Brentwood, near Washington (1818). The one in Brentwood, instead of being a hall of passage, was the chief reception room—and the grandest domestic example in Latrobe's *oeuvre* of a feature which he had first used in the Bank of Pennsylvania, his own favorite among all his designs.

Latrobe's last design was for a bank, the State Bank of Louisiana (118, 119). While he was working on it he must often have thought of another, much more important bank which he had failed to win in competition two years before, and which was even then being built to the design of one of his former pupils, William Strickland. But that is a matter which must wait for consideration later. Due for our attention now are four immigrant architects, three French and one English, who were never lucky or unlucky enough to be involved in the building of the Capitol.

J. F. Mangin and John McComb

The architectural competition for New York City Hall in 1802 produced twenty-six designs. Among them was one by Latrobe incorporating the central rotunda and other features of the Bank of Pennsylvania but with Corinthian porticoes instead of Ionic. To judge from the architect's perspective, it would have been something of an architectural understatement. It is easy to see why the city fathers preferred the much more decorative design by Mangin and McComb (120).

Joseph François Mangin came from a family of architects. He was in New York by 1794, when he was recommended to Washington as an engineering consultant for the fortifications; his earliest known work of architecture was the Park Street Theater, designed in collaboration with his brother Charles, which opened in 1795. John McComb, Jr., has been mentioned already as the architect of the New York presidential mansion, subsequently Government House.

118
*State Bank of Louisiana,
New Orleans, Louisiana.
Benjamin Henry Latrobe,
1820. Street view. The
parapet and dormers are
later additions.*

119
*State Bank of Louisiana,
New Orleans, Louisiana.
Plan of first floor.*

120
*New York City Hall, New
York. Joseph François
Mangin and John Mc-
Comb, Jr., 1802–11. Gen-
eral exterior.*

121
New York City Hall, New
York. Stair rotunda.

He and his father before him were among the most successful builder-architects in New York. Trained as masons and bricklayers, they often undertook the execution of their own designs; on other occasions—as in the case of the presidential mansion—they supplied designs which were executed by others.

The drawings submitted in the New York City Hall competition by Mangin and McComb were the work of the former, who must also have been responsible for the design of facades. The horizontal rustication, the windows with swags in panels above them, the projecting portico without a pediment, the openness of the facade above the portico, the sculpture in front of the cupola, and the cupola itself in its original form are French.

The plan, one suspects, was McComb's. The *parti* is Palladian and the grandest interior feature, the stair rotunda, clearly came from James Paine's Wardour Castle (1770–76) via that architect's *Plans, Elevations and Sections of Noblemen and Gentlemen's Houses* (121). Construction was supervised by McComb alone, who was also responsible for the detailed design of the interior. He made good use of his copy of Adam's *Works*; not only is the ornament exceptionally sophisticated but columns are used to create spaces within spaces and change the apparent shape of rooms, as often in Adam's work but rarely in his American followers'. He also redesigned the cupola, Neo-Classicizing it and its relation to the building below; in Mangin's competition design the skyline of the central section of the building was distinctly Rococo.

Maximilien Godefroy

There is nothing Rococo about any of the designs of Maximilien Godefroy; their stylistic affiliations are with the Neo-Classical architecture of post-Revolutionary France. Godefroy arrived in America in 1805, after a term of imprisonment on suspicion of being an enemy of the Napoleonic regime. Before the end of the year he joined the faculty of St. Mary's College, Baltimore; by the following March he had designed a new chapel for the college, thus beginning a new career as an architect—in France he had been a civil engineer, apparently concerned more with canal works than with building construction—at the age of forty.

St. Mary's Chapel is Gothic; it has a place in the history of the Gothic Revival and will be treated of under that head. In 1810 the reputation it brought Godefroy led to an invitation to submit a design for the monument to George Washington that the Maryland legislature had authorized. He submitted two, one a rotunda and the other a triumphal arch, but the Commission went to Robert Mills.

In 1815 he designed the monument erected to commemorate the Battle of Baltimore.

The Battle Monument may be described in general terms as a column standing on a high pedestal with griffins on the four corners and supporting a statue (here a personification of Baltimore). Omit the griffins (symbols of immortality whose eagles' heads made them seem specially American) and that could be a description of any one of scores of commemorative columns. What was new about the Battle Monument came from Godefroy's treatment of its two largest components, the pedestal and the column. The pedestal, as befits what is a cenotaph to the thirty-nine Baltimoreans who died in the battle as well as a monument to the victory, is in the form of a tomb. Its battered sides, tapered doorways, and cavetto cornice ornamented with winged solar disks make it an early example of Egyptian Revivalism. The column is what Godefroy himself described as fascial. This is to say, it is a representation of the ancient Roman lictor's fasces, which had come to symbolize republican unity, stylized and enormously enlarged but immediately recognizable and thus an architectural equivalent of those colossal statues of which the Neo-Classical age produced so many.

It was shortly before he laid the cornerstone of the Battle Monument that Godefroy was invited by Latrobe to collaborate in a design for the Baltimore Exchange. While the plan and the domed exchange room (already described) were Latrobe's, we have Latrobe's word for it that the main front "in its general effect" was Godefroy's. The collaboration was short-lived; before 1816 was out Latrobe was sole architect for the Baltimore Exchange. Meanwhile, Godefroy had been called to Richmond to improve the environs of the capitol. This planning commission led to two architectural ones, the more important being the revision of a design by Mills for a new Richmond courthouse. By making the building two-storied throughout instead of only in the center and setting an unpedimented Roman Doric portico with giant columns against either front he both monumentalized and Frenchified it.

Godefroy's last American building, the Unitarian Church in Baltimore (1817–18), has been called "a monument which might well have risen in the Paris of the 1790s, had the French Deists been addicted to building churches" (122).[4] The description is apt so far as the general form of the building is concerned, although in designing it Godefroy used a work that did not appear until the end of the 1790s, namely *Palais, maisons, et autres édifices modernes, dessinés à Rome* by the architects Percier and Fontaine. This was the first

122
Unitarian Church, Balti-
more, Maryland. Maxi-
milien Godefroy, 1817–
18. Facade. The Angel of
Truth in the pediment,
replaced by a modern
copy in 1960, is by Anto-
nio Capellano.

147

123
*Unitarian Church, Balti-
more, Maryland. Interior
as originally built.*

major French publication of Italian Renaissance architecture, and the
Unitarian Chapel, while quintessentially Neo-Classical in its composition of basic geometrical shapes, was the first nineteenth-century
building in America in which Renaissance forms and detail were
used, a single swallow more than thirty years ahead of the Renaissance Revival summer. Among the features owed to Percier and
Fontaine are the doorways within the porch; an account of the
building published soon after its dedication and probably written by
Godefroy himself describes them as imitations of the doors of the
Vatican with archivolts after the style of the Farnese Palace. The
arcaded porch or loggia was an Italianate feature that had been a
favorite with French architects since the 1780s. A building in which
it was combined with a pediment and which Godefroy could have
known was the Théâtre des Jeunes Artistes by J.-N. Sobre. In this,
the pediment stretched across the whole facade and the porch was an
opening in an otherwise unbroken wall; in the Unitarian Chapel the
pediment surmounts a central section breaking forward from the
main mass and square piers flank the outer columns of the porch so
as to make it a distinct portico. The difference shows Godefroy's
regard for character, or *caractère*, as defined by the eighteenth-
century French theorists he had read in the course of his architectural
self-education.

The central space inside the Unitarian Church was a square, fifty-
three feet and six inches on a side, under a hemispherical Pantheon-
type dome which rose from a circle produced by four pendentives
between four wide arches (123).[5] The spaces under the arches turned
the plan into a short-armed cross, the arm toward the entrance
containing the organ loft and the one opposite it being rounded off
as an apse. Again Renaissance detail appeared—in the impost mold-
ings under the arches, for example—while Greek architecture was
represented by columns of the Tower of the Winds order under the
organ loft.

J. J. Ramée and
William Jay

Godefroy left America, never to return, in 1819.[6] The American career of Joseph Jacques Ramée was little more than a third as long. Born, like Latrobe, in 1764, in 1792 Ramée found himself under the necessity of fleeing France and went to Hamburg, where he established a flourishing practice in landscape gardening and interior decoration as well as architecture. In 1811 the financier David Parish persuaded him to join him on his estate in northern New York. There Ramée designed a variety of buildings in the towns of Parishville and Rossie and landscaped the grounds of the Ogden mansion nearby. In 1813 Parish introduced him to Eliphalet Nott, president of Union College near Schenectady. Chartered in 1795, Union was one of the four largest colleges in the country and quite the most progressive.

The first building of Union College, by Philip Hooker of Albany, was an altogether conventional specimen of American collegiate architecture, of three stories with a central pedimented pavilion and a tall cupola. For the new site above the existing campus on which Nott had decided to build Ramée designed an entirely new kind of college complex (124). The focal structure was a Pantheon-like rotunda standing on the chord of a range of building, partly of one story and partly of three, resembling an omega on plan; in front of the rotunda there was a wide lawn flanked by buildings like back-to-back Ls and with its fourth side left open toward the country; the surroundings were to be landscaped in the English manner. Only two of the buildings, those flanking the lawn, were ever built to Ramée's design; stylistically they are rather conservative. Nevertheless, Union has a place in the history of collegiate architecture alongside the University of Virginia. And although Jefferson's concept of an academical village antedated Ramée's plan by eight or nine years, knowledge of the latter may well have inspired Latrobe's suggestion to Jefferson that gave the University of Virginia its rotunda. Ramée's other American works included designs for a commemorative arch to George Washington in Baltimore and for the Baltimore Exchange. The failure of the latter to win acceptance was evidently the cause of his return to France in 1816 after only five years in America.

William Jay was another architect whose stay in America was brief. In less than seven years he gave Savannah, Georgia, where he landed in 1817 at the age of 23 after serving his articles in the office of D. R. Roper in London, a handful of the most original Neo-Classical buildings on this side of the Atlantic. The austere geometry of the Scarborough House (1818) is reminiscent of Ledoux; behind its porch lies what has been called "one of the grandest spacial compositions in American domestic architecture," an atriumlike hall,

124
Union College, Schenec-
tady, New York. Joseph
Jacques Ramée, 1813.
Plan of buildings and
landscaping.

125
Scarborough House, Sa-
vannah, Georgia. William
Jay, 1818. Porch.

two stories high, with four Doric columns supporting a mezzanine. The porch columns of the Scarborough House are unfluted but support a complete Doric entablature (125); in Jay's Branch Bank of the United States (1820) the Doric columns were fluted but the entablature was devoid of triglyphs and the other customary details of the order. In the Telfair House (ca. 1820) the geometry of the subtly proportioned facade is relieved by a porch in the Corinthian of the Monument of Lysicrates; in the Bullock-Habersham House (1820) the same Athenian model was imitated in a circular porch, which led to a rectangular hall from whose floor a free-standing stair spiraled up inside a ring of six more Lysicratean columns.

Jay was as energetic as he was inventive. Practicing in Charleston as well as Savannah, he was a member of the Board of Public Works in South Carolina and a founder member of the South Carolina Academy of Arts. His return to England as a result of the financial depression suffered by the South in 1822 was a serious loss to American architecture.

Latrobe's Pupils

Latrobe's contribution to American architecture was not limited to his own buildings or confined to the span of his own short life. Many of the most important buildings that went up between his death and the Civil War were designed by architects trained in his office, the first American office in which young men were accepted with the status of pupil-assistants. Foremost among them were Robert Mills and William Strickland. The bulk of their work belongs to the period 1820–1850, when they were among the half-dozen most successful architects in the country, but their earlier designs are not without importance and should not be omitted from any account of Neo-Classicism during the Federal period.

Robert Mills was a native of Charleston, South Carolina, where he was born in 1781. After a brief spell as a draftsman with Hoban he was taken up by Jefferson and spent two years at Monticello. In 1803 he entered Latrobe's office, where he remained five years.[7] In 1808 he designed the circular Sansom Street Baptist Church in Philadelphia, with a wooden roof modelled on that of the Halle au Blés in Paris, a structure greatly admired by Jefferson. His first public commission after he left Latrobe was Washington Hall, Philadelphia. Designed in 1809 but not completed until 1816, this also was remarkable for its roof, which covered a hall that could hold nearly 6,000 people without intermediate supports; its facade, with a columnar screen in a domed niche, was inspired by Ledoux's Hôtel Guimard in Paris. Assisted by the understanding of construction that was one of Latrobe's greatest gifts to his pupils, in his early career

126
*Monumental Church,
Richmond, Virginia. Rob-
ert Mills, 1812. General
Exterior.*

Mills was something of a specialist in large auditoria, secular and ecclesiastical. The ecclesiastical ones included the Octagon Unitarian Church, Philadelphia (completed in 1813), the Monumental Church, Richmond (designed in 1812), which also is octagonal, and the First Baptist Chruch, Baltimore (1817–18), an Ionic Pantheon. The Monumental Church, the only survivor of these three, was the one into which Mills put most of himself (126). The simplifications of classical detail are perhaps more odd than original. But then Mills, for all his solid ability, was not the most original of architects. Nor did he have the sensibility of Latrobe's other star pupil, William Strickland.

Mills's junior by seven years, at fifteen Strickland was apprenticed to Latrobe by his father, a carpenter who worked on the Bank of Pennsylvania; the apprenticeship was terminated by Latrobe less than two years later when the boy absented himself without leave. In 1808, when he was twenty, Strickland designed the Masonic Hall, Philadelphia, which was completed in 1811 and destroyed by fire eight years later; Gothic, it had a wooden steeple, 180 feet high. He had few architectural commissions in the next ten years and supported himself for the most part by surveying, engraving, and scene painting. Strickland's day came in September, 1818, when he was proclaimed winner of the competition for the Bank of the United States in Philadelphia—his old master Latrobe taking the second premium. His design, which was executed in 1819–24, ushered in a new age in American architecture.

On May 13, 1818, *The Philadelphia Gazette and Daily Advertiser* carried an advertisement by the Board of Directors of the Bank of the United States inviting "architects of science and experience" to submit designs for a banking house to be erected on a site between Chestnut and Library streets. "The ground plan will include an area of about ten or eleven thousand square feet. . . . The building will be faced with marble, and have a portico on each front, resting upon a basement or platform of such altitude as will combine convenience of ascent with due proportion and effect. In this edifice, the Directors are desirous of exhibiting a chaste imitation of Grecian Architecture, in its simplest and least expensive form."

Clearly the Directors, in specifying a portico on each front, were thinking of Latrobe's Bank of Pennsylvania, designed twenty years before, while in desiring that the building should be Grecian "in its simplest and least expensive form" they were virtually stipulating that the order should be Doric. And the designs that they received from Latrobe and from his former pupil Strickland were both Doric and both *criticisms* (rather than imitations) of the earlier bank. But the criticisms were based on different premises. In Latrobe's design a high attic concealing a dome over the central banking hall supplies a secondary mass which would have given the building a much greater sense of weight than the Bank of Pennsylvania had. The architect seems to be saying that his earlier bank was not monumental enough; in any event, the changes are esthetically motivated. In Strickland's design, on the other hand, the barrel-vaulted banking hall was denied any but the most perfunctory expression on the exterior, and the pediments were joined by an unbroken roof to preserve the temple form of the whole, the implication being that his former master's bank was not Greek enough. Strickland's criteria, that is to say, were historical. So were those of the bank's directors, who found his design more "classic" (meaning more like a Greek temple) than Latrobe's. As a result, the Second Bank of the United States (from 1844 to 1932 the Customs House) became the first building of the Greek Revival that was to dominate the architectural scene in America for more than thirty years (127, 128, 129).

In theory, revivalism puts learning before sensibility and values deference to authority more highly than originality. The English Gothic Revival architect Augustus Welby Pugin wrote of himself in 1843: "Mr. Pugin, we believe, never claimed the least merit on the score of originality . . . but simply to revive . . . the glorious but till lately despised work of the Middle Ages." Yet the architectural revivals of the nineteenth century were saved from producing mere copies and became true styles because in practice the need for a

127
Second Bank of the
United States (later Cus-
toms House), Philadel-
phia, Pennsylvania.
William Strickland, 1818–
24. South portico.

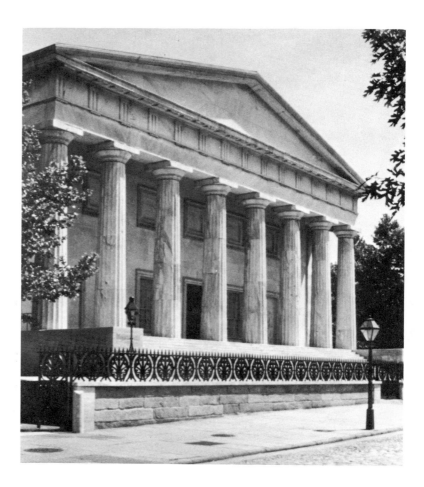

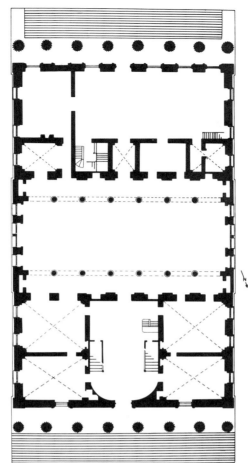

128
Second Bank of the
United States, Philadel-
phia, Pennsylvania. Plan
of first floor.

129
Second Bank of the
United States, Philadel-
phia, Pennsylvania.
Banking room.

O   6   12   18   24
FEET

degree of adaptation to modern requirements was always recognized and, however self-denying an architect's intentions, a personal sense of form has a way of asserting itself. Ignorance might also play a part. Strickland modeled the porticoes of the Second Bank of the United States on the Parthenon, reducing them to three-fifths the scale of the prototype. But those slight departures from the rectilinear and the vertical which go under the name of refinements and which give the temple an organic quality that it otherwise would not have are altogether absent from the bank—simply because Strickland did not know of them.[1] Consequently the Second Bank of the United States could never be mistaken for a real Greek temple from any viewpoint.

Capitols and Customs Houses

The Second Bank of the United State is amphiprostyle but not peripteral. As Strickland pointed out, lateral colonnades would have obscured the windows. It was Ithiel Town who solved the problem of how to preserve the trabeated system (at least in appearance) on the flanks of a temple-form building without denying light to its interior in his design for the Connecticut State House, which went up in 1827–31 within a stone's throw of his Gothic Trinity Church in New Haven. The order was again that of the Parthenon, although the porticoes were hexastyle only; along the side walls in the original design—though not in the executed one—were series of prominent antae, forming what may most handily be called pilastrades.

The pilastrade was a feature of both the state capitols designed by Town and Alexander Jackson Davis, his partner for the fifteen years 1829–44 (when their New York office was the biggest and busiest in the country). In other respects they differed significantly. The Indiana State Capitol, designed in 1831, had a dome and lantern rising from a high drum on an octagonal plinth midway between its octastyle porticoes. In the North Carolina Capitol, designed in 1833, the temple form has been abandoned for a cruciform plan and the porticoes stand on high rusticated basements; the dome rises directly from an octagonal plinth—as it also did in the Vermont State House, designed in 1832 by Ammi B. Young.

The placing of Roman domes upon buildings otherwise Greek did not escape criticism. In 1835 *The American Monthly Magazine* attacked Town and Davis's design of 1833 for the New York Customs House on the ground that its dome was "an excrescence, which, however elegant in itself, is utterly monstrous when added to a model of the present Grecian architecture." Again the criteria were historical; the dome was an expression of the largest space within and its lowering under the roof by the architect who supervised

130
Customs House (later
Sub-Treasury, now Fed-
eral Hall National Memo-
rial), New York City.
Town and Davis and
James Frazee, 1833–42.
South portico.

131
Customs House, New
York City. Plan.

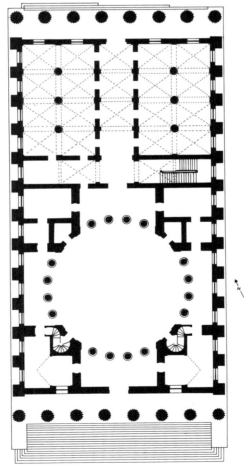

0 6 12 18 24
FEET

132
Ohio State Capitol, Co-
lumbus, Ohio. Thomas
Cole, 1838–61. View from
south.

construction, John Frazee, only intensified the conflict between interior and exterior that the use of the temple form made inevitable
(130, 131). A low dome crowned the Boston Customs House, built
in 1837–47 to Young's design. Young eschewed the pilastrades of
Town and Davis and used half-columns instead, thereby giving the
Boston building a massiveness and a richness of light and shade that
save it from being visually crushed by the skyscraper for which since
1915 it has served as a pedestal. The Ohio State Capitol at Columbus
has as its central feature a tall drum, sans dome (132). The complex
history of this, perhaps the finest of the pre-Civil War capitols,
began in 1838 with a competition of which Henry Walter of Cincinnati was declared the winner, with Martin E. Thompson, an associate
of Town and Davis, taking the second premium and Thomas Cole,
the landscape painter, the third. After asking Town and Davis to
synthesize the three prize-winning designs, the commissioners for
the building finally settled on Cole's, which was executed, with a few
changes, in the next twenty-four years. The unbroken rectangle of
the plan, the simplicity of the pilastraded elevations, and the unfluted
columns of the recessed porticoes recall the Neo-Classicism of an
earlier age.

The instructions to the architects competing for the Ohio capitol
suggested the use of the Greek Doric order, though ''not with a view

of governing exclusively in the choice." This was an expression of a widely held preference, for Doric was the rule for Greek Revival capitols; besides those already mentioned, the Arkansas State Capitol (Gideon Shryock, 1833, with modification by George Weigart), the Illinois State Capitol (John Rague, 1837), and the Iowa State Capitol (Rague, 1840), were Doric. Of the two most notable exceptions one appeared at the beginning and the other near the end of the revival. The first was the Ionic temple at Frankfort, Kentucky, designed in 1825—and so antedating Town's Connecticut State House—by Gideon Shryock of Lexington, whose builder-architect father had apprenticed him to Strickland for a year; it has a hexastyle portico of the order of the Temple of Athena Polias at Priene and a domed lantern lighting a double circular stair, leading to the legislative chambers on the second floor, which must have been inspired by the stair in New York City Hall. The other was the Tennessee State Capitol, built in 1845–59, in which Strickland made a great display of the Ionic of the Erechtheum in an octastyle portico at either end and an unpedimented hexastyle one on either flank, while catering to the mid-century taste for height which was among the causes of the demise of the Greek Revival with a square tower surmounted by a version of the Monument of Lysicrates (133, 134).

Porticoed Churches

For the first churches of the Greek Revival we must return to Philadelphia. Even before the Second Bank of the United States was finished two of temple form, both with hexastyle Ionic porticoes facing the street, had risen in that city: the first Presbyterian Church, in which the order was taken from the Temple on the Ilissus, and St. Andrew's Episcopal Church (now St. George's Greek Orthodox), with the delicately enriched Ionic of the Temple of Dionysus at Teos done in wood. They were designed, in 1820 and 1822, respectively, by John Haviland, a young English architect who had come to America from Russia in 1816 at the urging of John Quincy Adams. Most often remembered for his prisons (to be discussed later), Haviland was a prolific architect and a protean one even within the limitations of the Greek Revival; in Philadelphia his archaeologically imitative Ionic portico of St. Andrew's was followed in 1824 by the radically simplified Doric one of his Pennsylvania Institution for the Deaf and Dumb (now the Philadelphia College of Art), and that in 1825 by the Franklin Institute (now the Atwater Kent Museum), in which he employed the order of the Monument of Thrasyllus with four massive antae to give monumentality and a powerful sense of structure to a street front of little more than domestic scale.

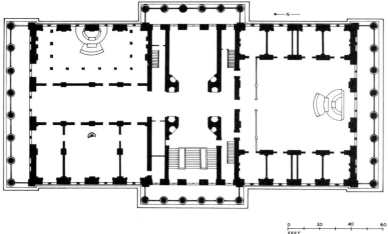

133
*Tennessee State Capitol,
Nashville, Tennessee.
William Strickland, 1845–
59. View from northeast.*

134
*Tennessee State Capitol,
Nashville, Tennessee.
Plan of principal floor.*

Haviland's *The Builder's Assistant*, published in Philadelphia in 1818, was the first American book to give the Greek orders; nine years later Asher Benjamin followed suit in the sixth edition of *The American Builder's Companion*. Moderately priced handbooks, substituting for the expensive volumes of Stuart and Revett's *Antiquities of Athens*—and also supplementing them, with examples of the application of Greek forms to modern functions—did for the builder-architects of the Greek Revival what the handbooks of William Salmon and others had done for their colonial predecessors a hundred years before. Among the most used were those of Minard Lafever, whose first, *The Young Builder's General Instructor*, appeared in 1829. It was Lafever who designed, in 1834, the ecclesiastical counterpart of the Second Bank of the United States. The First Reformed Dutch Church in Brooklyn was amphiprostyle and octastyle, like the bank, but the order was Ionic, after the Temple on the Ilissus; as in the bank, the side walls were plain; however, Lafever went one better than Strickland—or perhaps, counting the columns, one should say two better—by providing a vestibule or pronaos, distyle in antis, within the front portico.

Lafever's Dutch Church in Brooklyn had no steeple of any kind. In this it was exceptional; enthusiasm for Greek architecture rarely absolved an architect designing a church from the obligation of providing such a feature, "of Gothic extraction" though it was. The Greek Revival architect's problem was the problem that had been Wren's a century and a half before, with the added difficulty that it was now thought desirable to imitate specific prototypes as closely as possible. There were two Greek structures that could serve as such for church steeples, namely the cylindrical Monument of Lysicrates, of the fourth century B.C., and the octagonal Tower of the Winds, of the first. The Monument of Lysicrates was the more frequent choice. Among the churches on which it found a place—it was not, as we have seen already and shall see again, confined to churches—was the French Protestant Episcopal Church in New York (1832–34) by Town and Davis. But freely composed Greek versions of the Wren-Gibbs type of steeple were a common solution, and the St. Martin-in-the-Fields formula continued to be followed; a graceful example of the latter in New England is the Congregational Church at Madison, Connecticut (1838), and a showy one in the South is St. Paul's, Richmond, Virginia, completed to the design of Thomas S. Stewart of Philadelphia in 1845 (135). The interior of St. Paul's, Richmond, with its colonnaded apse, is an exception to the rule that Greek Revival church interiors are featureless and boxlike. Another, earlier exception is the interior of Old St. Louis Cathedral at St.

135
St. Paul's, Richmond,
Virginia. Thomas S.
Stewart, 1845. Steeple
and portico.

136
Unitarian Church,
Quincy, Massachusetts.
Alexander Parris, 1828.
Steeple and portico.

Louis, Missouri, which was completed in 1834 to the design of George Morton and Joseph C. Laveille. The facade and steeple of Old St. Louis Cathedral are also remarkably fine, with more of Latrobe and Wren than of the Greek Revival about them. Perhaps the finest facade and steeple combination in a strict (though simplified) Greek idiom is that of the Unitarian Church at Quincy, Massachusetts, built of the local granite in 1828 to the design of Alexander Parris, whose St. Paul's, Boston (1819), was the first Greek Revival church in New England (136).

Courthouses and Colleges

A building type whose Greek Revival examples may often be mistaken for churches at first glance, or even second, is the courthouse. The earliest courthouse of temple form was a modest affair designed in 1821 for Buckingham County, Virginia; it was not Greek but Roman, with a Tuscan portico, and the architect was Thomas Jefferson. It had no cupola, but most Greek Revival courthouses did. Sometimes they have what can only be described as steeples. The Hustings Courthouse at Petersburg, Virginia, built to the design of Calvin Pollard in 1838–40, has one that might well belong to a church, but for the statue of Justice on its summit; the order of the Tower of the Winds is used both in its first stage and in the portico, but H. W. Inwood's St. Pancras Church, London, must have been the immediate progenitor, while the clock stage comes from St. Anne's, Soho, by Latrobe's master, S. P. Cockerell (137).

It is said that the handsome Ionic courthouse at Dayton, Ohio, built in 1848–50, was the result of the revision by its architect, Howard Daniels, of a fully peripteral scheme proposed by a local amateur. The only full peripteral temple of the American Greek Revival actually built was not a temple of justice but a temple of learning, the Center Building of Girard College, Philadelphia (138).

The history of Girard College began with a competition held in 1832–33 for a school for orphans to be built in accordance with the terms of the will of the banker Stephen Girard. It was won by Thomas Ustick Walter, not long out of Strickland's office, with a simple Doric design. But the chairman of the trustees was Nicholas Biddle, another banker, who had traveled in Greece and believed that "the two great truths in the world" were "the Bible and Grecian architecture," and he had grander ideas which led him to persuade Walter to make a new and much more costly design, the City Councils to accept it, and his fellow trustees to divert funds intended by Girard for other purposes to its execution. The result was the colossal Corinthian temple, containing twelve classrooms on three

137
Hustings Courthouse, Petersburg, Virginia. Calvin Pollard, 1838–40. Tower and portico.

138
Girard College, Philadelphia, Pennsylvania. Thomas Ustick Walter, 1833–48. Founder's Hall.

floors and two stair halls, that was completed at the cost of over a million and a half dollars in 1848. It is still impressive for its scale as well as the beautiful execution of its detail; its "incorrect" proportions—for a Greek temple it is too short for its width—are due to the architect having to follow the dimensions on plan specified in Girard's will, which also specified the fireproof brick vaulting whose design shows Walter's mastery of masonry construction.

Although no other college or university had a Girard fortune at its disposal, the number of buildings for higher education that went up in the Grecian years was large. In mood they ranged from the austerity of the stern Doric library (later Manning Hall) at Brown University, designed by James Bucklin in 1833, to the cheerfulness of the unlearned mixture of Greek and Roman which has been on parade, so to speak, in Jeffersonian red and white, at Washington and Lee since 1842. An earlier group that, like Washington and Lee, owes much to its landscape setting is at Amherst, where plain dormitories flanking a chapel with a tetrastyle Paestum portico were built in 1821–27 to the design of Isaac Damon.

Buildings for Bureaucracy and Commerce

The architect who left the biggest mark on the government buildings of Washington, where the Greek Revival made its debut in the Ionic-porticoed City Hall (now District of Columbia Courthouse), designed by George Hadfield in 1820, was Robert Mills. The former pupil of Latrobe spent the twenties in his native Charleston, where he designed various buildings for the South Carolina Board of Public Works; the Record Office at Charleston, with its arched windows, unfluted Doric columns, plain entablature, and raking blocking course instead of a pediment, is a good example of the non-doctrinaire

Neo-Classical style of this period of his career. In 1830 Mills moved to Washington and three years later, repeating his Baltimore success of 1815, won the competition for the monument to be erected there to the first president. In 1836 he was appointed supervising architect for federal buildings, thus becoming responsible for the construction of the Treasury Building, the Patent Office (now the National Portrait Gallery), and the Post Office and Land Office (now the Tariff Commission). Although one William P. Elliot had already prepared designs for the first two, as built they are to be counted Mills's work. Both are vaulted in masonry throughout. The Treasury Building is Ionic; its immensely long colonnade is a piece of architectural rhetoric which is no less impressive for having been rather too often emulated by later architects in Washington. The National Portrait Gallery is Doric; the effect of its sixteen-column Parthenaic portico was much diminished when the steps were removed in a street-widening operation in 1936, but the cantilevered double stair behind it and the Lincoln Gallery on the third floor are still two of the finest features of their respective kinds in the city, or indeed in the country (139). The Tariff Commission is Corinthian, with long facades punctuated with columnar pavilions in the manner of Chambers's Somerset House; the recessed portico with coupled columns that answers the portico of the National Gallery across the street was designed by Walter, who succeeded Mills as supervising architect for federal buildings in 1851. Mills's Washington buildings can perhaps be best characterized in the phrase of a greater architect, Inigo Jones: "solid, proportionable according to the rules, masculine and unaffected"— all admirable qualities in the office buildings of a republic.

A commercial building that challenged comparison with anything built for the federal government was the Merchants' Exchange in New York, designed by Isaiah Rogers in 1836 (and so exactly contemporaneous with the Treasury Building). It too had an Ionic colonnade on a high podium; its exterior was of Quincy granite and the floors were carried by brick vaulting; the exchange room was a brick-domed rotunda eighty feet in diameter, with columns of a Corinthian order of Rogers's own invention set in antis in four recesses opening out of it. Its stern monumentality was in strong contrast to the elegance of the Merchants' Exchange in Philadelphia, designed by Strickland four years earlier, with its Lysicratean lantern rising from a hemitholos of the same order. The Boston Merchants' Exchange (completed in 1842), in which Rogers employed the temple portico formula but substituted antae for columns, was both monumental and rich. A New Englander who before opening his own office spent four years with Solomon Willard, Rogers would have a

139
*Patent Office (National
Portrait Gallery), Wash-
ington, District of Colum-
bia. Robert Mills, 1836.
Stairs.*

good claim to be regarded as the greatest commercial architect of his time even without his hotels (of which more shortly).

From among market buildings the Quincy Market in Boston, begun in 1825 to the design of Alexander Parris, may be singled out for mention on account of both its functional plan and its construction of large blocks of Quincy granite—stone skeleton construction, so to call it. Of the shopping arcade, which had appeared in France (where it is called a *passage*) around 1790, America had two examples before the twenties were out. The first was the Philadelphia Arcade, designed by John Haviland and built in 1827, the second the Providence Arcade, designed by Russell Warren and James Bucklin and completed in 1829 (140). The street fronts of the Philadelphia Arcade were opened up with arches, like the Burlington Arcade in London (1818–19); at Providence the glass-roofed interior is visible from the street through screens of Ionic columns.

The hotel is a building type that falls somewhere between the commercial and the domestic. The first American hotel to be so called was the City Hotel in New York, built in 1794–96; architecturally it was not distinctive. Much more of a hotel by nature though not in name was the seven-story Exchange Coffee House in Boston, designed by Asher Benjamin, built in 1806–09, and burnt in 1818. But it was Tremont House, Boston, built in 1828–32 to the design of Isaiah Rogers, that deserved the appellation, first given to it by Talbot Hamlin, of the first modern hotel in America (141, 142); with its spacious Doric porch, its circular lobby with the reception office opening off it, its seventy-by-thirty-foot dining room with a peristyle of fourteen Ionic columns, its sumptuous public rooms and its commodious private ones (from singles to suites), and not least its plumbing (with a row of eight water closets on the first floor and baths below them in the basement), it set a new standard. Its fame made Rogers the leading hotel architect of the next three-and-a-half decades. In 1834 he was commissioned to design Astor House, New York, with more than 300 rooms against the 170 in Tremont House and with plumbing carried through all three stories; among his many later hotels were the (second) St. Charles Hotel in New Orleans, Burnet House in Cincinnati, Galt House in Louisville, and Maxwell House in Nashville. There is some doubt as to whether the Charleston Hotel, opened in 1839, is his. In any case its Corinthian colonnade is a worthy fellow to the Ionic one of the New York Merchants' Exchange.

140
Providence Arcade, Providence, Rhode Island. Russell Warren and James Bucklin, 1828–29. Interior.

141
Tremont House, Boston, Massachusetts. Isaiah Rogers, 1828–32. Tremont Street front.

142
Tremont House, Boston, Massachusetts. Plan of first floor.

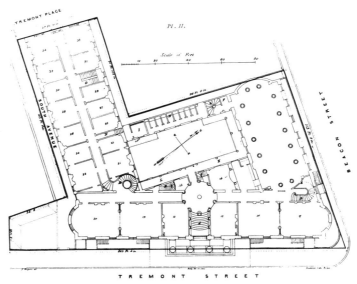

Houses Great and Small

The first temple house of the Greek Revival appeared in 1820 when George Hadfield transformed the Lee Mansion at Arlington, Virginia, by adding a porticoed center which overwhelmed the earlier structure (143); in choosing the order, Paestum Doric with unfluted columns, he had an eye to the effect of the house on its hill as seen across the Potomac from Washington. Five years later the Bowers House at Northampton, Massachusetts, was built to the design of Ithiel Town as an Ionic temple with low wings, their roofs at right angles to the roof of the two-storied center, which the wings seemed to penetrate—a scheme that became very common in the thirties, when it was popularized by Lafever's *Modern Builder's Guide.* Then in 1828–30 Town's partner Davis built the Russell House at Middletown, Connecticut, with a hexastyle Corinthian portico and no wings or other projections to compromise the temple form.

In the third and fourth decades of the century domestic temples went up everywhere. Among the grander ones, two that demand notice are Andalusia in Pennsylvania, where in 1833 T. U. Walter helped Nicholas Biddle bear witness to the great truth of Grecian architecture by wrapping the order of the Temple of Hephaestus at Athens around three sides of the house, and Berry Hill in Virginia, built in 1835–40, with an octastyle portico after the Parthenon which is approached between two porticoed dependencies. Size and quality were not necessarily commensurate, however, and many of the

143
Lee Mansion, Arlington, Virginia. George Hadfield, 1820. Portico.

144
Judge Wilson House, Ann Arbor, Michigan. 1843. General view.

145
Judge Wilson House, Ann Arbor, Michigan. Plan of first floor, with additions removed.

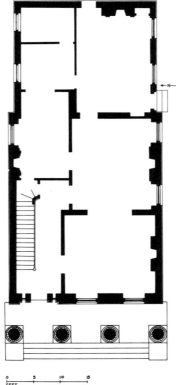

146
Uncle Sam Plantation, St.
James Parish, Louisiana.
Circa 1850. South front.

147
Uncle Sam Plantation, St.
James Parish, Louisiana.
Plan of first floor.

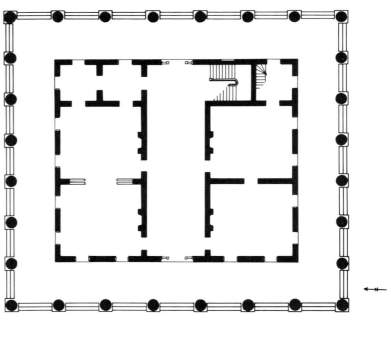

```
0      10      20      30
|   |   |   |   |   |   |
FEET
```

smaller temple houses, designed by builders of local fame only with the aid of their Benjamins and their Lafevers, deserve as much notice as the great show places (144, 145).

Characteristic and conspicious though they were, temple-form houses never constituted an absolute majority. More often Greek forms were used to dress up houses of traditional plan, with the long axis parallel to the front; a portico might be applied to the center of the front in the Palladian manner, or an order might be used without any pretense that it belonged to any part of a temple. The result could be original, as it is in the house that Hitchcock singles out for illustration in his international survey of nineteenth-century architecture: Elmhyrst at Newport, Rhode Island, which was designed by Russell Warren about 1833. Then there were the many houses in which a colonnaded porch ran the length of the front, and those in Louisiana and the Deep South for which Hitchcock coined the term "peripteral mode," with giant columns on all four sides (146). The peripteral mode was the result of classicizing the French colonial plantation house with its *galeries*; the earliest examples predated the Greek Revival, and as late as 1832 Oak Alley in St. James Parish was designed (by George Swainey) with Tuscan columns and Adamesque fanlights and dormers. Greenwood, in West Feliciana Parish, begun in 1830, would appear to have been the first Grecian plantation house in Louisiana. In many cases the designers of these houses are obscure or unknown. However, Ashland, in Ascension Parish, which was built in 1841 and with its square piers in the place of columns is one of the most impressive of them, is attributed to James Gallier, Sr., Irish by birth and English by training, whose work in New Orleans, where he arrived in 1835, includes the City Hall (1845–50). In the larger Greek Revival houses of this period a great interior space for formal entertainment was a general requirement that was often met by providing sliding doors between the dining room and the parlor, as was first done in New York city houses in the 1820s (147).

Externally, the city house of the period was distinguished from its Federal predecessor by the insistence on the principle of trabeation shown in its design; the oblong overdoor light took the place of the fanlight and window lintels were often emphasized by one means or another; the front might be crowned by a full entablature, often with windows in the frieze. If there was a porch, it might consist of two columns supporting a section of entablature; or antae, perhaps decorated with a form of the Greek fret, might be used instead of columns; patterns for both treatments were available in the books of Benjamin and Lafever. Attempts at giving row houses a monumental effect were few; the most ambitious was Lafayette Terrace, New

York, formerly attributed to A. J. Davis, which was built in 1832–33, of Westchester marble, with a Corinthian colonnade screening the two upper stories as in the Charleston Hotel.

The Egyptian Episode

From time to time an architect would forsake the acanthus for the lotus, the vertical wall for the battered, and produce a design which paid homage to a civilization that was already more than two thousand years old when the Parthenon was built. The tangible results were not numerous—they totalled about eighty—but they were often substantial and sometimes very substantial indeed.

The first architect to propose the use of Egyptian forms in America was, as might be expected, Latrobe; this was in a design for the Library of Congress in the Capitol made in 1808. Seven years later, as we saw, they were used by Godefroy in the Battle Monument in Baltimore. In 1825 the many-talented Willard (who had worked as a sculptor on Godefroy's Unitarian Church) began the construction, with granite from his own quarries at Quincy, of the first of the colossal obelisks, commemorating another battle, on Bunker Hill at Charlestown, Massachusetts. In 1833 Mills won the competition for the monument to George Washington in the federal city with an obelisk which, denuded of the Doric peristyle that concealed its base in the winning design, was to rise—though not until 1884—to the unprecedented height of 555 feet.

While the solidity and permanence of Egyptian architecture recommended its imitation for commemorative functions generally, the funerary purpose of so many of its remaining monuments made it seem especially appropriate in cemeteries, with results that range from the simple granite portals provided by Rogers for the Old Granary Burying Ground in Boston and the Touro Cemetery in Newport in 1840 and 1843 to the elaborate columnar gateway of the Grove Street Cemetery in New Haven, designed in 1845 by Henry Austin. As for churches, the only two in which Egyptian forms preponderate are the Whalers' Church at Sag Harbor, Long Island, which was built, probably to Lafever's design, in 1843–44, and the First Presbyterian Church at Nashville, by Strickland, built in 1848–51. But some Greek Revival churches—St. Paul's Richmond, for example—have Egyptian touches, while in the First Baptist Church at Essex, Connecticut (ca. 1845), battered walls are combined with an Adam Style cupola. In Philadelphia two Egyptian synagogues were built: the Mikveh Israel Synagogue on Cherry Street to Strickland's design early in the revival in 1822 and the Beth Israel Synagogue on Crown Street toward its end in 1849.

148
*New York City Halls of
Justice and House of De-
tention (The Tombs), New
York City. John Haviland,
1835–38. Portico on
Centre Street front.*

Egyptian forms were employed in a number of other types of building. Sometimes the choice seems reasonably apt, as in the case of the Medical College of Virginia at Richmond, designed in 1844 by Stewart, the architect of St. Paul's Church nearby, in which it was doubtless suggested by the traditional view of Egypt as the cradle of medicine. It is less easy to account for the Egyptian railroad station at New Bedford, Massachusetts, designed in 1840 by Russell Warren. Nor is the popularity of the style for prisons and courthouses easily explained.[2] The first two Egyptian prisons, both designed in 1832, were the Moyamensing Debtors' Prison, in Philadelphia, by Walter, and the New Jersey State Penitentiary, Trenton, by Haviland. In 1835 Haviland designed the New York City Halls of Justice and House of Detention, better known as The Tombs, which was unquestionably the most important work of the revival (148). Completed in 1838, the prison in The Tombs was planned on no less progressive lines than the Eastern State Penitentiary in Philadelphia to accommodate, like that earlier prison by Haviland (to be treated in our next chapter), the separate system as opposed to the "silent system," then in use in Auburn and Sing-Sing, under which prisoners worked together but were forbidden to talk or communicate with each other in any way; it was not as influential, however. In 1836 Haviland designed an Egyptian courthouse for Essex County, New Jersey, at Newark. His last Egyptian design, made in 1838, was a building for the Pennsylvania Fire Insurance Company in Philadelphia; it was John Rague, architect of the Illinois and Iowa capitols, who ten years later designed, in the City Jail of Dubuque, Iowa, the last building of any importance in which Egyptian forms were employed to go up before the Civil War.

The Egyptian Revival was never more than a part of, or an episode in, the Greek Revival. The frequency with which Egyptian and Greek forms were combined, if nothing else, shows that architects regarded Egyptian as a kind of proto-Greek rather than as an alternative style. The alternatives to Greek were supplied by later periods of history.

However sonorously Robert Adam might declare that "the buildings of the Ancients are in Architecture what the works of nature are with respect to the other arts . . . the models which we should imitate and the standards by which we ought to judge," his insistence on the architect's right to break "the rules," together with his emphasis on the "novelty and variety" (both *relative* qualities) of his own designs, opened the door to a kind of situational esthetics that could be used to justify the imitation of other buildings of the past than those of the Ancients. The recognition of an alternative kind of beauty to the classical in the Picturesque supplied further justification, while the growing historical consciousness and the associationist theory of Archibald Alison revolutionized the way in which people looked at architecture—including classical architecture, so that while to the eighteenth-century man of taste the Greek Doric column was ugly because it was "ill proportioned," to his nineteenth-century counterpart it was beautiful because it was Greek.

The Gothic Revival and the Picturesque

In England Gothic architecture had been esteemed for its associations long before Alison published his *Essays on the Nature and Principles of Taste* in 1790, and it was imitated for the sake of them, and for the relief from Palladianism it afforded, in the first phase of the Gothic Revival, the Gothic Rococo, of which Horace Walpole's Strawberry Hill, built piecemeal between 1749 and 1776, is the most famous product. Walpole called Gothic "picturesque" in 1760, but the second phase of the revival, Picturesque Gothic, was not initiated until Payne Knight, the leading theorist of the Picturesque movement—or *point of view,* as it is termed in the subtitle of Christopher Hussey's classic study of the subject—designed Downton Castle for himself in 1774 as the first house in Europe to be built in one campaign to an asymmetrical plan to harmonize with its landscape setting, in obedience to his rule that "houses should be irregular where all the accompaniments are irregular." Knight was followed, at a distance, by James Wyatt, who in Lee Priory (designed in 1782) and in the prodigious Fonthill Abbey (designed in 1795) employed an ecclesiastical vocabulary of forms in place of the military one employed at Downton—and preferred by the greatest of all the masters of the Picturesque, John Nash. The last masterpiece of Picturesque Gothic in England, the Houses of Parliament, was designed by Charles Barry in 1835; soon after that, owing in large part to the writings of Barry's collaborator Pugin, the Gothic Revival entered another phase.

The Picturesque was slow to cross the Atlantic. Although Haviland discussed its principles in *The Builder's Assistant,* published in 1818, neither he nor anyone else applied them in America until the thirties. The first buildings of the Gothic Revival in America (as in England) were classical in general conception and Gothic, or "Gothick," only in detail. The first of all—assuming that its predecessor of 1698 represented the survival rather than a revival of Gothic—was the second Trinity Church, New York, built in 1788–89. It was followed ten years later by Sedgeley, near Philadelphia, by Latrobe. The first Gothic Revival house in America, this was altogether classical in its symmetry and massing, with four corner pavilions linked by verandas; the architect himself was not pleased with it and such records as there are suggest that it was a rather peculiar affair. The last adjective might well occur to anyone confronted for the first time with another early Gothic Revival building already mentioned in these pages as Godefroy's first work of architecture: St. Mary's Chapel, Baltimore, designed in 1806 (149). Here again the proportions are classical—if any single medieval building influenced Godefroy, it was Nôtre-Dame de Paris, the most classical of the great Gothic cathedrals—while the second story of the facade is merely a screen wall, as in a Roman Baroque church, though stabilized by flying buttresses. Yet the way Godefroy has used arches of identical form in four different sizes shows that he had grasped an important principle of Gothic architecture antithetic to the rules of classicism, and the more one studies St. Mary's Chapel the clearer it becomes that its design merits an adjective which can be applied to few indeed of the buildings of the early Gothic Revival, in America or England—thoughtful.

Had Latrobe's Gothic design for Baltimore Cathedral been executed it would certainly have been the finest Gothic church of the first quarter of the century in America, if no more "correct" than most of the rest; forced by the lack of books to design "from memory" Latrobe used his sensibility to greater effect in it than in any of his later Gothic designs. These were three in number: the Bank of Philadelphia (1807), Christ Church, Washington (1808), and St. Paul's, Alexandria (1816). The bank was a brick box with a pointed arch over the entrance and other token Gothic detail outside and a fan vault, of plaster, over the banking hall inside; the Washington church has the distinction of containing the earliest iron columns in American architecture, supporting the roof; the one in Alexandria, which was botched by the builder, cannot be said to be distinguished for anything in particular. More attractive than any of these was the Federal Street Church in Boston, designed in 1809 by Bulfinch—his one Gothic building and the first Gothic Revival church in New England. Its steeple, with pinnacles on the four corners of the tower

and a needle spire growing out of two octagonal stages with gablets
and pointed arches, was a translation into Gothick (rather than a
retranslation into Gothic) of the Wren-type steeple, such as that of
Old North; the galleried interior, with slender clustered columns
between the nave and aisles and ogee arches framing the tables of
the Commandments behind the pulpit, was of a purely eighteenth-
century character.

The year 1809 saw both of the architects of New York City Hall
designing Gothic churches in that city—Mangin St. Patrick's, Mott
Street, and McComb the Presbyterian Church on Wall Street. Both
buildings have gone, as has also Town's Trinity Church, New Haven
(1814), but the second Gothic Revival church in New England, dating
from 1810, survives. St. John's Cathedral, Providence, was designed
by John Holden Greene, who combined pointed windows with, in
the porch and front, a "Gothic order" of the kind that had been
offered first in the mid-eighteenth-century books of Batty Langley
and later by William Pain. It all seems very anachronistic until one
remembers how few books on Gothic architecture were then available, and that the first serious study of Gothic detail, Thomas Rick-
man's *Attempt to Discriminate the Styles of English Architecture*,
did not appear until 1817.

Gothic was rarely employed for secular purposes before 1830. The
design for Columbia College, New York, made in 1814 by James

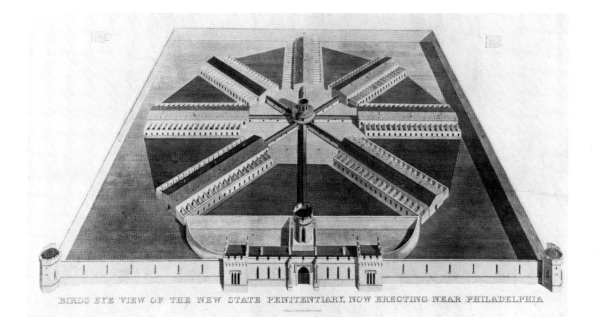

BIRDS EYE VIEW OF THE NEW STATE PENITENTIARY NOW ERECTING NEAR PHILADELPHIA

150
Eastern State Peniten-
tiary, Philadelphia, Penn-
sylvania. John Haviland,
1823–29. From an en-
graving by C. G. Childs.

Renwick, Sr., may be mentioned, though nothing came of it, as the first Gothic collegiate design; the first Gothic Revival building for higher education was Kenyon College at Gambier, Ohio, begun in 1827, and the first of architectural distinction New York University, built in 1833–35 by Town and Davis. In the 1820s enthusiasm for the Grecian led to a decline in the number of Gothic church designs, though in 1822 Strickland himself returned to Gothic—it will be recalled that his first design, the Philadelphia Masonic Hall, was Gothic—for St. Stephen's, Philadelphia, a plain structure to which he gave presence with a high screen-wall facade flanked by octagonal towers. In 1827–30 the Georgia Capitol at Milledgeville (built 1805–07) was gothicized. But the most important Gothic building of the twenties—and arguably the most important American building of that decade—was the Eastern State Penitentiary in Philadelphia, built in 1823–29 to John Haviland's design (150). A stone wall with a tower at each corner enclosed a square of 650 feet, which was entered through the crenellated governor's house, complete with portcullis, in the middle of one side. Seven cellblocks for separate confinement, each cell with a tiny exercise yard attached, radiated from a round center building. "The first American building to have real influence abroad," as Hitchcock has pointed out, the Eastern State Penitentiary established the superiority of the radial prison over the panopticon— of which the Western State Penitentiary at Pittsburgh, designed by Strickland in 1820, was a contemporary example—in the eyes of penologists both in America and in Europe.

In 1832 Alexander Jackson Davis designed a large Gothic country house near Baltimore for a client, Robert Gilmor, who had recently visited Sir Walter Scott, whose books did so much to promote Romantic medievalism in America. The plan of Glen Ellen was essentially classical, with two axes crossing in a rotunda and only slight adjustments in the interests of "irregularity." The octagonal tower at one corner which gave its outline an overall asymmetry was hardly massive enough to prevail over the individual symmetries of the elevations, and there was still much of the Gothic Rococo in the small-scale intricacy of the detail. For all that, Glen Ellen must be accounted the first major work of Picturesque Gothic in America. Davis went on to design many more Gothic houses, large and small, in which he developed a complete mastery of the compositional principles of the Picturesque. The finest is Lyndhurst, at Tarrytown, New York, which he designed for General William Paulding and his son in 1838, when it was called Knoll, and greatly enlarged for another owner, George Merritt, in 1865–67 (151, 152). In both the plan and the elevations the symmetry of the parts is absorbed by the irregularity of the whole, while the detail is distinguished from that of Glen Ellen by its authenticity as well as its greater solidity, having been taken from Pugin's *Examples of Gothic Architecture.* Of Davis's smaller houses the Delamater Cottage at Rhinebeck, New York (1844), and the Rotch House at New Bedford, Massachusetts (1848), may be named. Both are symmetrical and have high central gables, ornamental bargeboards ("gingerbread"), spacious verandas, and Gothic detail of the least learned sort. Davis supplied his friend Andrew Jackson Downing—horticulturalist, landscape gardener, architectural theorist, and popularizer of the Picturesque—with designs for his immensely successful and influential books; one for a house of this type in *Cottage Residences,* where it is described as "A Cottage in the English or Rural Gothic Style," may well be the most frequently adopted house design ever published.

Many other architects designed Gothic houses in the twenty-five years before the Civil War; Richard Upjohn, John McMurtry, and James Renwick, Jr., are among the better known names. Upjohn at least showed himself the equal of Davis in the genre when in 1839 he designed Kingscote, at Newport, Rhode Island, the first of the summer houses or "cottages" that were to give that resort of the very rich its unique character (153, 154, 155). But Davis was the dominant figure and the greatest influence in the Picturesque Gothic episode. Most of its unattributed products could be labelled "school of Davis," and it comes as no surprise to learn that the architect in 1847–50 of the Gothic capitol at Baton Rouge, Louisiana, James Harrison Dakin, was trained in the Town and Davis office.

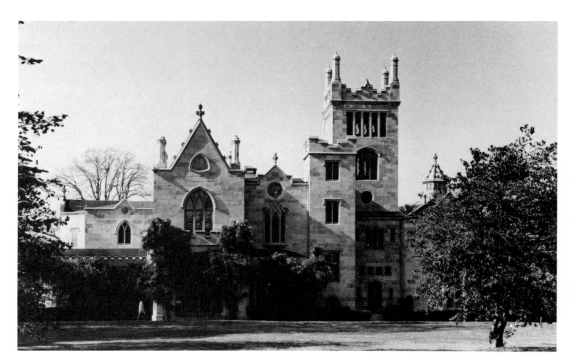

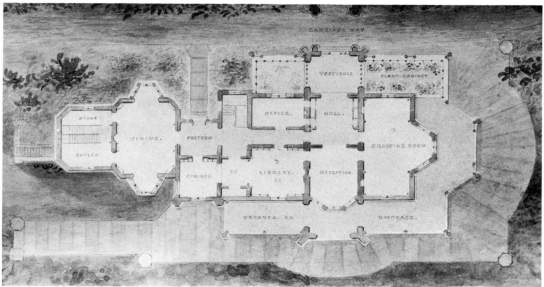

151
Lyndhurst, Tarrytown, New York. Alexander Jackson Davis, 1838 and 1865–67. East front.

152
Lyndhurst, Tarrytown, New York. Plan of first floor. Everything to the left (north) of the stair, together with the porte-cochère on the east front, was built in 1865–67.

153
Kingscote, Newport, Rhode Island. Richard Upjohn, 1839–41. Entrance front from southwest. (Addition to left by Stanford White, 1880–81.)

154
Kingscote, Newport, Rhode Island. Original plan of first floor.

155
Kingscote, Newport, Rhode Island. Hall.

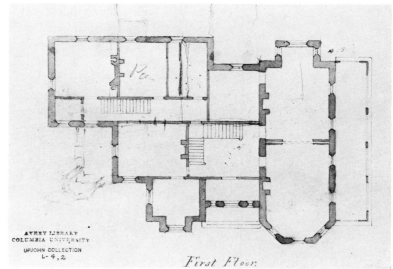

The Italian Villa Style   In 1837 the Scottish-born architect John Notman designed a house at Burlington, New Jersey, for the Rt. Rev. George Washington Doane, Bishop of New Jersey, of a type that was new to America, although it had been well established in England for a couple of decades. The Italian villa, as it was called, was the result of the discovery, around 1800, of the Picturesque qualities of the "vernacular" or anonymous architecture of the Italian countryside; John Nash was the architect of the first English example in 1802. Downing, who published Bishop Doane's house in his book on landscape gardening in 1841 and designs for Italian villas in both of his later books, thought that "as a rural style" the Italian was "inferior to pointed and high-roofed modes" but nevertheless "remarkable for expressing the elegant culture and variety of accomplishment of the retired citizen or man of the world"; the English architect Francis Goodwin pointed out that it permitted "many freedoms which in a more finished and consistent style would not unjustly incur censure"; the American architect Samuel Sloan wrote that "the irregular outline" demanded by the Picturesque was "formed without difficulty," the "predominant figure" being the rectangle, of which many were "introduced and so disposed as to break in upon each other." It is not surprising that with all these advantages the Italian Villa Style soon became the rival in domestic design of the so much trickier Gothic, and was even on occasion—as when Upjohn designed Utica City Hall in 1852—employed for public buildings.

Notman, Upjohn, Davis, and Austin were the leading practitioners of the style. For another Italian villa by Notman, Prospect at Princeton, New Jersey (1849), much larger than Bishop Doane's, may be named. Upjohn's first, and perhaps finest, was the Edward King House at Newport, Rhode Island, built in 1845–47, in the plan of which irregularity is achieved without sacrifice of axial discipline (156, 157). Homewood Villa, Baltimore (1851), is a mirror-image copy of the King House. In the E. B. Litchfield House at Brooklyn (1855) Upjohn moved the tower from its customary corner position to the center of the entrance front over a vestibule to the hall, which ran back the whole depth of the house with stairs at the far end, supported the arches of the loggia with columns instead of piers, and gave the second story an emphatically Renaissance character, with classical architraves framing the windows and triangular pediments surmounting several of them. Davis's chief works in the style came in the fifties, although he had exhibited an Italian villa design in 1835. His Haskell House at Belleville (1851), Munn House at Utica (1854), and E. C. Litchfield House at Brooklyn (1854) shared the motif of a three-story octagonal tower with a more slender square

156
Edward King House,
Newport, Rhode Island.
Richard Upjohn, 1845–47.
Entrance front.

157
Edward King House,
Newport, Rhode Island.
Plan of first floor.

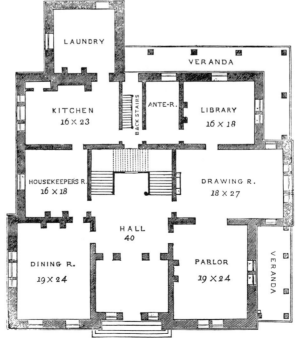

158
Morse-Libby House, Port-
land, Maine. Attributed
to Henry Austin, 1859–
63. Street front.

tower of four stories attached; in most Italian villas the only polygonal elements were bay windows, though Henry A. Sykes combined two octagons with singularly happy effect in the observatory and "cabinet" (natural history museum) of Amherst College (1847–48). Henry Austin's Norton House at New Haven, designed in 1849, shows the style at its plainest; the walls are smooth planes, the windows are simple apertures, and there are no quoins to soften the geometry of the component parts. When he came to design the Morse-Libby House at Portland ten years later Austin showed that his taste had changed with the times (158).[1] Richness, not simplicity, was now the ideal, and height and verticality were sought in contrast to the opposite qualities of the Greek Revival buildings that had dominated the scene for so long. Hence the rusticated quoins of the Morse-Libby House, the Baroque plasticity of its window pediments and the ornamental brackets supporting them, the great projection of its eaves, and its tall proportions. In all but its lack of certain forms and mannerisms with which postwar architects were to show their devotion to "reality," it is a High Victorian design.

Richard Upjohn and Ecclesiological Gothic

While Bishop Doane's villa at Burlington was going up, the first church of the architect he was nine years later to commission to design his church there was rising 500 miles to the north. The church was St. John's, Bangor, Maine; the architect was an English cabinetmaker and joiner who had landed in New York at the age of twenty-seven in 1829, Richard Upjohn, whom we now meet in his most important historical role,[2] as initiator in America of that development in ecclesiastical architecture which, because of the emphasis placed by its theorists on the moral qualities they perceived in Gothic, may be called Ethical Gothic—or alternatively, from the name given to their studies by a group of Cambridge undergraduates whom a common interest in medieval churches brought together in 1836, Ecclesiological Gothic. Not that St. John's, Bangor, would have satisfied the ecclesiologists; for although its detail was much more convincing, archaeologically, than that of any previous Gothic Revival church in America, its nave was lined with galleries (which they hated), it had no chancel (a feature they insisted on), and—worst of all—the whole thing was of wood. But a lithographed view of it, according to a credible story, was the cause of Upjohn being asked, in 1839, to superintend repairs to Trinity Church, New York, and subsequently to design a new church, the third on the site, which stands to this day (159).

As finished in 1846 Upjohn's Trinity was externally a smaller and somewhat simplified version of an ideal church of which Pugin, the most aggressive theorist of Ethical Gothic, had published a perspective in his *True Principles of Pointed or Christian Architecture* in 1841. Inside, there were no galleries, and there was a raised chancel of two full bays—a feature which, as Upjohn's biographer puts it, "to many smacked of popery," and which the architect, as a devout Episcopalian imbued with ecclesiological ideas, had to fight hard for. Neither Pugin nor the ecclesiologists of the Cambridge Camden Society could have approved of the plaster vaults, but they were ordered by the building committee in place of the timber roofs intended by Upjohn; as for the style of the whole, although by the time the building was completed Perpendicular had been rejected by Pugin and the ecclesiologists in favor of Decorated or "Middle Pointed," it had been acceptable when Upjohn made the design. All in all, with its noble proportions and consistent detail Trinity was a fine exemplar for the new movement.

New York was not without churches in the ecclesiologists' favorite style for long. In 1843 James Renwick, Jr., then only twenty-five, designed Grace Church in Decorated, and in 1844 Upjohn followed suit with the Church of the Holy Communion. In other respects the

159
Trinity Church, New York City. Richard Upjohn, 1839–46. View from southeast.

two buildings had little in common, for the Church of the Holy Communion was as simple as Grace Church is highly wrought. Both had transepts, but while the steeple of Grace Church stands axially at the end of the nave, like that of Trinity, the tower of the Church of the Holy Communion stood beside it. The latter arrangement, repeated more often than not in Upjohn's later churches, is certainly the more picturesque—but only incidentally, for ecclesiological theory was functional, stressing liturgical requirements and symbolism, rather than esthetic, while Pugin had stated in *True Principles* that it was a great defect when a building was *"designed to be picturesque"*—the italics are his—and, again in italics, that *"the picturesque effect of the ancient buildings results from the ingenious methods by which the old builders overcame local and constructive difficulties."*

Two of the largest and most elaborate of the Gothic churches of the forties were Holy Trinity, Brooklyn Heights, by Minard Lafever, and Calvary Church, New York, by Renwick. Both were built in 1844–47. As first designed Holy Trinity was Perpendicular, but Lafever went over to Decorated in the course of the work. For Calvary Renwick employed Early English or "First Pointed," as did Upjohn in the much smaller church which he designed for Bishop Doane in 1846. The latter, St. Mary's, Burlington, is of great importance in the history of the Gothic Revival in America, for here for the first time an architect developed his design from measured drawings of a medieval church (160). St. John's, Shottesbrook, in Berkshire, was the model; Upjohn introduced certain simplifications—the use of Early English was one, for Shottesbrook is Decorated—and gave St. Mary's what one comes to recognize as the stamp of his personal style. In the same year, 1846, in Philadelphia, work began on a church that followed a medieval model much more closely, with the aid of drawings provided by the Cambridge Camden Society, which had long been anxious to promote its doctrines in America (which its journal, *The Ecclesiologist*, was apt to refer to as "the colonies"). This was the church of St. James the Less (161); the model was St. Michael's, Longstanton, Cambridgeshire, built circa 1230. Although some slight alterations were made in England by the architect G. G. Place and the contractor added a vestry and an extra bay to the nave, St. James the Less was a copy of St. Michael's rather than an adaptation or an imitation in the old sense—and in ecclesiological eyes all the better for that. During its construction and furnishing the donor, Robert Ralston, corresponded with Benjamin Webb, one of the two founders of the Cambridge Camden Society. No expense was spared and in the end it cost just five times

160
St. Mary's, Burlington, New Jersey. Richard Upjohn, 1846–48. View from east.

161
St. James the Less, Phila-
delphia, Pennsylvania.
G. G. Place, 1846–50. In-
terior, looking east.

the amount of the original estimate. Its influence was considerable, one of those who felt it being Upjohn, as appears most obviously in his Calvary Church at Stonington, Connecticut (1847–49).

In 1847 the Cambridge Camden Society sent to Philadelphia drawings of All Saints, Brighton, the latest work of R. C. Carpenter, its favorite architect at the time, in response to a request by Ralston for a pattern to guide John Notman, who had been commissioned to design a large church by the vestry of St. Mark's parish. The triple roof of Carpenter's church with its deep valleys would not have survived many American winter snows; so Notman adopted St. Stephen's, Westminster, by Benjamin Ferrey, which had also been begun that year and was known to him from an illustration in the *Illustrated London News*, as his model instead. St. Mark's is a fine building, and it led to Notman being much sought after as an architect of churches; one of his most successful, Emmanuel Church at Cumberland, Maryland, built in 1850–51, was modelled, with the aid of an illustration in *The Ecclesiologist,* on another Brighton church by Carpenter, St. Paul's (162).

There was never a more English architecture in America than the Gothic Revival of the 1840s and 1850s; even the German hall church which Robert Cary Long, Jr., designed in 1841 for the German Redemptorist Fathers in Baltimore, St. Alphonsus, is clothed in English detail—as is the interior of St. Patrick's Cathedral, New York (1857–79), Renwick's version (Anglicized also in plan and proportions) of Cologne. Yet it produced one group of buildings for which there is no English analogue. In the fifties Upjohn designed a number of town churches, of which St. Paul's, Buffalo (1850–51), was the biggest (and in the architect's opinion the best), and a larger number of country churches. Many of the latter are of wood, and the frankness with which the fact is acknowledged and the boldness with which Gothic forms are modified to suit the material show that there had been a revolution in architectural thought since Ware declared that it was the honour of the architect that the form should triumph over the material (163). Pugin, more than any other one writer, had brought this revolution about. In America the new principles were championed by Downing in *The Architecture of Country Houses,* first published in 1850. "To build a house of wood so exactly in imitation of stone as to lead the spectator to suppose it stone, is a paltry artifice, at variance with all truthfulness," wrote Downing, and: "We greatly prefer the vertical to the horizontal boarding. The main timbers which enter into the frame of a wooden house and support the structure, are vertical, and hence the vertical boarding properly signifies to the eye a wooden house." Upjohn used vertical

162
Emmanuel Church, Cumberland, Maryland. John Notman, 1850–51. View from east.

163
St. John Chrysostom's, Delafield, Wisconsin. Richard Upjohn, 1851–53. Church and bell tower from west.

164
The Chalet, Newport, Rhode Island. Leopold Eidlitz, 1854. General view.

boarding in his wooden churches, as Davis had a little earlier in his wooden cottages. Here we have the beginning of that American structuralism in wood which in the fifties was further developed in such buildings as that striking example of what Downing considered "the most picturesque of all dwellings built of wood," The Chalet at Newport (1854) by Leopold Eidlitz, which in the sixties and seventies occupied a central place in the architectural scene, and which in more recent decades has shown itself to have an enduring vitality (164).[3]

Romanesque Revival

In the later 1840s, while the Gothic Revival was coming under the influence of the English ecclesiological movement, an alternative medieval style was gaining ground; in the 1850s it overtook Gothic, and most of the churches of that decade, as well as many public buildings, are round-arched. This revival of the Romanesque was different from any comparable phenomenon we have encountered in that it was not of English origin or inspiration. In England Neo-Romanesque buildings were hardly numerous enough to warrant one's speaking of a Romanesque Revival, and none of them has been shown to have been imitated on this side of the Atlantic; what was English in the products of the American Romanesque Revival—and much was—came out of archaeological publications. In Germany, however, there had been a flourishing Romanesque Revival since about 1830, and even if this did not give the initial impetus to the American one it certainly influenced it. Not only is there evidence of a familiarity with the round-arched works of von Gärtner and Schinkel in designs by the Prague-born (but Upjohn-trained) Leopold Eidlitz but the Rhode Islander Thomas Tefft must have been referring to something that many people knew of when in 1851 he wrote: "The round arch school of Germany is employing much invention and originality in their designs and we hazard but little in predicting a favorable result." For most Americans at the time the Germans were the cultural leaders of Europe.

Romanesque, as the mid-nineteenth century saw it, had qualities of just the kind to recommend its use in America. An itemization of those of one regional style by the English architect John Shaw could be applied to Romanesque as a whole: "Lombard Architecture," Shaw wrote, "contains in an eminent degree the qualities now so important. These appear to be first, economy; secondly, rapidity of execution; thirdly, strict simplicity combined with high capability of ornament; fourthly, durability; fifthly, beauty." One might change the order—since he was writing to a bishop about the provision of churches in the East End of London, Shaw naturally put economy first—but one could but agree that Romanesque did indeed possess those advantages. Its simplicity was particularly welcome in a country where the level of skill in stone-cutting required that direct imitations like Notman's Gothic churches in Philadelphia and at Cumberland be considerably simpler in detail than their English models. Robert Dale Owen, in his *Hints on Public Architecture* (1849), emphasized that Romanesque, or "Norman," had "fewer members and less complication of details" than Gothic, while the author of *Plans for Churches,* published by the Congregational Church in 1853, went a step further in recommending what he called "the modernized Romanesque," which was "based upon the supposition that the Romanesque . . . progressed as such instead of turning into Gothic" and was "remarkable for the simplicity of its moulding." And then, besides possessing these practical advantages, Romanesque could be shown to be preferable to Gothic on religious and political grounds. Thanks to a typical sophistry of the associative sense, Protestants regarded it as free from the taint of popery—which Gothic, in the eyes of many, never could be. As for the politics of the style, Owen was cautious but definite: "Its entire expression is less ostentatious, and if political character may be ascribed to Architecture, more republican."

The first building of the Romanesque Revival was the Church of the Pilgrims, Brooklyn, which went up in 1844–46; the architect was Upjohn. It was a plain structure, with arcaded corbel tables under the eaves as the only enrichment; the gabled facade was flanked on the left by a low tower with a concave pyramidal roof and on the right by a high one with an upper stage terminating in four gables (in the manner of the towers of the German abbey church of Corvey, for example), from which rose a spire with a curious wavy outline. It cannot have been an altogether successful design—the first historian of the revival characterized Upjohn's approach here as tentative—but it might be called a prophetic one because arcaded corbel tables, pairs of unmatched towers, and spires were to adorn scores or even hundreds of later churches. The arcaded corbel table was of course incontrovertibly Romanesque, having been employed by several regional schools in the eleventh and twelfth centuries; American architects evidently regarded it as the hallmark of the style and it would be hard to find a Romanesque design of any pretensions without it. On the other hand there was little medieval precedent for unmatched towers flanking a facade (165); whether they were a concession to economy justified by the Picturesque esthetic or a concession to the Picturesque with welcome economic consequences is a question which doubtless should in some cases be answered one way and in others the other. As for spires, they were not really Romanesque at all. But besides being time-honored components of churches and universally understood symbols they appealed to the competitive spirit—a congregation would pride itself on having the highest spire in its city or neighborhood, and many of them rose to more than 200 feet—and those who thought like the author of the Congregational Church's manual could have argued that if the Romanesque had not turned into Gothic it would have produced spires in due course.

In 1845 work began on Upjohn's second Romanesque building, the chapel of Bowdoin College at Brunswick, Maine. It is of an emphatically German character, with two matching spire-crowned towers; what appear to be aisles held classrooms, while the nave, the chapel proper, was arranged like an English college chapel with banked-up rows of seats on either side facing each other across the central space. (Romanesque Revival churches as a class had spacious but characterless preaching-hall interiors, often galleried.) Before the decade was over three more architects we have met in other connections designed Romanesque churches: James Renwick, the Church of the Puritans, New York (1846); Leopold Eidlitz, with assistance from a young Bavarian architect, Otto Blesch, St. George's on Stuyvesant Square, New York (1846); and Henry Austin the Congregational Church at Kent, Connecticut (1848). The Eidlitz and Blesch

165
*Old Stone Church, Cleve-
land, Ohio. Charles
Heard, circa 1855. West
front.*

166
*Smithsonian Institution,
Washington, District of
Columbia. James Ren-
wick, Jr., 1848–49. View
from west.*

building, whose two towers were surmounted by openwork spires, was purely German; the other two were at least as German as they were anything else. The stylistic terminology of the time was far from exact; any Romanesque building was liable to be called Lombard, while any that did not have the characteristics of the regional style of Lombardy was liable to be called Norman. Churches that we would call Lombard today began to appear in the fifties; the finest remaining one, which would be even finer had its campanile been built, is St. Paul's, Baltimore (1852–56), by Upjohn. As for a church that we would call Norman today, the finest is perhaps Holy Trinity, Rittenhouse Square, Philadelphia, designed by Notman in 1857, spireless—a spire was planned—though it is.

Downing included a "villa in the Norman style"—"this is not a house to please a practical, common-sense man"—in *The Architecture of Country Houses* in 1850, and in 1851 Sloan built one, Bartram Hall, near Philadelphia; but Romanesque had a rather less than moderate success as a domestic style. A select list of secular buildings of the Romanesque Revival would include Tefft's Union Station at Providence (begun in 1848), Eidlitz's City Hall at Springfield (1854–55), and St. Luke's Hospital, New York (1856) by John W. Ritch; it would be headed by the Smithsonian Institution in Washington, designed by Renwick in 1846 and built in 1848–49, to which pride of place is due as not only the first public building of the revival but also its one masterpiece (166). Admittedly, the detail of the Smithsonian is mechanical and repetitive, and for all that it is built of solid brownstone the building has a seeming fragility that reminds one of the early Gothic Revival. (Hitchcock has likened it to "an enormous garden fabrick.") Yet seen from the right distance across the leaf-strewn sward of the Mall on a mellow autumn day it could make the most hardened classicist a temporary convert to the Picturesque.

Renaissance Revival   Although as time went on more and more architects abandoned Greek for one or another of the styles discussed so far in this chapter for individual commissions, none of them was a real threat to the Greek Revival; only an alternative classical style, which with a Roman revival out of the question had to be (in the terminology of the time) "modern," could be that. Downing was one of the first to attack the Greek Revival, in 1842, on the grounds that "the taste for Grecian temples" tended "to destroy expression of purpose" and also for the Picturesque reason that its buildings were generally white and "no painter of landscapes, that has possessed a name, was ever guilty of displaying in his pictures a glaring white house." Then in 1844 the young Boston architect Arthur Gilman, writing anonymously in the *North American Review*, described Greek buildings as the "offspring of a remote age, an antagonistic religion, an obsolete form of government, and a widely different state of society than our own" and proposed the adoption of "the style of Bramante, of Palladio, and Michael Angelo," or the *"palazzo* style." In the next year, 1845, the first two buildings of the Renaissance Revival were begun, soon to be joined by so many more than in 1854 a writer in *Putnam's Monthly* could state: "The Grecian taste . . . has within the last few years been succeeded and almost entirely superseded, both here and in England, by the revival of the Italian style."

The Renaissance Revival was no less an English import than Palladianism had been, with the illustrated magazines now providing the chief means of transatlantic conveyance. In England Charles Barry had been the first to use the cinquecento *palazzo* formula in the Travellers' Club, built in 1829–32, which he followed up with the larger, Farnese-inspired Reform Club of 1836–40. It is therefore no surprise that one of the first two buildings of the revival in America should have been a clubhouse, the Athenaeum of Philadelphia, designed by Notman (167). To say that Notman's clubhouse will stand comparison with Barry's is to say much, but by no means too much. The heightening of the second floor or *piano nobile* (as in Peruzzi's Palazzo Massimi, one of seven Italian *palazzi* named by Gilman for "a true greatness of manner") is a telling difference, justified functionally by the placing of the library on that floor. It is easy to sense what welcome relief (in two senses) the balcony and crowning *cornicione* provided after all the flat fronts of the Adam Style and the Greek Revival.

167
Athenaeum of Philadel-
phia, Philadelphia, Penn-
sylvania. John Notman,
1845–47. Washington
Square front.

There is still some question about the identity of the architect of the other American *palazzo* begun in 1845; there is none at all about the impression it made. This was Stewart's Downtown Store in New York, of a more generalized Renaissance Style than the Athenaeum but much bigger and faced with gleaming Westchester marble. There were plenty of English precedents for the application of the *palazzo* formula to commercial buildings; the first had appeared in the late thirties. But Stewart's was the first commercial building to demonstrate a great practical advantage of the mode: extensibility. Greek buildings were finite forms; they could not be enlarged. *Palazzi* could be and in 1850 Stewart's was, thus starting a tradition that may be followed down to Sullivan's Carson Pirie Scott & Company store.

More than a fair share of the buildings Putnam's writer might have pointed to in 1854 were designed by Thomas Thomas, an English architect who had established his practice in New York in the thirties. He and his son, Griffith, were the most successful commercial specialists of the fifties and sixties; their works already included the large and plain Moffat Building (1847–48), the large and ornamental Lord & Taylor Store (1852–53), and the smaller Chemical Bank (1850–51) and Broadway Bank (1852–53), both of which were interesting for their architects' attempt to give vertical emphasis to narrow fronts. All these were more or less Roman or Florentine in style; the richer Venetian or Sansovinesque Style (first used in England in 1847 by Sydney Smirke in the Carlton Club) made its American *début* in Baltimore, in the Sun Building (1851). Designed by the architect R. G. Hatfield in collaboration with James Bogardus, a former engraver who in 1848 had built a factory in New York for the production of iron building components, this had two fronts entirely of iron, cast in sections and bolted together.[4] In 1854 Bogardus produced a second edition of the Sun Building for Harper Brothers in New York. In these two buildings iron was used not only for the ease with which elaborate ornament could be mass-produced (as it had been for decades) and for the very open facades that it permitted but also for its structural advantages. For behind their cast-iron fronts were complete iron frames—the columns of cast, the beams of wrought iron—that were capable of supporting themselves and the floors without the aid of the brick walls at the sides or back. They are thus early examples—very early for America—of the internal skeleton or "cage" structure. In 1855 Bogardus put up the first metal-frame structure in which the brickwork was no more than an infilling—a shot tower for the McCullough Shot & Lead Company in New York—and thus anticipated the first use of this type of construction in Chicago by nearly thirty years. It was a building

168
Haughwout Store, New York City. J. P. Gaynor, 1857. Broadway facade.

169
Customs House (Post Office), Georgetown, District of Columbia. Ammi B. Young, 1857. Principal front.

manufactured by Bogardus's chief rival in the iron building industry, Daniel Badger, the Sansovinesque Haughwout Store in New York, that had the distinction of being the first commercial building equipped with that other essential of the modern skyscraper, the passenger elevator (168).

The impact of the Renaissance Revival on the design of public buildings was not long delayed. During Ammi B. Young's tenure of the federal post of Supervising Architect of the Office of Construction (1852–62) most new post offices and customs houses were of Renaissance character; the post office at Windsor, Vermont, and the customs house (now post office) at Georgetown, District of Columbia, are among the surviving examples (169). In the domestic field, the astylar *palazzo* mode was obviously suitable for large town houses; the first in which it was adopted seems to have been the Herman Thorne House on West Sixteenth Street, New York, built in 1846–48, which was much praised in the press at the time though no one thought fit to mention the name of its architect. In 1859 *The Builder*, the leading English architectural magazine, told its readers: ''In the city of New York, avenues are springing up lined not with houses, but with palaces. . . . Neither London nor Paris, with all the accumulations of wealth of a thousand years, can show such a street as Fifth Avenue.'' Most of the palaces were *palazzi*.

Although the first buildings of the revival in both England and America were academic imitations of a High Renaissance type, ar-

170
*United States Capitol,
Washington, District of
Columbia. Dome. Thomas
Ustick Walter, 1855–65.
View from southeast.*

chitects were soon imitating, in the freest manner, anything dating from the early fifteenth to the late sixteenth century. Some, in their search for "modern" (as distinct from "ancient" models), moved on to the seventeenth century and even the eighteenth—as did the first American to propose a renaissance revival, Gilman, the exterior of whose Arlington Street Church in Boston (1859–61) is almost purely Gibbsian. In ecclesiastical design a one-man Wren revival was initiated by Minard Lafever as early as 1846–48 in the Church of the Holy Apostles, New York, and carried on by him in the Reformed Church on the Heights, Brooklyn (1850–51), the Reformed Protestant Dutch Church, Kingston, and the Pearl Street Congregational Church, Hartford (both 1851–52). The biggest tribute to Wren, however, was paid by Thomas Ustick Walter, when in 1855 it fell to him to design a new dome for the United States Capitol and he responded with a paraphrase in iron of the masterpiece of construction in masonry, timber, and lead that crowns the cathedral of the bishop of whose diocese a vast tract of the North American continent once formed a part (170).

Notes

Foreword   1. W. F. Deknatel, quoted by B. Zevi, *Towards an Organic Architecture* (London: Faber & Faber, 1950), p. 126.

1   1. Forman, *The Architecture of the Old South*, p. 28.

2. In the English colonies piazza (Italian for an open space or square in a town) was the common designation of any kind of porch—in the South it still is. This was a result of Inigo Jones's giving to the great square he planned for the Earl of Bedford in 1631 the name of Covent Garden Piazza. Londoners transferred the outlandish new term from the square to what was for them the most novel feature of the development, the arcaded walks under the houses bounding it on two sides.

3. The *galerie* seems to have come into general use in the 1740s. In 1751 the plantation owner Jean de Pradel wrote to his brothers in France of his new house, Monplaisir: "It will be one hundred and sixteen feet in length by forty-eight in width, including the galleries which will surround the house. What a great convenience these galleries are in this country!"

4. See J. Evans, *Monastic Architecture in France from the Renaissance to the Revolution* (Cambridge: Cambridge University Press, 1964), figs. 388, 390, 541. The resemblance between the stair at New Orleans and the one at Auberive is striking but can only be coincidental, since the former was retained from the building of 1727–34 and Auberive was not built until circa 1750.

5. The resemblance was more marked before 1847, when the balustrades over the cornices of the Cabildo and Presbytère were removed and mansard roofs added.

2   1. J. A. Baird, Jr., *The Churches of Mexico 1530–1810* (Berkeley and Los Angeles: University of California Press, 1962), p. 5.

2. The present woodwork of the *portal* dates from a restoration in 1909.

3. When the friar's house was in the usual position its flat roof could be used as a halfway platform for hoisting the materials for the roof of the church.

4. In 1776, when Fray Dominguez visited and reported on the church, there were three windows in the south wall.

5. Today the effect can still be experienced at Isleta, Trampas, and Ranchos de Taos. Most transverse clerestories have been blocked up at one time or another because of their tendency to leak.

6. The *presidio* church of San Miguel, Santa Fe, is one of the few with eastern sanctuaries; the church at Pecos was another.

7. The *retablo* is dated 1780 in an inscription on the back; the decoration of the walls of the sanctuary is presumably coeval. The murals in the nave must be much later. Similar but less extensive paintings in the nave at Acoma were whitewashed over circa 1970.

8. H. de la Croix, *Military Considerations in City Planning: Fortifications* (New York: Braziller, 1972), p. 44.

9. The churches of the other two missions near San Antonio, San Francisco de la Espada and San Juan Capistrano, have been too thoroughly reconstructed to count as eighteenth-century buildings. The Moorish arch of the

doorway of San Francisco is not without interest, although its voussoirs were "incorrectly reassembled in a restoration." P. Goeldner, *Texas Catalog: Historic American Buildings Survey* (San Antonio: Trinity University Press, 1976), p. 193.

10. For example, the *portadas* of La Valenciana near Guanajuato and of the parish church of Lagos de Moreno in Jalisco; see Baird, *The Churches of Mexico 1530–1810*, plates 153 and 146.

11. It was rebuilt once before, incorrectly, in 1884.

3 1. The best brief account of these books is in R. Wittkower, *Palladio and Palladianism* (New York: George Braziller, 1974), chapter 7.

2. The area had been settled in the seventeenth century by planters from Barbados.

3. For what it really was, see Wittkower, *Palladio and Palladianism*, pp. 79–85.

4. The plan of Coleshill must have crossed the Atlantic be some other means than a book, for it was not published in one until 1771, when it appeared in the continuation of *Vitruvius Britannicus* by J. Woolfe and J. Gandon.

4 1. The portico was not built until 1785–87, and then of wood instead of stone; Harrison's design is said to have been followed faithfully. The balustrade was originally continued around the roof of the nave.

2. The Swanenburch House, Halfweg.

3. "The Capitol is a light and airy structure, with a portico in front of two orders, the lower of which, being Doric, is tolerably just in its proportions and ornaments, save only that the intercolonnations are too large. The upper is Ionic, much too small for that on which it is mounted, its ornaments not proper to the order, nor proportioned within themselves. It is crowned with a pediment, which is too high for its span." (*Notes on the State of Virginia,* p. 152).

4. A "penitentiary house" containing sixteen cells for solitary confinement was built to the rear of Smith's building in 1791

5. Mount Airy was gutted by fire in 1844.

6. The craftsmen who did the decorations in the dining room at Mount Vernon were Lamphier and Sears; they were probably from Philadelphia.

5 1. The detailed treatment of Monticello I was Palladian. The uninterrupted templelike roof between the pediments, its most Neo-Classical feature, had Anglo-Palladian precedent in Colen Campbell's Wanstead, built in 1715–20.

2. Jefferson may also have been influenced by seeing a painting by Hubert Robert ("Robert des Ruines"), *La Réunion des Plus Célèbres Monuments Antiques de la France*, with the Maison Carrée in the foreground, which was exhibited in the Salon du Louvre when he was in Paris in 1785.

3. In 1807 Bulfinch had rebuilt the spire of Old North, blown down in a gale three years before, reducing the total height of the steeple from 191 feet to 175 feet.

4. So called because the first operation with ether used as an anaesthetic was performed in it on October 6, 1846.

6 1. He won the Gold Medal at the Royal Academy Schools in 1781 and in 1790 received the first Travelling Scholarship in Architecture awarded by the Academy.

2. As in the Walnut Street Prison, Philadelphia.

3. When it was dedicated in 1821, Baltimore Cathedral lacked its portico, and its east end terminated in an apse, flanked by square rooms, abutting the piers under the dome. The present portico was completed in 1865 by Latrobe's son, John H. B. Latrobe, and the domed choir was added in 1890, in accordance with Latrobe's plan, which had been truncated for reasons of economy. (The choir being equal in length to the nave is one of the clearest evidences of the relationship to Wren's St. Paul's.) The onion domes on the belfries date from 1832 and were not designed by Latrobe.

4. H.-R. Hitchcock, *Architecture: Nineteenth and Twentieth Centuries*, p. 7.

5. The interior was altered radically in 1893.

6. He went first to London, where he spent seven years; his only building there, as well as another in which elements of a competition design by him were incorporated, has been destroyed. In 1827 he returned to France, where he ended his career as Architect of the Department of Mayenne.

7. Mills already had independent commissions when he joined Latrobe, and it was in connection with one of them that Latrobe wrote him a letter which contains a classic description of the situation of the professional architect in America at the time: "The profession of architecture has been hitherto in the hands of two sorts of men. The first, of those, who from travelling or from books have acquired some knowledge of the theory of the art, but know nothing of its practice; the second, of those who know nothing but the practice, and whose early life being spent in labor, and in the habits of a laborious life, have had no opportunity of acquiring the theory. The complaisance of these two sets of men to each other, renders it difficult for the Architect to get in between them, for the building mechanic finds his account in the ignorance of the *Gentleman-architect*, as the latter does in the submissive deportment which interest dictates to the former" (T. F. Hamlin, *Benjamin Henry Latrobe*, p. 586).

7 1. Under the head of curvature, only the entasis of the columns of the Parthenon had yet been observed, for the first time in 1810; their inclination—inward, so that their vertical axes meet about a mile above the earth's surface—went unnoticed until 1829, and the curvature of the stylobate and entablature until 1837.

2. An explanation is offered by R. G. Carrott, *The Egyptian Revival*, pp. 120–21.

8 1. Assuming that the traditional but apparently undocumented attribution is correct.

2. In the History of architecture as an art, that is. Upjohn also has an important place in the history of the architectural profession. In his office on February 23, 1857, the meeting that led to the founding of The American Institute of Architects was held. Including Upjohn and his son Richard M. Upjohn, fourteen architects were present; twelve more were invited to subsequent meetings, and the institute was incorporated two months later. Upjohn was President of the AIA for its first eighteen years.

3. The most important nineteenth-century technical innovation in building in wood, the balloon frame, was first used for St. Mary's Church, Chicago, by the Connecticut architect and builder A. D. Taylor in 1833. It was unknown in the East until the end of the fifties, when it was described first in a New York newspaper in 1857 and then, with illustrations, in *Carpentry Made Easy* by William Bell (Philadelphia, 1858). In the sixties it was called "Chicago construction." It would be hard to exaggerate the importance of the part that the balloon frame, which required only know-how (as distinct from skill) and lent itself to the prefabrication of buildings, played in the westward movement and the urbanization of the Middle West. But its effect on architectural design was negligible.

4. The first iron-fronted building in America was erected on Washington Street, Boston, in 1842 by Daniel Badger. The Miners' Bank at Pottsville, Pennsylvania, built in 1829 to Haviland's design, was a masonry structure faced with iron plates, like the Narva Triumphal Arch in St. Petersburg, which was completed in 1816, the year in which Haviland left Russia for America. Russia was a leader in iron technology; there was an all-iron house in St. Petersburg by 1765, when it was visited by Casanova (Giacomo Casanova, *History of My Life*, translated and edited by W. R. Trask (New York: Harcourt, Brace & World, 1966–71), X, p. 132). The earliest known iron columns in America are (as already noted) in Christ Church, Washington, completed to Latrobe's design in 1808; in 1820 Strickland used iron columns in the Chestnut Street Theatre, Philadelphia. The first iron roof was also, it would seem, due to Latrobe, who covered Nassau Hall, Princeton, with one in 1803 when he renovated the building after a fire. Iron was also used for fire-proofing. A building in which it proved its worth for this purpose was Mills's Record Office in Charleston, whose window frames, sashes, and shutters of iron, combined with the brick vaults supporting the floors and the copper sheathing of the wooden roof structure, enabled it to survive the fire at the beginning of the Civil War.

9

1. Owen Jones published two volumes on the Alhambra (1842 and 1845) before his *Grammar of Ornament* (1856). In 1850–51 he served as color consultant for Paxton's Crystal Palace, whose supports and girders were painted red, yellow, and pale blue.

2. Ruskin's architectural Lamp of Truth did "not admit iron as a constructive material," although, like other mid-Victorians, Ruskin vaguely prophesied "the time is probably near when a new system of architectural laws will be developed, adapted entirely to metallic construction."

3. Charles Eliot Norton, a key member of the building committee, was the first professor of fine art at Harvard (1875–98), just as Ruskin, whom Norton knew well, had been at Oxford. Norton's belief in the idea of collegiate architecture as an influence on youth has its parallel in Jefferson's thoughts in designing the University of Virginia. Despite the enduring effects of architecture, the selected competitors for Memorial Hall were given only twenty-five days in which to prepare their designs. Norton, without giving specific reasons, did not like the final building. Wight and Russell Sturgis would have been more sympathetic architects, but then they were not graduates of Harvard College.

4. Later, in 1864, William Robert Ware opened an *atelier* of his own in Boston. The following year he was asked to form an architectural department at MIT. Actual instruction did not begin until 1868, in Rogers Hall in Boston. The second school of architecture was founded at the University of Illinois in 1867. Subsequently schools were established at Cornell in 1871, Syracuse in 1873, Michigan in 1876, and Columbia in 1880, the last also under Ware.

5. Durand, professor of architecture at the Paris Ecole Polytechnique, published two volumes summarizing French theory and practice (1802–1805). His emphasis on repetition of elements forced a joint clarity of plans and elevations.

10 1. The term skyscraper first appeared in print in 1890: "A new system has found much favor here, and is being generally followed now in the construction of mammoth buildings known as 'Sky-scrapers,' which has given Chicago a new celebrity." John J. Flinn, *Chicago: A History, an Encyclopedia and a Guide*, p. 129.

2. The firm name Burnham and Root was not changed until 1894 when it became D. H. Burnham and Co., which it remained until Burnham's death in 1912. In his *Autobiography* Wright tells of Burnham's offer to him of an expense-paid Beaux-Arts training, which Wright refused.

3. Raft foundations proved unreliable. Portions of the Monadnock have settled more than twenty inches. Today's practice is to sink concrete caissons down to bedrock, which in Chicago lies more than 100 feet below ground level. The first use of caissons in Chicago building was under the west party wall of the Chicago Stock Exchange, completed in 1894. William Sooy Smith was the engineer; Adler and Sullivan were the architects. Pneumatic caissons were first developed by English and French engineers in the mid-nineteenth century.

4. The first use of terra-cotta for sheathing a facade was in 1889–90 in Burnham and Root's second Rand McNally Building. It soon became popular for tall buildings everywhere, the Woolworth Building in New York being the largest example.

5. Interior courts were frequent delights in nineteenth-century buildings of all sorts. Some examples are the Palace Hotel in San Francisco (1874–75), the second John Shillito Store in Cincinnati (1878), the Old Pension Building in Washington, D.C. (1883), the thirteen-story Chamber of Commerce Building in Chicago (1888–89), the Brown Palace Hotel in Denver (1892), and the Bradbury Building in Los Angeles (1893).

6. Even before the building was completed Adler and Sullivan moved into the tower, the loftiest office suite in Chicago at that time. Here Frank Lloyd Wright assisted Sullivan on the final decorative details of the Auditorium Building.

7. Holabird and Roche received the 1898 Gage commission for a trio of buildings on South Michigan Avenue, of eight, seven, and six stories. For the tallest, at the north, a millinery establishment, Sullivan was asked to design the facade, which included a four-foot band of translucent glass above the clear glass windows of each grouping to diffuse the glare for the benefit of close needlework. Sullivan's facade was increased in 1902 by the addition of four stories, which were according to the same design as the lower stories.

8. The first use of Chicago construction in New York was in the Tower Building by Bradford Gilbert (1888–89).

9. Prior to 1916 the building code of New York City merely limited the weight of a building on rock foundation to fifteen tons per square foot. On this basis it would have been theoretically possible to erect on a 200-foot square plot an office building 2,000 feet high.

11 1. To Wells it was "inconceivable . . . how any civilized architect [could] design in the Romanesque or Gothic styles." The story goes that Wells declined a partnership in the firm saying, with sly humor, that he could not with self-respect sign his name to such mediocre work. Wells served as a draftsman in the firm for ten years. He died in 1889.

2. The French educational model was so highly esteemed that in the following year McKim instigated plans for an architectural study center in Rome. After a trial, the American Academy was founded in 1898 to provide a graduate experience for architects, sculptors, and painters.

3. This vaulting method was introduced to America in 1881 with the arrival of the Spaniard Rafael Guastavino. He had perfected the traditional Catalan tile vault with an improved mortar, essential because the principle of adhesion rather than compression is the source of its strength. Tiles are laid in horizontal layers; centering is not required. McKim, Mead and White used Guastavino vaulting in the Boston Public Library, Madison Square Presbyterian Church, and the rebuilding of Jefferson's library at the University of Virginia.

4. Vaughan never returned to England. From his Boston base he continued to receive commissions for ecclesiastical work, notably St. Paul's School Chapel in Concord, New Hampshire, completed in 1888 (except for the tower), and the Cathedral Church of St. Peter and St. Paul in Washington, D.C., a joint commission received with Bodley in 1907. The cathedral was incomplete at the time of Vaughn's death in 1917 and remains so.

5. Cram was perhaps more the antiquarian than the modern medievalist he claimed to be. He was quite proud that the hammer-beam trusses of his Princeton dining hall had no hidden steel. He advocated, to no avail, Latin for the services in the Princeton chapel and boasted that on his estate he built a chapel first, a garage second.

6. Although never enunciated, there seems to have been an understood apportionment of styles to various sects. Gothic and Colonial were acceptable for Protestants of all types; earlier medieval styles, both Lombard and Tuscan, with a permitted touch of Byzantine, were principally for Roman Catholics; synagogues opted for Moorish and Byzantine combinations. Newer, freer cults were a problem. The Christian Scientists seemed to find most inspiration under a Pantheon-like dome.

12 1. Wright was born in 1867 but claimed 1869 in *An Autobiography*, published in 1943. The willful error is perpetuated on his grave marker at Spring Green, Wisconsin.

2. Wright had equal admiration for Dankmar Adler and went out of his way to make known the injustice of underrating Adler's contribution to the firm. (See "Recollections," 10 July 1940, letter from Wright to The Art Institute

of Chicago. **Burnham Library, The Art Institute of Chicago.**) Wright believed that Adler, not Sullivan, deserved the credit for the dictum form follows function.

3. Wright to Ashbee, 26 September 1910: "Do not say that I deny my love for Japanese art has influenced me—I admit that it has but claim to have digested it—"

4. The discipline of Wright's interlocking forms and geometrical massing has been traced to the Froebel "gifts." These were constructive games of maple blocks and colored papers to be arranged against a linear grid that encouraged an instinctive order in the creative act. See Grant Manson, "Wright in the Nursery: The Influence of Froebel Education on the Work of Frank Lloyd Wright," *Architectural Review* CXIII (June 1953): 114–123.

5. When Wright returned to the United States in 1911, he established himself at Spring Green and began to build Taliesin. He revived his architectural practice using a downtown Chicago office but this ended when he sailed for Japan in the winter of 1915–16 to begin work on the Imperial Hotel.

6. The West Coast, unlike the Midwest, was not given to pronouncements on architecture or essays in print. An exception is the modest book by Charles A. Keeler, *The Simple Home,* San Francisco, 1904. Illustrated were various Berkeley houses, including his own by Maybeck.

13   1. Louis Sullivan, "The Chicago Tribune Competition," *Architectural Record* LIII (February 1923): 151–157. Saarinen's proposal was not wholly new; his Helsinki Railroad Station, designed in 1904, incorporated a tower of similar design.

2. In the midst of the Depression most Americans could not afford a Streamline Moderne house, but they might content themselves with household items designed by Raymond Loewy, Russel Wright, Donald Deskey, and Henry Dreyfus.

3. A likely source for the PSFS Building is the Tagblatt Turm in Stuttgart (1927–28) by E. Otto Osswald, which was published in the February 1929 issue of *Architectural Record.*

4. The exhibition and the accompanying catalog did include Wright's work and that of other Americans because a numerical balance between Europeans and Americans was a condition of the museum trustees' approval.

5. A symptom of an impending academic phase of the modern movement was the founding in 1928 of the Congrès Internationaux d'Architecture Moderne (CIAM). Through its meetings and publications it began to codify the loose theories of the twenties.

14   1. Promontory Apartments was the first of numerous projects done in association with the developer Herbert Greenwald, whose dedication to Mies places him among the important patrons of modern architecture. He died in 1959 in a plane crash.

2. At a time when temperate glances backward were inadmissible, Johnson freely confessed in print a number of historical sources of inspiration for his glass house. See "House at New Canaan . . ." *Architectural Review* CVIII (**September** 1950): 152–160.

3. Mies van der Rohe, "Frank Lloyd Wright," 1940. An appreciation written for the unpublished catalog of the Frank Lloyd Wright Exhibition held at the Museum of Modern Art, New York. Reprinted in P. Johnson, *Mies van der Rohe* (New York, 1947): 195–196.

4. In 1913 Wright's son John recommended the sculptor Alfonso Iannelli as an assistant for the Midway Gardens project. Iannelli accepted Wright's offer, leaving San Diego, where he had been working with John Wright, and spent eight months in Chicago alongside of Richard W. Bock, who had previously done sculpture for Wright's Oak Park studio. Together they executed Wright's designs for sculptured figures and four large stair towers for Midway Gardens. Iannelli later regretted that he did not accept Wright's offer to continue with the Imperial Hotel project in Japan, but he did return to the Midwest to collaborate with Purcell and Elmslie and also with Barry Byrne.

5. Wright's solution for urban problems was to eliminate the city altogether by substituting a decentralized, agrarian society. His answer, Broadacre City, was first outlined in his book, *The Disappearing City* (William Farquhar Payson, 1932). A model of Broadacre City was exhibited at Rockefeller Center in New York in April 1935.

6. Knowing Wright's animosity and fearful of his wit, the American Institute of Architects, which Wright had dubbed the "Arbitrary Institute of Appearances," delayed awarding its Gold Medal to him until 1949.

7. The Ralph Jester House design was built in Arizona at Taliesin West in 1972 as a residence for Bruce Pfeiffer, archivist for the Frank Lloyd Wright Foundation. Concrete was substituted for the intended curved plywood walls.

15 1. "The Skyline," *New Yorker*, XXIII, October 11, 1947. Mumford's recognition of a Bay Region style was reinforced by a 1949 exhibition entitled "Domestic Architecture of the San Francisco Bay Region," held at the San Francisco Museum of Art.

2. The Eames House is one of a series that constituted the Case Study House program organized by John Entenza, editor of the Los Angeles-based *Arts and Architecture*. Between 1945 and 1962 the magazine acted as client in commissioning houses by such Californians as Pierre Koenig; Craig Ellwood; Buff, Straub and Hensman; and Killingsworth, Brady and Smith.

3. Saarinen was one of four jury members for the international competition of 1956 for the Sydney Opera House. Jorn Utzon's winning entry, while impractical structurally and functionally, was nonetheless chosen for its evocative image of billowing, saillike forms. Utzon's scheme may have influenced Saarinen, who was at work on the TWA design at the time. Yet Saarinen had long been interested in curvilinear shapes, as seen in his plastic shell chair of 1948, the Aspen music tent of 1949, and the St. Louis Jefferson Memorial Arch, designed in 1948 and completed in 1964.

4. Netsch's chapel is the exception to his Miesian architecture at the Air Force Academy. For the chapel at the Illinois Institute of Technology Mies chose to differentiate the design in a comparatively subtle way, substituting brick bearing walls for the steel frame he used elsewhere.

5. Edward Stone began his career in the thirties as an advocate of the International Style. A testimonial example of this is the Museum of Modern

Art in New York of 1939, for which Stone was associated with Philip L. Goodwin.

6. The phrase New Brutalism first appeared in print in December 1953. The first building to which it was applied was the Hunstanton School in England by Peter and Alison Smithson, designed in 1949 and completed in 1954. However, the Hunstanton School is a studiously crude version of Mies van der Rohe's work and is visually unrelated to the raw concrete and exposed brickwork of Le Corbusier's Maisons Jaoul, which became the basis of Brutalism as a style despite its proponents' regard of Brutalism as an ethic rather than an esthetic of building.

7. The beauty of primitive and vernacular buildings, particularly in their village context, was being rediscovered in the late forties and fifties. It was formally acknowledged by an exhibition sponsored by the Museum of Modern Art, the substance of which is contained in *Architecture without Architects* by Bernard Rudofsky (1964). Sympathy for nonpedigreed architecture was indicative of dissatisfaction with formal architecture. Some architects, John Johansen and Frederick Kiesler among them, proposed a revival of the primitive experience by returning to cavelike forms of shelter.

8. Rogers was a consultant and supervising architect for Wellesley College for many years. Day and Klauder were the architects of adjacent Founders and Green Hall.

16 1. The slenderizing of curtain-wall mullions together with minimized detailing of the corners and roof lines began in Denmark in two works of Arne Jacobsen: the offices for Jespersen and Sons in Copenhagen and the town hall at Rødovre, both completed in 1956.

2. The city of Columbus, Indiana, is a microcosm of recent architecture. Largely through the patronage of J. Irwin Miller, president of Cummins Engine Company, the Cummins Engine Foundation has paid architectural fees for new schools and other buildings by distinguished architects. The diversity of the sixties and seventies is illustrated by a church by Harry Weese, a library by I. M. Pei, and a school by Mitchell-Giurgola Associates.

3. Because it is largely visible, the steel structure is carefully designed. The major girder, spanning 80 feet between the "silo" supports, is five feet from the recessed glass walls. Secondary beams welded to this girder at 10-foot intervals are exposed inside as well as out. The suggestion of a trellis that shades the glass comes from the Deere and Company Administrative Center at Moline, Illinois (1962–64), designed by Saarinen and executed by Roche and Dinkeloo.

4. The Yale Art Gallery commission was secured by George Howe, who was then chairman of the Department of Architecture, for his former Philadelphia associate. Kahn first came to Yale in 1947 as a visiting critic and remained ten years before returning to Philadelphia to resume practice and hold a professorship at the University of Pennsylvania.

Sources of Illustrations

1 1. Adam Thoroughgood House, Princess Anne County, Virginia. Virginia State Library.

2. Boardman House, Saugus, Massachusetts. Marcus Whiffen.

3. Boardman House, Saugus, Massachusetts. Historical American Building Survey (HABS), Library of Congress. Redrawn by Cynthia Cobb.

4. John Ward House, Salem, Massachusetts. Sandak, Inc.

5. Bacon's Castle, Surry County, Virginia. HABS, Library of Congress.

6. Bacon's Castle, Surry County, Virginia. HABS, Library of Congress. Redrawn by Cynthia Cobb.

7. McIntire Garrison House, Scotland, Maine. HABS, Library of Congress.

8. McIntire Garrison House, Scotland, Maine. HABS, Library of Congress. Redrawn by Cynthia Cobb.

9. Second Meeting House, Sudbury, Massachusetts. Wesleyan University Press.

10. Old Ship Meeting House, Hingham, Massachusetts. Wesleyan University Press.

11. Old Brick Church (St. Luke's), Isle of Wight County, Virginia. Marcus Whiffen.

12. Old Brick Church (St. Luke's), Isle of Wight County, Virginia. HABS, Library of Congress. Redrawn by Cynthia Cobb.

13. Capitol, Williamsburg, Virginia. Colonial Williamsburg Foundation.

14. Stadthuys (City Tavern), New Amsterdam. New-York Historical Society.

15. Dyckman House, New York City. HABS, Library of Congress.

16. Dyckman House, New York City. HABS, Library of Congress. Redrawn by Cynthia Cobb.

17. The Cloister (Klosters), Ephrata, Pennsylvania. HABS, Library of Congress.

18. Cahokia Courthouse, Cahokia, Illinois. HABS, Library of Congress.

19. Parlange, Pointe Coupée Parish, Louisiana. HABS, Library of Congress.

20. Parlange, Pointe Coupée Parish, Louisiana. HABS, Library of Congress. Redrawn by Cynthia Cobb.

21. St. Louis Cathedral, New Orleans, Louisiana. Maryland Historical Society.

22. Cabildo, New Orleans, Louisiana. Marcus Whiffen.

2 23. Palace of the Governors, Santa Fe, New Mexico. Marcus Whiffen.

24. San Estevan, Acoma, New Mexico. HABS, Library of Congress.

25. San Estevan, Acoma, New Mexico. HABS, Library of Congress. Redrawn by Cynthia Cobb.

26. Santo Tomás, Trampas, New Mexico. Marcus Whiffen.

27. San Francisco, Ranchos de Taos, New Mexico. Marcus Whiffen.

28. San Francisco, Ranchos de Taos, New Mexico. HABS, Library of Congress. Redrawn by Cynthia Cobb.

29. San José, Laguna, New Mexico. Marcus Whiffen.

30. San José, Laguna, New Mexico. Marcus Whiffen.

31. Castillo de San Marcos (Fort Marion), St. Augustine, Florida. HABS, Library of Congress.

32. Castillo de San Marcos (Fort Marion), St. Augustine, Florida. HABS, Library of Congress. Redrawn by Cynthia Cobb.

33. Nuestra Señora de la Purisima Concepcion de Acuna, San Antonio, Texas. Marcus Whiffen.

34. Nuestra Señora de la Purisima Concepcion de Acuna, San Antonio, Texas. HABS, Library of Congress. Redrawn by Cynthia Cobb.

35. San Antonio de Valero (The Alamo), San Antonio, Texas. HABS, Library of Congress.

36. San José y San Miguel de Aguayo, San Antonio, Texas. Marcus Whiffen.

37. San Xavier del Bac, near Tucson, Arizona. Marcus Whiffen.

38. San Xavier del Bac, near Tucson, Arizona. HABS, Library of Congress. Redrawn by Cynthia Cobb.

39. San Xavier del Bac, near Tucson, Arizona. HABS, Library of Congress.

40. San Carlos Borromeo, Carmel, California. G. E. Kidder Smith, *A Pictorial History of Architecture in America.*

41. San Luis Rey de Francia, near Oceanside, California. Marcus Whiffen.

42. San Luis Rey de Francia, near Oceanside, California. HABS, Library of Congress. Redrawn by Cynthia Cobb.

43. Santa Barbara, Santa Barbara, California. HABS, Library of Congress.

44. Governor's Palace, Williamsburg, Virginia. Colonial Williamsburg Foundation.

45. McPhedris-Warner House, Portsmouth, New Hampshire. Detroit Photographic Company Collection, Library of Congress.

46. College of William and Mary, Williamsburg, Virginia. Colonial Williamsburg Foundation.

47. President's House, College of William and Mary, Williamsburg, Virginia. Colonial Williamsburg Foundation. Redrawn by Cynthia Cobb.

48. Westover, Charles City County, Virginia. Marcus Whiffen.

49. St. James's, Goose Creek, South Carolina. Marcus Whiffen.

50. Christ Church, Lancaster County, Virginia. Marcus Whiffen.

51. St. Philip's, Charleston, South Carolina. Courtesy of The Henry Francis du Pont Winterthur Museum.

52. Old North Church (Christ Church), Boston, Massachusetts. Courtesy of The Society for the Preservation of New England Antiquities.

53. Old North Church (Christ Church), Boston, Massachusetts. G. E. Kidder Smith, *A Pictorial History of Architecture in America.*

54. Old South Meeting House, Boston, Massachusetts. Courtesy of The Society for the Preservation of New England Antiquities.

55. Stratford Hall, Westmoreland County, Virginia. Courtesy of The Robert E. Lee Memorial Association.

56. Stratford Hall, Westmoreland County, Virginia. HABS, Library of Congress. Redrawn by Cynthia Cobb.

57. Whitehall, Newport, Rhode Island. Courtesy of The Preservation Society of Newport County.

3

58. Westover, Charles City County, Virginia. Marcus Whiffen.

59. Mulberry, St. John's Parish, South Carolina. Carnegie Survey of the Architecture of the South by Frances Benjamin Johnston, Library of Congress.

60. Drayton Hall, Charleston, South Carolina. G. E. Kidder Smith, *A Pictorial History of Architecture in America.*

61. Drayton Hall, Charleston, South Carolina. Carnegie Survey of the Architecture of the South by Frances Benjamin Johnston, Library of Congress.

62. Drayton Hall, Charleston, South Carolina. HABS, Library of Congress. Redrawn by Cynthia Cobb.

63. Old Colony House, Newport, Rhode Island. John Hopf.

64. Christ Church, Philadelphia, Pennsylvania. G. E. Kidder Smith, *A Pictorial History of Architecture in America.*

65. Christ Church, Philadelphia, Pennsylvania. G. E. Kidder Smith, *A Pictorial History of Architecture in America.*

4   66. Redwood Library, Newport, Rhode Island. Courtesy of The Preservation Society of Newport County.

67. King's Chapel, Boston, Massachusetts. Sandak, Inc.

68. Brick Market, Newport, Rhode Island. John Hopf.

69. Christ Church, Cambridge, Massachusetts. HABS, Library of Congress.

70. St. Michael's, Charleston, South Carolina. Courtesy of William H. Pierson, Jr.

71. St. Michael's, Charleston, South Carolina. HABS, Library of Congress. Redrawn by Cynthia Cobb.

72. First Baptist Meeting House, Providence, Rhode Island. Sandak, Inc.

73. Shirley Place, Roxbury, Massachusetts. *Old-Time New England.*

74. Shirley Place, Roxbury, Massachusetts. *Old-Time New England.*

75. Carter's Grove, James City County, Virginia. HABS, Library of Congress. Redrawn by Cynthia Cobb.

76. Carter's Grove, James City County, Virginia. Colonial Williamsburg Foundation.

77. Gunston Hall, Fairfax County, Virginia. Courtesy of The Board of Regents, Gunston Hall.

78. Mount Airy, Richmond County, Virginia. Marcus Whiffen.

79. Vassall-Longfellow House, Cambridge, Massachusetts. 1759. HABS, Library of Congress.

80. Whitehall, Anne Arundel County, Maryland. Sandak, Inc.

81. Miles Brewton House, Charleston, South Carolina. Marcus Whiffen.

82. Cliveden, Germantown, Pennsylvania. HABS, Library of Congress.

83. Cliveden, Germantown, Pennsylvania. J. P. Sims and C. Willing, *Old Philadelphia Colonial Details.* Redrawn by Cynthia Cobb.

84. Chase-Lloyd House, Annapolis, Maryland. HABS, Library of Congress.

85. Hammond-Harwood House, Annapolis, Maryland. HABS, Library of Congress.

115. St. Mary's Cathedral, Baltimore, Maryland. Sandak, Inc.

116. St. Mary's Cathedral, Baltimore, Maryland. Courtesy of William H. Pierson, Jr. Redrawn by Cynthia Cobb.

117. St. Mary's Cathedral, Baltimore, Maryland. Courtesy of William H. Pierson, Jr.

118. State Bank of Louisiana, New Orleans, Louisiana. HABS, Library of Congress.

119. State Bank of Louisiana, New Orleans, Louisiana. HABS, Library of Congress. Redrawn by Cynthia Cobb.

120. New York City Hall, New York. Detroit Photographic Company Collection, Library of Congress.

121. New York City Hall, New York. Sandak, Inc.

122. Unitarian Church, Baltimore, Maryland. Marcus Whiffen.

123. Unitarian Church, Baltimore, Maryland. Engraving by W. Goodacre, Maryland Historical Society.

124. Union College, Schenectady, New York. Courtesy of Union College.

125. Scarborough House, Savannah, Georgia. Carnegie Survey of the Architecture of the South by Frances Benjamin Johnston, Library of Congress.

126. Monumental Church, Richmond, Virginia. Courtesy of William H. Pierson, Jr.

7 127. Second Bank of the United States (Customs House), Philadelphia, Pennsylvania. Marcus Whiffen.

128. Second Bank of the United States (Customs House), Philadelphia, Pennsylvania. HABS, Library of Congress. Redrawn by Cynthia Cobb.

129. Second Bank of the United States (Customs House), Philadelphia, Pennsylvania. Sandak, Inc.

130. Customs House (Federal Hall National Memorial), New York City. National Park Service.

131. Customs House (Federal Hall National Memorial), New York City. HABS, Library of Congress. Redrawn by Cynthia Cobb.

132. Ohio State Capitol, Columbus, Ohio. Wayne Andrews.

133. Tennessee State Capitol, Nashville, Tennessee. G. E. Kidder Smith, *A Pictorial History of Architecture in America.*

134. Tennessee State Capitol, Nashville, Tennessee. HABS, Library of Congress. Redrawn by Cynthia Cobb.

135. St. Paul's, Richmond, Virginia. Marcus Whiffen.

136. Unitarian Church (Stone Temple), Quincy, Massachusetts. Wayne Andrews.

137. Hustings Courthouse, Petersburg, Virginia. Marcus Whiffen.

138. Girard College, Philadelphia, Pennsylvania. Sandak, Inc.

139. Patent Office (National Portrait Gallery), Washington, District of Columbia. HABS, Library of Congress.

140. Providence Arcade, Providence, Rhode Island. Marcus Whiffen.

141. Tremont House, Boston, Massachusetts. W. H. Eliot, *A Description of Tremont House.*

142. Tremont House, Boston, Massachusetts. W. H. Eliot, *A Description of Tremont House.*

143. Lee Mansion, Arlington, Virginia. Virginia State Library.

144. Judge Wilson House, Ann Arbor, Michigan. 1843. Hedrich-Blessing.

145. Judge Wilson House, Ann Arbor, Michigan. HABS, Library of Congress. Redrawn by Cynthia Cobb.

146. Uncle Sam Plantation, St. James Parish, Louisiana. Carnegie Survey of the Architecture of the South by Frances Benjamin Johnston, Library of Congress.

147. Uncle Sam Plantation, St. James Parish, Louisiana. HABS, Library of Congress. Redrawn by Cynthia Cobb.

148. New York City Halls of Justice and House of Detention (The Tombs), New York City. Metropolitan Museum of Art.

149. St. Mary's Chapel, Baltimore, Maryland. HABS, Library of Congress.

150. Eastern State Penitentiary, Philadelphia, Pennsylvania. Historical Society of Pennsylvania.

151. Lyndhurst, Tarrytown, New York. G. E. Kidder Smith, *A Pictorial History of Architecture in America.*

152. Lyndhurst, Tarrytown, New York. Metropolitan Museum of Art.

153. Kingscote, Newport, Rhode Island. Courtesy of The Preservation Society of Newport County.

154. Kingscote, Newport, Rhode Island. Upjohn Collection, Avery Architectural Library, Columbia University.

155. Kingscote, Newport, Rhode Island. Courtesy of The Preservation Society of Newport County.

156. Edward King House, Newport, Rhode Island. Courtesy of The Preservation Society of Newport County.

157. Edward King House, Newport, Rhode Island. A. J. Downing, *The Architecture of County Houses.*

158. Morse-Libby House, Portland, Maine. HABS, Library of Congress.

159. Trinity Church, New York City. Municipal Art Society of New York.

160. St. Mary's, Burlington, New Jersey. HABS, Library of Congress.

161. St. James the Less, Philadelphia, Pennsylvania. Courtesy of Phoebe B. Stanton.

162. Emmanuel Church, Cumberland, Maryland. Courtesy of Phoebe B. Stanton.

163. St. John Chrysostom's, Delafield, Wisconsin. HABS, Library of Congress.

164. The Chalet, Newport, Rhode Island. Courtesy of The Preservation Society of Newport County.

165. Old Stone Church, Cleveland, Ohio. HABS, Library of Congress.

166. Smithsonian Institution, Washington, District of Columbia. Detroit Photographic Company Collection, Library of Congress.

167. Athenaeum of Philadelphia, Philadelphia, Pennsylvania. HABS, Library of Congress.

168. Haughwout Store, New York City. Cervin Robinson.

169. Customs House (Post Office), Georgetown, District of Columbia. HABS, Library of Congress.

170. United States Capitol, Washington, District of Columbia. Sandak, Inc.

9   171. Boston City Hall, Boston, Massachusetts. HABS, Library of Congress.

172. State, War and Navy Building (Executive Office Building), Washington, District of Columbia. HABS, Library of Congress.

173. All Souls' Unitarian Church, New York City. New-York Historical Society.

174. National Academy of Design, New York City. Museum of the City of New York.

175. Museum of Fine Arts, Boston, Massachusetts. *American Architect and Building News.*

176. Nott Memorial Library (Alumni Hall), Union College, Schenectady, New York. Courtesy of Union College.

177. Church of the Holy Trinity, New York City. The Huntington Library, San Marino, California.

178. Memorial Hall, Harvard University, Cambridge, Massachusetts. Western Reserve Historical Society.

179. Pennsylvania Academy of the Fine Arts, Philadelphia, Pennsylvania. HABS, Library of Congress.

180. Provident Life and Trust Company, Philadelphia, Pennsylvania. Historical Society of Philadelphia.

181. Trinity Church, Boston, Massachusetts. G. E. Kidder Smith, *A Pictorial History of Architecture in America.*

182. Trinity Church, Boston, Massachusetts. Mrs. Schuyler Van Rensselaer, *Henry Hobson Richardson and His Works.*

183. Crane Memorial Library, Quincy, Massachusetts. Sandak, Inc.

184. Crane Memorial Library, Quincy, Massachusetts. Redrawn by Michael Riley.

185. Sever Hall, Harvard University, Cambridge, Massachusetts. The Museum of Modern Art, New York.

186. Allegheny County Court House, Pittsburgh, Pennsylvania. The Museum of Modern Art, New York.

187. Allegheny County Court House, Pittsburgh, Pennsylvania. Redrawn by Pamela Meyer.

188. Marshall Field Wholesale Store, Chicago, Illinois. Chicago Historical Society.

189. Stanford University, Palo Alto, California. Stanford University Archives.

190. Lenox Library, New York City. Museum of the City of New York.

191. W. K. Vanderbilt House, New York City. Brown Brothers.

192. Biltmore, Asheville, North Carolina. HABS, Library of Congress.

10   193. Western Union Building, New York City. New-York Historical Society.

194. Tribune Building, New York City. Museum of the City of New York.

195. New York Produce Exchange, New York City. New-York Historical Society.

196. First Leiter Building, Chicago, Illinois. Art Institute of Chicago.

197. Home Insurance Company Building, Chicago, Illinois. Chicago Historical Society.

198. The Rookery, Chicago, Illinois. Author's collection.

199. The Rookery, Chicago, Illinois. Chicago Historical Society.

200. Monadnock Building, Chicago, Illinois. HABS, Library of Congress. Photograph by Jack E. Boucher.

201. Monadnock Building, Chicago, Illinois. Redrawn by Donald L. Looney.

202. Tacoma Building, Chicago, Illinois. Chicago Historical Society.

203. Reliance Building, Chicago, Illinois. Chicago Historical Society.

204. Guaranty Loan Building (New York Metropolitan Life Building), Minneapolis, Minnesota. *Minneapolis Tribune.*

205. Proposal for a twenty-eight-story building. Northwest Architectural Archive, University of Minnesota.

206. Auditorium Theater and Hotel Building, Chicago, Illinois. The Museum of Modern Art, New York.

207. Wainwright Building, St. Louis, Missouri. Hedrich-Blessing.

208. Wainwright Building, St. Louis, Missouri. Redrawn by Gregory Hankins.

209. Guaranty Building (Prudential Building), Buffalo, New York. HABS, Library of Congress.

210. Buildings of the Gage Group, Chicago, Illinois. Chicago Municipal Library.

211. Carson Pirie Scott & Co., Chicago, Illinois. G. E. Kidder Smith, *A Pictorial History of Architecture in America.*

212. Project for Fraternity Temple, Chicago, Illinois. The Museum of Modern Art, New York.

213. American Surety Building, New York City. Museum of the City of New York.

214. Woolworth Building, New York City. G. E. Kidder Smith, *A Pictorial History of Architecture in America.*

11   215. Villard Houses, New York City. Museum of the City of New York.

216. Boston Public Library, Boston, Massachusetts. HABS, Library of Congress.

217. Morgan Library, New York City. *A Monograph of the Work of McKim, Mead and White, 1879–1915.*

218. Court of Honor, World's Columbian Exposition, Chicago, Illinois. Chicago Historical Society.

219. Palace of Fine Arts, World's Columbian Exposition, Chicago, Illinois. Philip Turner.

220. Lincoln Monument, Washington, District of Columbia. Library of Congress.

221. Pennsylvania Station, New York City. Redrawn by Gerald Leco, Graciela Lopez, and Stanford Smith.

222. Pennsylvania Station, New York City. Museum of the City of New York.

223. Pennsylvania Station, New York City. Museum of the City of New York.

224. Grand Central Terminal, New York City. Landmarks Preservation Commission, New York.

225. City Hall, San Francisco, California. Gabriel Moulin Studios.

226. New York Public Library, New York City. New-York Historical Society.

227. Castle Hill, Ipswich, Massachusetts. The Trustees of Reservations, Milton, Massachusetts.

228. Vizcaya, Miami, Florida. Courtesy of Dade County Art Museum.

229. All Saints' Church, Ashmont, Boston, Massachusetts. Courtesy of Boston Public Library, Print Department.

230. Cadet Chapel, United States Military Academy, West Point, New York. Boston Public Library, Print Department.

231. St. Thomas's Church, New York City. Museum of the City of New York.

232. St. Catherine's Church, Somerville, Massachusetts. Courtesy of Kennedy and Kennedy, Architects.

233. Competition Drawing: Nebraska State Capitol. Courtesy of American Institute of Architects.

234. Nebraska State Capitol, Lincoln, Nebraska. G. E. Kidder Smith, *A Pictorial History of Architecture in America.*

235. Indianapolis Public Library, Indianapolis, Indiana. Art Alliance Press, Philadelphia.

236. Watts Sherman House, Newport, Rhode Island. Wayne Andrews.

237. Isaac Bell House, Newport, Rhode Island. Sheldon, *Artistic Country Seats.*

238. Isaac Bell House, Newport, Rhode Island. Redrawn by Todd Heringer.

239. Richard Ashurst House, Overbrook, Pennsylvania. Sheldon, *Artistic Country Seats.*

240. William Kent House, Tuxedo Park, New York. Sheldon, *Artistic Country Seats.*

241. Mrs. F. M. Stoughton House, Cambridge, Massachusetts. Mrs. Schuyler Van Rensselaer, *Henry Hobson Richardson and His Works.*

242. W. H. Winslow House, River Forest, Illinois. Marcus Whiffen.

243. Warren Hickox House, Kankakee, Illinois. Courtesy of the Archives of the Frank Lloyd Wright Memorial Foundation.

244. Ward Willits House, Highland Park, Illinois. Sandak, Inc.

245. Ward Willits House, Highland Park, Illinois. *Frank Lloyd Wright: Ausgeführte Bauten.*

246. Darwin D. Martin House, Buffalo, New York. *Frank Lloyd Wright: Ausgeführte Bauten.*

247. Avery Coonley House, Riverside, Illinois. *Frank Lloyd Wright: Ausgeführte Bauten.*

248. Frederick C. Robie House, Chicago, Illinois. HABS, Library of Congress.

249. Frederick C. Robie House, Chicago, Illinois. *Frank Lloyd Wright: Ausgeführte Bauten.*

250. Larkin Building, Buffalo, New York. *Frank Lloyd Wright: Ausgeführte Bauten.*

251. Unity Temple, Oak Park, Illinois. *Frank Lloyd Wright: Ausgeführte Bauten.*

252. Porter House and Waybur House, San Francisco, California. © Morley Baer, from *Bay Area Houses.*

253. George H. Boke House, Berkeley, California. Charles Keeler, *The Simple Home.*

254. First Church of Christ, Scientist, Berkeley, California. College of Environmental Design, University of California, Berkeley.

255. David B. Gamble House, Pasadena, California. Marvin Rand.

256. David B. Gamble House, Pasadena, California. Redrawn by Georgia Kajer.

257. Walter L. Dodge House, Los Angeles, California. Marvin Rand.

13   258. Competition Drawing, Chicago Tribune Tower. *The International Competition for a New Administration Building for the Chicago Tribune MCMXXII.*

259. Tribune Tower, Chicago, Illinois. Hedrich-Blessing.

260. Christ Lutheran Church, Minneapolis, Minnesota. G. E. Kidder Smith, *A Pictorial History of Architecture in America.*

261. Crow Island School, Winnetka, Illinois. Hedrich-Blessing.

262. New York Telephone (Barclay-Vesey) Building, New York City. Cervin Robinson.

263. Chrysler Building, New York City. G. E. Kidder Smith, *A Pictorial History of Architecture in America.*

264. Zoning Envelope Diagrams. Hugh Ferriss, *Pencil Points.*

265. Daily News Building, New York City. Cervin Robinson.

266. Rockefeller Center, New York City. Thomas Airviews, Courtesy of Rockefeller Center, Inc.

267. Johnson Wax Administration Building, Racine, Wisconsin. Marcus Whiffen.

268. Johnson Wax Administration Building, Racine, Wisconsin. Courtesy of Johnson Wax.

269. Schindler-Chase House, Los Angeles, California. Redrawn by Jerome Stastny.

270. Philip Lovell Beach House, Newport Beach, California. Architectural Archives UCSB Art Museum, University of California, Santa Barbara.

271. Philip Lovell House, Los Angeles, California. Julius Shulman.

272. PSFS Building, Philadelphia, Pennsylvania. Redrawn by Ronald James Bartlo.

273. PSFS Building, Philadelphia, Pennsylvania. Courtesy PSFS, Philadelphia.

305. Dulles International Airport, Chantilly, Virginia. Courtesy Revere Copper and Brass.

306. Chapel, United States Air Force Academy, Colorado Springs, Colorado. Courtesy Skidmore, Owings & Merrill.

307. St. Mary's Cathedral, San Francisco, California. Gabriel Moulin Studios.

308. Thomas McNulty House, Lincoln, Massachusetts. Redrawn by Oscar Burgueno.

309. Stuart Pharmaceutical Company, Pasadena, California. Julius Shulman.

310. McGregor Memorial Conference Center, Wayne State University, Detroit, Michigan. Courtesy of Wayne State University.

311. Sheldon Memorial Art Gallery, University of Nebraska, Lincoln, Nebraska. Esto, Ezra Stoller.

312. Lincoln Center for the Performing Arts, New York City. Courtesy of Lincoln Center for the Performing Arts, Inc. Photograph by Bob Serating.

313. Carpenter Visual Arts Center, Harvard University, Cambridge, Massachusetts. Julius Shulman.

314. Boston City Hall, Boston, Massachusetts. G. E. Kidder Smith, *A Pictorial History of Architecture in America.*

315. Art and Architecture Building, Yale University, New Haven, Connecticut. Julius Shulman.

316. Art and Architecture Building, Yale University, New Haven, Connecticut. Courtesy Paul Rudolph.

317. St. John's Abbey Church, Collegeville, Minnesota. Hedrich-Blessing. Courtesy of Marcel Breuer Associates.

318. Mummers Theater, Oklahoma City, Oklahoma. Balthazar Korab.

319. Guild House, Philadelphia, Pennsylvania. Courtesy Venturi and Rauch.

320. Sea Ranch Condominium, Sea Ranch, California. © Morley Baer, from *Bay Area Houses.*

321. Kresge College, University of California, Santa Cruz, G. E. Kidder Smith, *A Pictorial History of Architecture in America.*

16 322. Blue Cross-Blue Shield of Maryland, Towson, Maryland. G. E. Kidder Smith, *A Pictorial History of Architecture in America.*

323. Investors Diversified Services Building, Minneapolis, Minnesota. Courtesy Johnson and Burgee, Photograph by Richard W. Payne.

324. Bronx Developmental Center, New York City. Esto, Ezra Stoller.

325. Beinecke Rare Book Library, Yale University, New Haven, Connecticut. G. E. Kidder Smith, *A Pictorial History of Architecture in America.*

326. Marina City, Chicago, Illinois. Redrawn by Alan Maglaughlin.

327. Raymond Hilliard Housing, Chicago, Illinois. Orlando Cabanban.

328. John Hancock Center, Chicago, Illinois. Hedrich-Blessing.

329. Sears Tower, Chicago, Illinois. Orlando Cabanban.

330. Federal Reserve Bank Building, Minneapolis, Minnesota. Balthazar Korab.

331. Gund Hall, Harvard University, Cambridge, Massachusetts. Steve Rosenthal.

332. House in Old Westbury, Long Island, New York. Retoria, Y. Futagawa.

333. Behavioral Science Center, Circle Campus, University of Illinois, Chicago, Illinois. Orlando Cabanban.

334. East Building, National Gallery of Art, Washington, District of Columbia. National Gallery of Art.

335. Christian Science Center, Boston, Massachusetts. G. E. Kidder Smith, *A Pictorial History of Architecture in America.*

336. Knights of Columbus, New Haven, Connecticut, New Haven. G. E. Kidder Smith, *A Pictorial History of Architecture in America.*

337. Veterans Memorial Coliseum, New Haven, Connecticut. G. E. Kidder Smith, *A Pictorial History of Architecture in America.*

338. College Life Insurance Company, Indianapolis, Indiana. Retoria, Y. Futagawa.

339. Richards Medical Research and Biology Buildings, University of Pennsylvania, Philadelphia, Pennsylvania, John Lautman.

340. Richards Medical Research and Biology Buildings, University of Pennsylvania, Philadelphia, Pennsylvania. Redrawn by Henry C. Mahlstedt.

341. Salk Institute of Biological Studies, La Jolla, California. Jim Cox.

342. First Unitarian Church, Rochester, New York. John Ebstel.

343. First Unitarian Church, Rochester, New York. Redrawn by Jeffrey Sessions.

344. Library, Phillips Exeter Academy, Exeter, New Hampshire. Photograph by Herndon Associates with permission of the Trustees of Phillips Exeter Academy.

345. Kimbell Art Museum, Fort Worth, Texas. Courtesy of Kimbell Art Museum. Photograph by Bob Wharton.

Select Bibliography

Books published before 1895 are not included in this bibliography. Refer to H.-R. Hitchcock, *American Architectural Books: A List of Books, Portfolios and Pamphlets Published in America before 1895 on Architecture and Related Subjects* for a complete bibliographical listing of these books. A comprehensive bibliography of writings on the period covered in part I is F. J. Roos, Jr., *Bibliography of Early American Architecture: Writings on Architecture Constructed Before 1860 in Eastern and Central United States* (Urbana: University of Illinois Press, 1968). For part II there are the guides to information sources by L. Wodehouse, *American Architects from the Civil War to the First World War* (Detroit: Gale Research Company, 1976) and *American Architects from the First World War to Present* (Detroit: Gale Research Company, 1977).

Adams, E. B., and Chavez, F. A., editors. *The Missions of New Mexico, 1776: A Description by Fray Francisco Atanasio Dominguez with Other Contemporary Documents.* Albuquerque: University of New Mexico Press, 1956. Reprinted in 1975.

Adams, W. H., editor. *Jefferson and the Arts: An Extended View.* Washington, D.C.: National Gallery of Art, 1976.

Alexander, R. *The Architecture of Maximilian Godefroy.* Baltimore: Johns Hopkins University Press, 1975.

American Philosophical Society. *Historic Philadelphia from the Founding until the Early Nineteenth Century.* Issued as Vol. XLIII, Part 1, of the *Transactions* of the American Philosophical Society, 1953.

Andrews, W. "Alexander Jackson Davis." *Architectural Review* CIX (May 1951): 307–312.

Andrews, W. *Architecture, Ambition, and Americans.* New York: Free Press, 1947. Revised edition, 1978.

Architectural Book Publishing Company. *A Monograph of the Work of McKim, Mead and White.* 4 vols. New York, 1915–25.

Baigell, M. "James Hoban and the First Bank of the United States." *Journal of the Society of Architectural Historians [JSAH]* XXVIII (May 1969): 135–136.

Baigell, M. "John Haviland in Philadelphia 1818–1826." *JSAH* XXV (October 1966): 197–208.

Baldwin, C. C. *Stanford White.* New York, 1931. Reprinted by Da Capo Press, New York, 1971.

Banham, R. *The Architecture of the Well-Tempered Environment.* Chicago: University of Chicago Press, 1973.

Beirne, R. R., and Scarff, J. H. *William Buckland, 1734–1774, Architect of Virginia and Maryland.* Annapolis: Maryland Historical Society, 1958.

Bridenbaugh, C. *Peter Harrison: First American Architect.* Chapel Hill: University of North Carolina Press, 1949.

Briggs, M. S. *The Homes of the Pilgrim Fathers in England and America.* London and New York: Oxford University Press, 1932.

Brooks, H. A. *The Prairie School: Frank Lloyd Wright and His Midwest Contemporaries.* Toronto: University of Toronto Press, 1972.

Brown, G. *History of the United States Capitol*. 2 volumes. Washington: Government Printing Office, 1900, 1902.

Burchard, J., and Bush-Brown, A. *The Architecture of America: A Social and Cultural History*. Boston: Little, Brown and Co., 1961.

Burnham, A. "The New York Architecture of Richard Morris Hunt." *JSAH* XI (May 1952): 9–14.

Cardwell, K. H. *Bernard Maybeck: Artisan, Architect, Artist*. Santa Barbara and Salt Lake City: Peregrine Smith, 1977.

Carrott, R. G. *The Egyptian Revival: Its Sources, Monuments, and Meaning*. Berkeley: University of California Press, 1978.

Carter, P. *Mies van der Rohe at Work*. New York: Praeger, 1974.

Chicago Tribune. The International Competition for a New Administration Building for the Chicago Tribune MCMXXII. Chicago, 1923.

Christ-Janer, A. *Eliel Saarinen*. Chicago: University of Chicago Press, 1948. Reprinted in 1979.

Condit, C. W. *American Building: Materials and Techniques from the Beginning of the Colonial Settlements to the Present*. Chicago: University of Chicago Press, 1969.

Condit, C. W. *The Chicago School of Architecture*. Chicago: University of Chicago Press, 1964.

Cook, J. *The Architecture of Bruce Goff*. New York: Harper and Row, 1978.

Cook, J. W., and Klotz, H. *Conversations with Architects*. New York: Praeger, 1973.

Coolidge, J. *Mill and Mansion: A Study of Architecture and Society in Lowell, Massachusetts, 1820–1865*. New York: Russell and Russell, 1942.

Coolidge, J. "Peter Harrison's First Design for King's Chapel, Boston." In *De Artibus Opuscula XL: Essays in Honor of Erwin Panofsky*, edited by M. Meiss, pp. 64–75. New York: New York University Press, 1961.

Cortissoz, R. *Monograph of the Work of Charles A. Platt*. New York: Architectural Book Publishing Company, 1913.

Cummings, A. L. "The Foster-Hutchinson House." *Old-Time New England* LIV (January–March 1964): 59–76.

Cummings, A. L. *The Framed Houses of Massachusetts Bay, 1625–1725*. Cambridge: Harvard University Press, 1979.

Danz, E. *Architecture of Skidmore, Owings & Merrill, 1950–1962*. New York: Praeger, 1963.

Donnelly, M. C. *The New England Meeting House of the Seventeenth Century*. Middletown, Conn.: Wesleyan University Press, 1968.

Dorsey, S. P. *Early English Churches in America 1607–1807*. New York: Oxford University Press, 1952.

Downing, A., and Scully, V. J., Jr. *The Architectural Heritage of Newport, Rhode Island*. Cambridge: Harvard University Press, 1952. Second edition published by Clarkson N. Potter, New York, 1970.

Drexler, A., editor. *The Architecture of the Ecole des Beaux-Arts*. New York: Museum of Modern Art, 1977.

Early, J. *Romanticism and American Architecture*. New York: A. S. Barnes, 1965.

Eaton, L. K. *Landscape Artist in America: the Life and Work of Jens Jensen.* Chicago: University of Chicago Press, 1964.

Edgell, G. H. *The American Architecture of Today.* New York: C. Scribner's Sons, 1928. Reprinted by AMS Press.

Ferriss, H. *The Metropolis of Tomorrow.* New York: I. Washburn, 1929.

Fitch, J. M. *American Building: The Historical Forces that Shaped It.* Boston: Houghton Mifflin Co., 1966. Second edition published by Schocken Books, New York, 1973.

Fitch, J. M. *Walter Gropius.* New York: George Braziller, 1960.

Floyd, M. H. "A Terra-Cotta Cornerstone for Copley Square: Museum of Fine Arts, Boston, 1870–1876, by Sturgis and Brigham." *JSAH* XXXII (May 1973): 83–103.

Forman, H. C. *The Architecture of the Old South.* Cambridge: Harvard University Press, 1948. Reprinted by Russell and Russell, 1969.

Frary, I. T. *Early Homes of Ohio.* Richmond: Garrett and Massie, 1936.

Frary, I. T. *Thomas Jefferson, Architect and Builder.* Richmond: Garrett and Massie, 1950.

Y. Futagawa, editor. *Kevin Roche, John Dinkeloo and Associates 1962–1975.* New York: Architectural Book Publishing Company, 1977.

Gallagher, H. M. P. *Robert Mills, Architect of the Washington Monument.* New York: Columbia University Press, 1935. Reprinted by AMS Press, 1975.

Garvan, A. N. B. *Architecture and Town Planning in Colonial Connecticut.* New Haven: Yale University Press, 1951.

Gebhard, D. *Schindler.* New York: Viking Press, 1971.

Giedion S. *Space, Time and Architecture.* Cambridge: Harvard University Press, 1946. Fifth revised and enlarged edition, 1979.

Gilchrist, A. A. "Additions to *William Strickland, Architect and Engineer, 1788–1854.* Supplement to *JSAH* XIII (October 1954).

Gilchrist, A. A. "John McComb, Sr. and Jr., in New York, 1784–1799." *JSAH* XXXI (March 1972): 10–21.

Gowans, A. *Images of American Living: Four Centuries of Architecture and Furniture as Cultural Expression.* Philadelphia: Lippincott, 1964.

Granger, A. H. *Charles Follen McKim: A Study of His Life and Work.* Boston: Houghton Mifflin Company, 1913.

Grube, O. W.; Pran, P. C.; and Schultz, F. *One Hundred Years of Architecture in Chicago.* Chicago: Follett, 1976.

Hamlin, T. F. *Benjamin Henry Latrobe.* New York: Oxford University Press, 1955.

Hamlin, T. F. *Greek Revival Architecture in America.* New York: Oxford University Press, 1944.

Heyer, P. *Architects on Architecture.* New York: Walker & Co., 1966.

Hines, T. S. *Burnham of Chicago: Architect and Planner.* New York: Oxford University Press, 1974.

Hitchcock, H.-R. *American Architectural Books: A List of Books, Portfolios and Pamphlets Published in America before 1895 on Architecture and Related Subjects.* Minneapolis: University of Minnesota, 1965.

Hitchcock, H.-R. *The Architecture of H. H. Richardson and His Times.* New York: Museum of Modern Art, 1936. Revised edition published by Anchor Books, Hamden, 1961.

Hitchcock, H.-R. *Architecture: Nineteenth and Twentieth Centuries.* London and Baltimore: Penguin Books, 1958. Fourth edition, 1977.

Hitchcock, H.-R. *Rhode Island Architecture.* Providence: Rhode Island Museum Press, 1939.

Hitchcock, H.-R. "Ruskin and American Architecture, or Regeneration Long Delayed." In *Concerning Architecture*, edited by J. Summerson, pp. 166–208. London and Baltimore: Allen Lane, 1968.

Hitchcock, H.-R., and Johnson, P. *The International Style: Architecture since 1922.* New York: W. W. Norton and Company, 1932.

Hitchcock, H.-R., and Seale, W. *Temples of Democracy: The State Capitols of the U.S.A.* New York: Harcourt Brace Jovanovich, 1976.

Hoffmann, D. *The Architecture of John Wellborn Root.* Baltimore: Johns Hopkins University Press, 1973.

Jacobus, J. *Twentieth-century Architecture: The Middle Years 1940–65.* New York: Praeger, 1966.

Jencks, C. A. *The Language of Post-Modern Architecture.* New York: Rizzoli, 1977.

Johnson, P. *Mies van der Rohe.* New York: Museum of Modern Art, 1947.

Johnson, P. *Writings.* New York: Oxford University Press, 1979.

Johnston, N. B. "John Haviland, Jailor to the World." *JSAH* XXIII (May 1964): 101–106.

Hunter, W. H., Jr., editor. *The Architecture of Baltimore: a Pictorial History.* Baltimore: Peale Museum, 1953.

Jordy, W. H. *American Buildings and Their Architects: The Impact of European Modernism in the Mid-Twentieth Century*, Vol. 4. Garden City, N.Y.: Doubleday & Co., 1976.

Jordy, W. H. *American Buildings and Their Architects: Progressive and Academic Ideals at the Turn of the Century*, Vol. 3. Garden City, N.Y.: Doubleday & Co., 1976.

Jordy, W. H. "Veterans Memorial Coliseum, New Haven, Connecticut." *Architectural Review* CLIII (April 1973): 228–232.

Kaufmann, E., Jr., editor. *The Rise of an American Architecture.* New York: Praeger in association with the Metropolitan Museum of Art, 1970.

Kelly, J. F. *Early Connecticut Meetinghouses.* New York: Columbia University Press, 1948.

Kelly, J. F. *The Early Domestic Architecture of Connecticut.* New Haven: Yale University Press, 1924.

Kimball, S. F. *American Architecture.* Indianapolis and New York, 1928.

Kimball, S. F. *Domestic Architecture of the American Colonies and of the Early Republic.* New York: C. Scribner's Sons, 1922. Reprinted by Dover Publications, 1966.

Kimball, S. F. "Gunston Hall." *JSAH* XIII (May 1954): 3–8.

Kimball, S. F. "Jefferson and the Public Buildings of Virginia: I—Williamsburg, 1770–1776." *Huntington Library Quarterly* XII (February 1949): 115–120.

Kimball, S. F. "Jefferson and the Public Buildings of Virginia: II—Richmond, 1779–1780." *Huntington Library Quarterly* XII (May 1949): 303–310.

Kimball, S. F. *Mr. Samuel McIntire, Carver, Architect of Salem.* Portland: The Southworth-Anthoensen Press, 1940.

Kimball, S. F. *Thomas Jefferson, Architect.* Boston: Riverside Press, 1916.

Kirker, H. *The Architecture of Charles Bulfinch.* Cambridge: Harvard University Press, 1977.

Komendant, A. E. *Eighteen Years with Architect Louis I. Kahn.* Englewood, N.J.: Aloray, 1975.

Kramer, E. W. "Detlef Lienau, An Architect of the Brown Decades." *JSAH* XIV (March 1955): 18–25.

Krinsky, C. H. *Rockefeller Center.* New York: Oxford University Press, 1978.

Kubler, G. *The Religious Architecture of New Mexico in the Colonial Period and Since the American Occupation.* Colorado Springs: Taylor Museum, 1940. Fourth edition published by the University of New Mexico Press, 1972.

Lancaster, C. *The Japanese Influence in America.* New York: W. H. Rawle, 1963.

Lancaster, C. "New York City Hall Stair Rotunda Reconsidered." *JSAH* XXIX (March 1970): 33–39.

Landy, J. *The Architecture of Minard Lafever.* New York: Columbia University Press, 1970.

Lehmann, K. *Thomas Jefferson, American Humanist.* New York: Macmillan Co., 1947.

Lockwood, C. "The Italianate Dwelling House in New York City." *JSAH* XXXI (May 1972): 141–151.

Maginnis, C. *The Work of Cram and Ferguson.* New York: Pencil Points Press, 1929.

Manson, G. C. *Frank Lloyd Wright to 1910: The First Golden Age.* New York: Reinhold, 1958.

Makinson, R. L. *Greene and Greene: Architecture as a Fine Art.* Salt Lake City and Santa Barbara: Peregrine Smith, 1977.

McCallum, I. R. M. *Architecture, U.S.A.* London: Architectural Press, 1959.

McCoy, E. *Five California Architects.* New York: Reinhold, 1960.

McCoy, E. *Richard Neutra.* New York: George Braziller, 1960.

McHale, J. *Buckminster Fuller.* New York: George Braziller, 1962.

McKee, H. J. "St. Michael's Church, Charleston, 1752–1762: Some Notes on Materials and Construction." *JSAH* XXIII (March 1964): 39–42.

Meeks, C. L. V. "Henry Austin and the Italian Villa." *Art Bulletin* (June 1948): 145–149.

Meeks, C. L. V. *The Railroad Station*. New Haven: Yale University Press, 1956.

Meeks, C. L. V. "Romanesque before Richardson in the United States." *Art Bulletin* XXXV (March 1953): 17–33.

Mendelsohn, E. *Amerika: Bilderbuch eines Architekten*. Berlin: R. Mosse, 1926.

Metcalf, P. "Boston Before Bulfinch: Harrison's King's Chapel." *JSAH* XIII (March 1954): 11–14.

Michels, E. "Late Nineteenth Century Published American Perspective Drawing." *JSAH* XXXI (December 1972): 291–308.

Middleton, W. D. *Grand Central . . . The World's Greatest Railway Terminal*, San Marino, Calif.: Golden West Book, 1977.

Miller, J., II. "The Designs for the Washington Monument in Baltimore." *JSAH* XXIII (March 1964): 19–28.

Moholy-Nagy, S. *The Architecture of Paul Rudolph*. New York: Praeger, 1970.

Moore, C. *The Life and Times of Charles Follen McKim*. Boston: Houghton Mifflin, 1929.

Moore, C.; Allen, G.; and Lyndon, D. *The Place of Houses*. New York: Holt, Rinehart & Winston, 1974.

Morrison, H. S. *Early American Architecture from the First Colonial Settlement to the National Period*. New York: Oxford University Press, 1952.

Morrison, H. S. *Louis Sullivan: Prophet of Modern Architecture*. New York: Museum of Modern Art, 1935. Reprinted by Greenwood Press, Westport, 1971.

Mujica, F. *History of the Skyscraper*. New York: Archaeology and Architecture Press, 1930.

Mumford, L. *The Brown Decades*. New York: Harcourt, Brace and Company, 1931. Second revised edition published by Dover Publications, New York, 1955.

Mumford, L. *Roots of Contemporary American Architecture*. New York: Reinhold, 1952. Second edition republished with updated biographical sketches by Dover Publications, New York, 1972.

Mumford, L. *The South in Architecture*. New York: Harcourt, Brace and Company, 1941.

Mumford, L. *Sticks and Stones*. New York: Boni and Liveright, 1924. Second revised edition published by Dover Publications, New York, 1955.

Museum of Modern Art. *Modern Architecture: International Exhibition*. New York, 1932.

Nelson, G. *The Industrial Architecture of Albert Kahn*. New York: Architectural Book Publishing Company, 1939.

Neutra, R. *Wie Baut Amerika*. Stuttgart: J. Hoffman, 1927.

Newcomb, R. *Architecture in Old Kentucky*. Urbana: University of Illinois Press, 1953.

Newcomb, R. *Architecture of the Old North-West Territory*. Chicago: University of Chicago Press, 1950.

Newcomb, R. *The Old Mission Churches and Historic Houses of California*. Philadelphia and London: J. B. Lippincott Company, 1925.

Newton, R. H. *Town & Davis, Architects*. New York: Columbia University Press, 1942.

Nichols, F. D. *The Early Architecture of Georgia*. Chapel Hill: University of North Carolina Press, 1957.

Noffsinger, J. P. *The Influence of the Ecole des Beaux-Arts on the Architects of the United States*. Washington: Catholic University of America Press, 1955.

Norton, P. F. *Latrobe, Jefferson, and the National Capitol*. New York: Garland Publishing, 1977.

O'Gorman, J. F. *The Architecture of Frank Furness*. Philadelphia: Philadelphia Museum of Art, 1973.

O'Gorman, J. F. *Henry Hobson Richardson and his Office*. Cambridge: MIT Press, 1974.

Orr, C. *Addison Mizner: Architect of Dreams and Realities*. Palm Beach: The Gallery, 1977.

Park, H. *A List of Architectural Books Available in America Before the Revolution*. Los Angeles: Hennessey & Ingalls, 1973.

Perrin, R. W. E. "'Fachwerkbau' Houses in Wisconsin." *JSAH* XVIII (March 1959): 29–33.

Peterson, C. E., editor. *Building Early America*. Radnor: Chilton Book Company, 1976.

Pickens, B. "Mr. Jefferson as a Revolutionary Architect." *JSAH* XXXIV (December 1975): 257–279.

Pickens, B. "Wyatt's Pantheon, the State House in Boston and a New View of Bulfinch." *JSAH* (May 1970): 124–131.

Pierson, W. H., Jr. *American Buildings and Their Architects: The Colonial and Neo-Classical Styles*, Vol. 1. Garden City, N.Y.: Doubleday & Co., 1970.

Pierson, W. H., Jr. *American Buildings and Their Architects: The Corporate and Early Gothic Styles*, Vol. 2. Garden City, N.Y.: Doubleday & Co., 1978.

Place, C. A. *Charles Bulfinch, Architect and Citizen*. Boston and New York: Houghton Mifflin, 1925.

Portman, J. C., Jr., and Barnett, J. *The Architect as Developer*. New York: McGraw-Hill Book Co., 1976.

Pratt, R. *David Adler: The Architect and his Work*. New York: M. Evans & Co., 1971.

Randall, F. A. *A History of the Development of Building Construction in Chicago*. Urbana: University of Illinois Press, 1949.

Robinson, C., and Bletter, R. H. *Skyscraper Style: Art Deco*. New York: Oxford University Press, 1975.

Roper, L. W. *FLO: A Biography of Frederick Law Olmsted.* Baltimore: Johns Hopkins University Press, 1974.

Rose, H. W. *The Colonial Houses of Worship in America.* New York: Hastings House, 1963.

Roth, L. M. *The Architecture of McKim, Mead and White, 1870–1920, A Building List.* New York: Garland Publishing, 1978.

Rutledge, A. W. "The Second St. Philip's, Charleston, 1710–1835." *JSAH* XVIII (October 1959): 112–114.

Saarinen, A. B., editor. *Eero Saarinen on His Work.* New Haven: Yale University Press, 1962.

Schless, N. H. "Dutch Influence on the Governor's Palace, Williamsburg." *JSAH* XXVIII (December 1969): 254–270.

Schless, N. H. "Peter Harrison, the Touro Synagogue, and the Wren City Church." *Winterthur Portfolio 8* (1973): 187–200.

Schuyler, M. *American Architecture and Other Writings.* W. H. Jordy and R. Coe, editors. 2 vols. Cambridge: Harvard University Press, 1961.

Scully, V. J., Jr. *American Architecture and Urbanism.* New York: Praeger, 1969.

Scully, V. J., Jr. *Frank Lloyd Wright.* New York: George Braziller, 1960.

Scully, V. J., Jr. *Louis I. Kahn.* New York: George Braziller, 1962.

Scully, V. J., Jr. *Modern Architecture: The Architecture of Democracy.* New York: George Braziller, 1961.

Scully, V. J., Jr. "Romantic Rationalism and the Expression of Structure in Wood: Downing, Wheeler, Gardner, and the 'Stick Style,' 1840–1876." *Art Bulletin* XXXV (June 1953): 121–142.

Scully, V. J., Jr. *The Shingle Style.* New Haven: Yale University Press, 1955.

Shurtleff, H. R. *The Log Cabin Myth.* Cambridge: Harvard University Press, 1939.

Smith, G. E. K. *A Pictorial History of Architecture in America.* 2 vols. New York: W. W. Norton & Co., 1976.

Smith, N. K. *Frank Lloyd Wright: A Study in Architectural Content.* Englewood Cliffs: Prentice-Hall, 1966.

Stanton, P. B. *The Gothic Revival and American Church Architecture.* Baltimore: Johns Hopkins University Press, 1968.

Stebbins, T. E., Jr. "Richardson and Trinity Church: The Evolution of a Building." *JSAH* XXVII (December 1968): 281–298.

Stern, R. A. M. *George Howe: Toward a Modern American Architecture.* New Haven: Yale University Press, 1975.

Stickley, G. *Craftsman Homes.* New York: The Craftsman Publishing Company, 1909.

Stillman, D. "New York City Hall: Competition and Execution." *JSAH* XXIII (October 1964): 129–142.

Stoddard, R. "A Reconstruction of Charles Bulfinch's First Federal Street Theater, Boston." *Winterthur Portfolio 6* (1970).

Stoney, S. G. *Plantations of the Carolina Low Country.* Charleston: The Carolina Art Association, 1938.

Sturges, W. K. "Arthur Little and the Colonial Revival." *JSAH* XXXII (May 1973): 147–163.

Sullivan, L. H. *The Autobiography of an Idea.* New York: W. W. Norton and Company, 1924. Reprinted by P. Smith, New York, 1949.

Sullivan, L. H. "The Chicago Tribune Competition." *Architectural Record* LIII (February 1923): 151–157.

Sullivan, L. H. *Kindergarten Chats and Other Writings.* New York: Wittenborn, Schultz, 1947.

Summerson, J. N. *Architecture in Britain 1530 to 1830.* London and Baltimore: Penguin Books, 1953. Sixth revised edition, 1977.

Sweeney, R. L. *Frank Lloyd Wright: An Annotated Bibliography.* Los Angeles: Hennessey & Ingalls, 1978.

Tallmadge, T. E. *Architecture in Old Chicago.* Chicago: University of Chicago Press, 1941.

Tallmadge, T. E. *The Story of Architecture in America.* New York: W. W. Norton and Company. Enlarged and revised edition, 1936.

Tatum, G. B. *Penn's Great Town: 250 Years of Philadelphia Architecture.* Philadelphia: University of Pennsylvania Press, 1961.

Taut, B. *Modern Architecture.* London: The Studio, 1929.

Torres, L. "Federal Hall Revisited." *JSAH* XXIX (December 1970): 327–338.

Torres, L. "John Frazee and the New York Custom House." *JSAH* XXII (October 1964): 143–150.

Tselos, D. "The Enigma of Buffington's Skyscraper." *Art Bulletin* XXVI (March 1944): 3–12.

Tselos, D. "Exotic Influences in the Architecture of Frank Lloyd Wright." *Magazine of Art* XLVI (April 1953): 160–169, 184.

Tunnard, C., and Reed, H. H. *American Skyline.* Boston: Houghton Mifflin, 1955.

Turner, P. V. *The Founders and the Architects: The Design of Stanford University.* Palo Alto: Department of Art, Stanford University, 1976.

Upjohn, E. M. *Richard Upjohn, Architect and Churchman.* New York: Columbia University Press, 1939.

Van Brunt, H. *Architecture and Society: Collected Essays of Henry Van Brunt.* Cambridge: Harvard University Press, 1969.

Van Derpool, J. G. "The Restoration of St. Luke's, Smithfield, Virginia." *JSAH* XVIII (March 1958): 12–18.

Van Zanten, D. T. "Jacob Wrey Mould: Echoes of Owen Jones and the High Victorian Styles in New York, 1853–1865." *JSAH* XXVIII (March 1969): 41–57.

Venturi, R. *Complexity and Contradiction in Architecture.* New York: Museum of Modern Art, 1966. Revised edition, 1977.

Waterman, T. T. *The Dwellings of Colonial America.* Chapel Hill: University of North Carolina Press, 1950.

Waterman, T. T. *The Mansions of Virginia.* Chapel Hill: University of North Carolina Press, 1946.

Waterman, T. T., and Barrows, J. A. *Domestic Colonial Architecture of Tidewater Virginia.* New York: C. Scribner's Sons, 1932.

Weisman, W. "The Commercial Architecture of George B. Post." *JSAH* XXXI (October 1972): 176–203.

Weisman, W. "Commercial Palaces of New York: 1845–1875." *Art Bulletin* XXXVI (December 1954): 285–302.

Weslager, C. A. *The Log Cabin in America: From Pioneer Days to the Present.* New Brunswick: Rutgers University Press, 1969.

Whiffen, M. *American Architecture Since 1780: A Guide to the Styles.* Cambridge: MIT Press, 1969.

Whiffen, M. "The Early County Courthouses of Virginia," *JSAH* XVIII (March 1959): 1–10.

Whiffen, M. *The Eighteenth-Century Houses of Williamsburg, Colonial Capital of Virginia.* Williamsburg: Colonial Williamsburg, 1960.

Whiffen, M. *The Public Buildings of Williamsburg, Colonial Capital of Virginia.* Williamsburg: Colonial Williamsburg, 1958.

Whiffen, M. "Some Virginia House Plans Reconsidered." *JSAH* XVI (May 1957): 17–19.

Whitaker, C. H., editor. *Bertram Grosvenor Goodhue, Architect and Master of Many Arts.* New York: Press of the American Institute of Architects, 1925.

White, T. B. *Paul Philippe Cret: Architect and Teacher.* Philadelphia: Art Alliance Press, 1974.

White, T. B., editor. *Philadelphia Architecture in the Nineteenth Century.* Philadelphia: University of Pennsylvania Press, 1953.

Wight, P. B. "Reminiscences of Russell Sturgis." *Architectural Record* XXVI (August 1909): 123–131.

Wilson, S., Jr. "Louisiana Drawings by Alexandre de Batz." *JSAH* XXII (May 1963): 75–89.

Wilson, S., Jr. "Religious Architecture in French Colonial Louisiana." *Winterthur Portfolio 8* (1973): 63–106.

Wilson, S., Jr., and Huber, L. V. *The Cabildo on Jackson Square.* New Orleans: Friends of the Cabildo, 1970.

Withey, H. F., and Rathburn, E. *Biographical Dictionary of American Architects (Deceased).* Los Angeles: New Age Publishing Company, 1956.

Wodehouse, L. "Alfred B. Mullett and his French Style Government Buildings." *JSAH* XXXI (March 1972): 22–37.

Wodehouse, L. "Ammi Burnham Young, 1798–1874." *JSAH* XXV (December 1966): 268–286.

Woodbridge, S., editor. *Bay Area Houses.* New York: Oxford University Press, 1976.

Wrenn, G. L. "'A Return to Solid and Classical Principles,' Arthur D. Gilman, 1859." *JSAH* XX (December 1961): 191–193.

Wright, F. L. *Ausgeführte Bauten und Entwürfe von Frank Lloyd Wright.* Berlin: Wasmuth, 1910. Reprinted as *Buildings, Plans and Designs*, Horizon Press, 1963. Also as *Studies and Executed Buildings by Frank Lloyd Wright*, Prairie School Press, 1975.

Wright, F. L. *An Autobiography.* London and New York: Longmans, Green and Company, 1932. Second edition published by Duell, Sloan and Pearce, New York, 1943.

Wright, F. L. *Frank Lloyd Wright: Ausgeführte Bauten.* Berlin: Wasmuth, 1911. Reprinted as *Frank Lloyd Wright: The Early Work*, Horizon Press, 1968.

Index

References to notes are distinguished by *n*, followed by the number of the chapter and that of the note, in that order. An asterisk indicates that the building has been destroyed. Buildings are indexed by city or county. Italicized page numbers refer to illustrations.

Index